NHTI Library
Concord's Community College
Concord, NH 03301

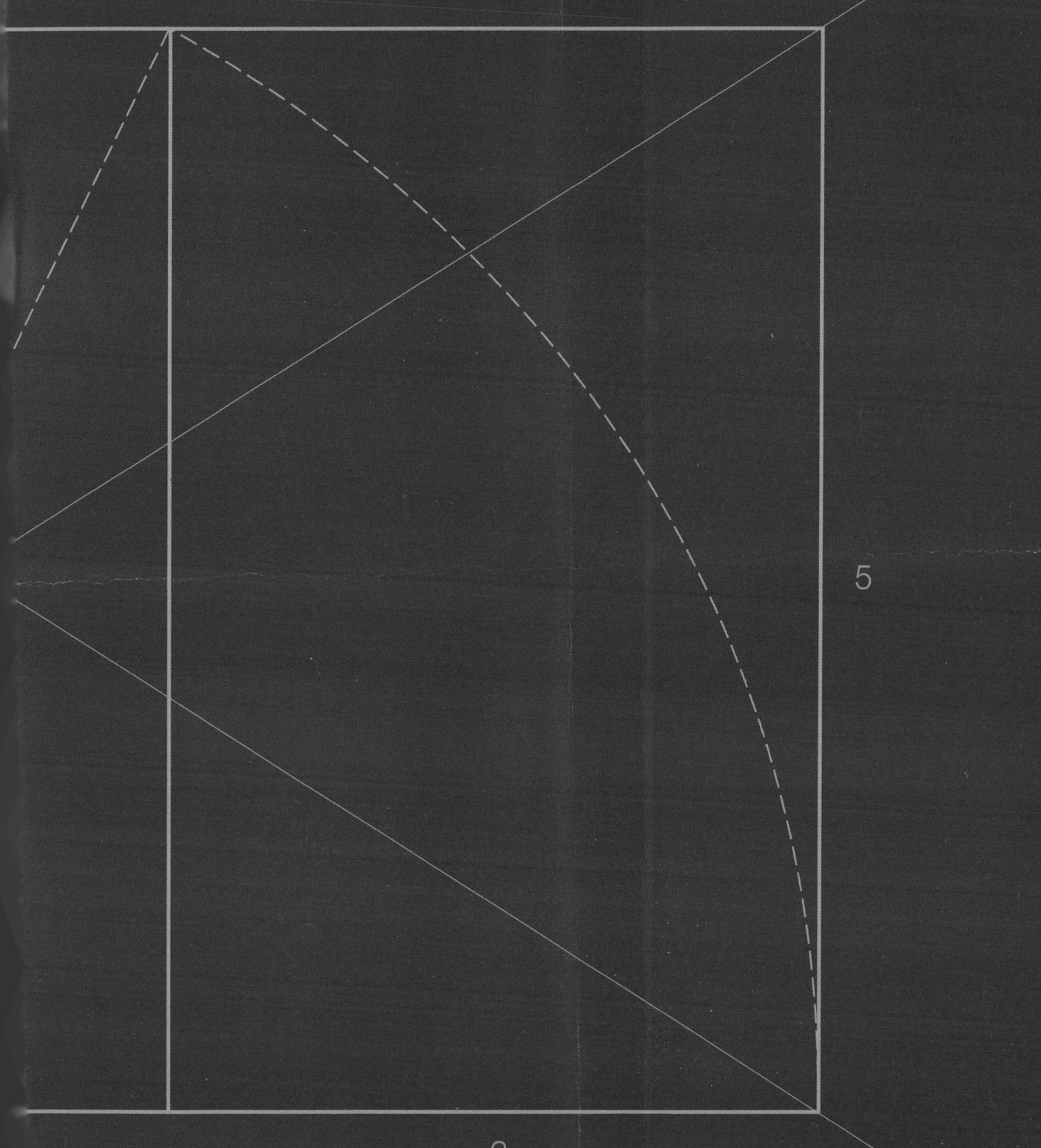

5

3

55   89   144   233   377   610   987

MAN
BETWEEN EARTH AND SKY

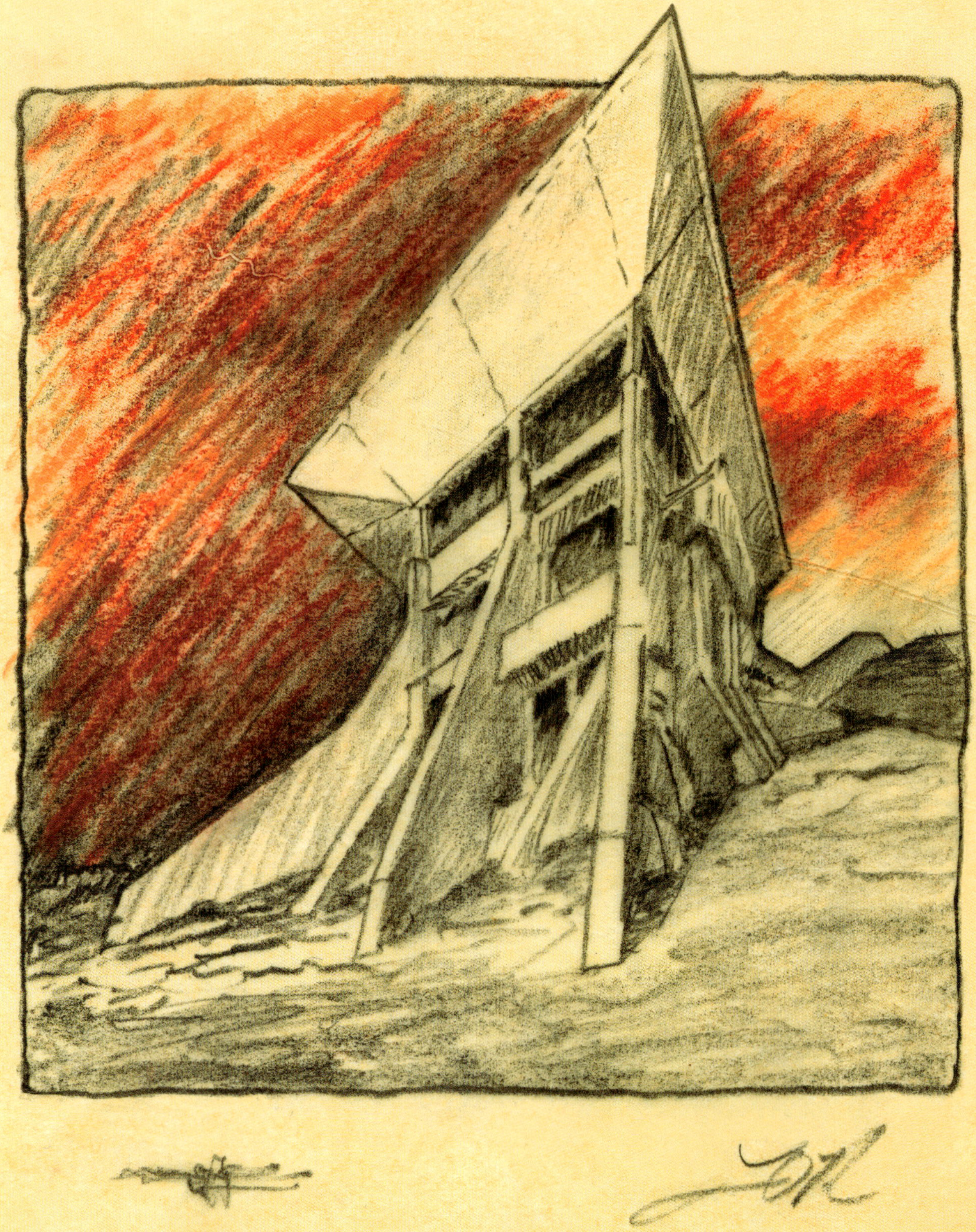

MAN
BETWEEN EARTH AND SKY

A SYMBOLIC AWARENESS OF
ARCHITECTURE
THROUGH A PROCESS OF **CREATIVITY**

Louis O. Roberts

LOUIS O. ROBERTS

OCTAVIO PUBLISHING
Carmel, California   2009

Copyright © 2009 Louis O. Roberts

First Edition

ISBN 978-0-9822407-0-0 Soft
ISBN 978-0-9822407-1-7 Hard

Library of Congress Control Number: 2008910991

All rights reserved. No part of this work covered by the copyright hereon may be reproduced or used in any form or by any means – graphic, electronic, or mechanical, including photocopying, recording, taping, or information storage and retrieval systems- without written permission of the copyright owner.

Graphic Design by Louis O. Roberts
Type Font: Helvetica Neue
Cover Portrait by Nancy R. Roberts
Cover & Title Images: Oakland Hills Residence

All creative works, drawings, photographs
and diagrams (covered under copyright)
are by the author except where noted.

Octavio Publishing
Post Office Box 221322
Carmel, California 93922

16 15 14 13 12 11 10 9 8 7 6 5 4 3 2 1

Cataloging Data

Roberts, Louis O.
Man Between Earth and Sky: A Symbolic
Awareness of Architecture Through a Process
of Creativity / Louis O. Roberts.

Includes bibliographical references and index.
1. Architectural design 2. Philosophy of architecture.
3. Symbolism in architecture. 4. Architecture – Environmental aspects 5. Creative thinking. I. Title
          2009   720'

www.louisoroberts.com

To the future of the human continuum

and to Nancy who has contributed
greatly to its flow

CONTENTS

Reference Code

Book Layers

Architectural Vision

Origins	18-28
Central Idea	44-57
Symbolism	9, 58-63, 70
Vision	9-10, 24, 27, 44-57, 70-75
Architecture	9, 14, 38, 70, 184, 195
Evolution	97-169
Precedents	24-27, 170-183
Concepts	201-203, 196-197
Expressions	2, 14-15, 210-248
Forms	2, 9, 14-15

Creative Process

Childhood	12, 18-23
Uniqueness	8, 10 17-18, 28
Unconscious	8, 38
Vision	9, 26, 64-69
Creativity	10, 12, 18, 40, 60, 84, 201
Principles	40-43, 194-204
Considerations	201-204
Tools	197-198, 257
Faith	88-95
Intuition	8, 88-95
Commitment	88-95
Flexibility	190, 196
Execution	98-169, 206-253

Balanced World

Nature	9, 12, 31, 33, 34-35
Man	8, 30-31, 34-35, 257
Existence	30, 34, 84-87, 257
Society	34-35
Continuum	30-43
Philosophy	30, 76-87
Wholeness	8, 30, 94-95, 190

Prelude

1	Title
2	Title Image
3	Title Page
4	Copyright
5	Dedication
6	Contents
8	Preface
9	Introduction
12	Foreword
14	Vision Images

I Idea

Origin

18	Beginning
24	Awareness
28	Uniqueness

Overview

30	Continuum
34	World / Society
38	Art / Architecture

Vision

44	Central Idea
58	Symbolism
64	Perception
70	Architecture

Philosophy

76	Wisdom / Knowledge
80	Life / Meaning
84	Existence

Actualization

88	Faith / Intuition / Commitment
94	Wholeness

II Evolution

Discovery
- 98 Early Expressions
- 106 Gathering Fragments

Direction
- 110 Sources / Influences
- 134 Emerging Path

Development
- 144 Exploring Ideas
- 160 Studies / Drawings

Precedents
- 170 Reinforcing Philosophies
- 180 Related Structures

Synthesis
- 184 Essence
- 190 Flexible / Fluid

III Reality

Principles
- 194 Human Architectural Design

Expressions
- 206 Architecture — Natural Forms
- 210 Architecture — Ancient Forms
- 216 Architecture — Earth Connected
- 224 Architecture — Earth and Sky
- 246 Urban Planning — Elements
- 250 Objects — Furniture
- 252 Objects — Sculpture
- 254 Objects — Mechanical

Conclusion

- 256 Conclusion
- 258 Appendix
- 260 Bibliography
- 263 Credits
- 264 Acknowledge
- 266 Index

PREFACE

Gathering over a lifetime
bits and pieces of wisdom,
knowledge and information

Following intuition
Pursuing things of interest
Letting ideas flow
in multiple directions

Running counter to current
trends of specialization

Unconsciously knowing
that all things have meaning and are interconnected

Following the laws
of reason and science
The more one absorbs,
the longer it takes
to assimilate,
process and filter
through the uniqueness
of the human psyche

Eventually pulling diverse
thoughts and ideas
together to create
a comprehensive under-
standing of the whole

For clarification
and a record of having
lived and thought
The time arrives to
commit to paper and
make of ideas a reality

To demystify what has
been beyond reach
To distill things
to their simplest terms

To open pathways
to the unconscious
To have access
to the unknown

Contributing to a
balanced environment
for man in the universe

A place where he is
fulfilled and at peace

INTRODUCTION

Architecture, Creativity and a Balanced World are the major themes explored in this book, each layered one upon the other to make a whole. This exploration began in the form of a personal notebook, evolving and expanding over time to include not only a vision of architecture, but also the creative process of making this or any vision a reality. The philosophical and physical ramifications of this architectural approach, utilizing the self-fulfilling aspects of the creative process, contribute to balancing human activity with the natural environment.

When we are not in nature, our primordial home, we are in architecture. *Architecture*, as I envision it, is a restatement of nature – of the earth and the sky. *Symbolic imagery* is the language of this *vision*, and as such, the architecture has a universal appeal originating from visual codes accumulated over eons of time in the human psyche. The *symbolic* puts us back in touch with our primordial roots. This is an architecture of belonging – to the earth, to the place, to the human spirit.

Architecture affects both our external and internal life more than any other man-made entity. It is with us and surrounds us for most of our existence. Architecture is the stage set for our life and can, when created on a poetic level, embody a spirit of comfort, peace, security or exhilaration depending on the type and use of the structure. Buildings can be designed to create various atmospheres that influence us in profound ways – from the interior of a Craftsman Style house to the view across the harbor of the Sydney Opera House, to the experience of walking the exterior wall of the Guggenheim Museum in Bilbao, Spain.

Architecture is an art for all men to learn because all are concerned with it. John Ruskin, 19th century architectural philosopher / critic.

We not only live with architecture, but create it, adding to the overall fabric of our environment. For this reason alone, it would be advantageous to know as much about architecture as possible.

Aside from its place in our everyday life, architecture is a major art form, and has been referred to as "the mother of the arts." As such, certain important artistic issues are covered in this book, the core of which, deals with *creativity*, and in turn *form*, *aesthetics* and *vision*. They are all interconnected. *Form* is an expression of content. Form evolves out of the forces acting on it from within and from without – to be what it wants to be, guided by the artist's vision and skilled hand. An essential part of content is the person doing the creating – the whole person affects the architecture – his unique way of seeing the world together with his core beliefs. The form derived from content and the artist's view of reality invariably expresses itself as our perception of physical and psychological beauty. This is the *aesthetic* factor – that which fulfills and uplifts our spirit – the ultimate goal.

The essence of creativity is *vision*. Vision is an extension of one's uniqueness. This is one of the most important messages in the following pages. The three part structure of this book, *Idea, Evolution, Reality*, is based on *vision*:

The **Idea** behind the vision
The **Evolution** of the vision
The **Reality** of the vision

Vision is what each person contributes to the world. This was aptly stated by Carl Jung, "The only thing you contribute in this world is your uniqueness or individuality – all the rest is rehashed information."

As my vision became more clearly defined, I began to see its manifestations almost everywhere; in nature, in found objects, in ancient man-made structures and monuments. These images / things I recorded over time in the form of notes, drawings, models and photographs. With the finding and documenting of each one came an excitement that pulled me into the realm of total absorption. I was discovering treasure – treasure of my own creation.

When reading this book, one can extract *me* and extract *architecture* and in their place inject *himself* and *anything creative* he wants to do. The creative process in general is the same – but specifically different because we are each unique. One must explore the depths of his own psyche to find his direction.

In writing about art, architecture, and creativity, I prefer to leave things flexible and open to any possibility. Creativity is not a science. There are no prescribed methods that will take us step-by-step through the process, as there are with math and physics. Because of that, this book has some ambiguity intrinsic to the nature of the subject. Being comfortable with ambiguity is an essential part of creativity.

I have attempted to include as many tangibles as possible, allowing the reader to begin exercising his or her creative capabilities. Everyone has the potential to tap into his genius – his spirit – to utilize the natural talents and abilities inherent in each of us. It is not important where one starts, but how far one goes in the pursuit.

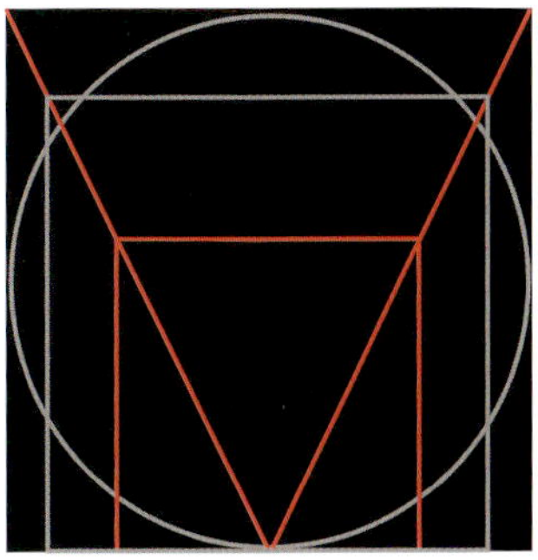

FOREWORD

The foreword is what comes before – in this case forty years before. I recently discovered in a notebook from my last semester in college, the following free verse I wrote touching on many of the ideas expressed in this book: *uniqueness, calling, evolution, nature, wholeness and architecture*. Our future direction is sometimes evident in the youthful ideas we leave behind.

You cannot be a follower and still arrive at yourself

Followers seldom evolve to individual greatness

One is generated by his own path, which began with his first moment of being

We do not reach the age of twenty as the same person

From the time of our beginning, we have innate characteristics

I might have noticed the texture and sound of cinders

Under my feet at the age of three

Even if you were to have a similar experience it might not fit

In the sequential order for you that developed my path to this point

The sequence is of prime importance

It makes one ready for the next step

The step that will be taken or the step that will go by unrecorded

That step may be lost for eternity

The New England countryside was of such an inspirational nature

I feel I could never pay it due homage

If I could make architecture for others as those woods were to me

The excitement of being captured within their depths

What a comfort to retreat in them

To be filled by their unknown forces

Discovery and adventure unfolded with every leaf

All interwoven in a network that could be no other way

One day I had to leave with only the hope that I would return a better person

I set out for the Midwest to the land of the Illinois

After eighteen years my path had lead me to that place

I was not starting anew with architecture

I had begun it with my being

My path was predestined

Every step led me to my arrival

I am now passing through the mill of knowledge

I take in all I can

All feeding steps to my path

I learn about this thing and that one

I expose myself to the happenings of all around me

From the depths of the ocean to the infinity of space

All is part of me

Relativity is of me and my time

Science unfolds to me what I must reflect to you

I will grow from its nourishment

And return to nature with all my new knowledge

My path has led me thus far

I give to it my direction in the future

I cannot be led to follow the paths of others

I evolved through different circumstances

And cannot arrive at the same point in life as others

I have arrived at myself and I must always be there

My path will always be true to me through time and circumstances

The bond between me and my self will remain unbroken

VISION IMAGES

Architectural expressions of earth and sky

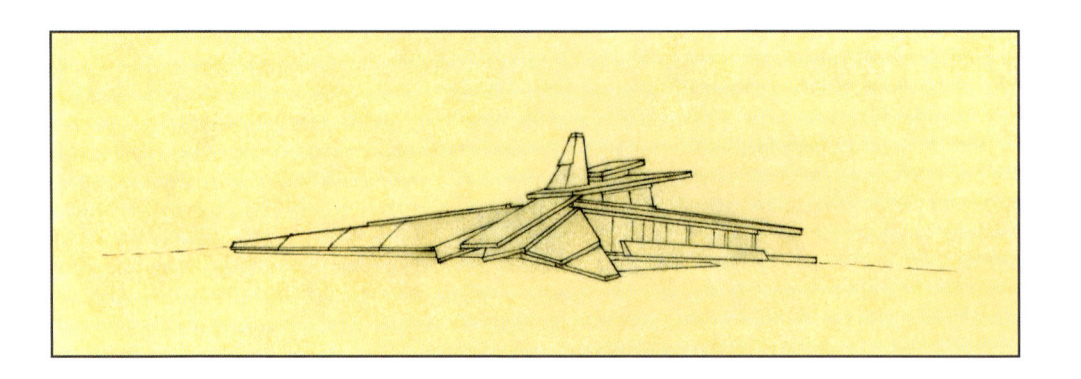

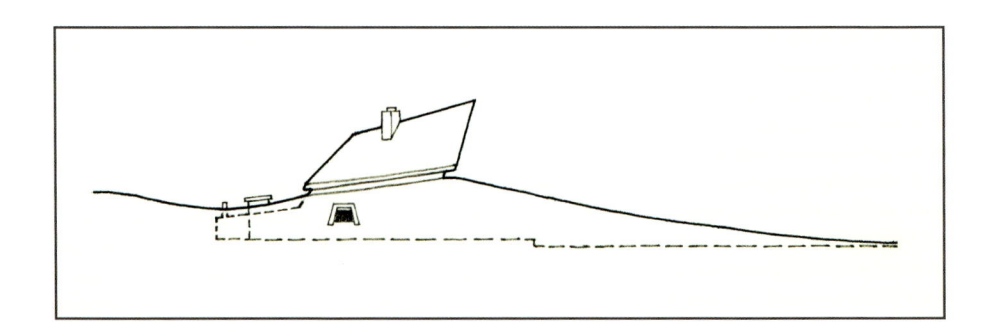

14   PRELUDE

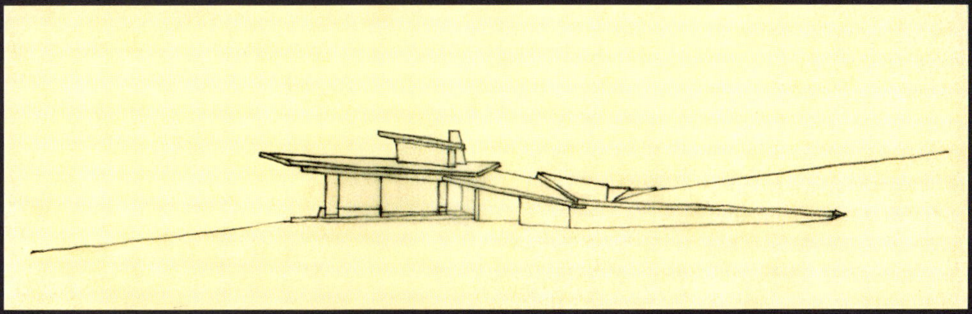

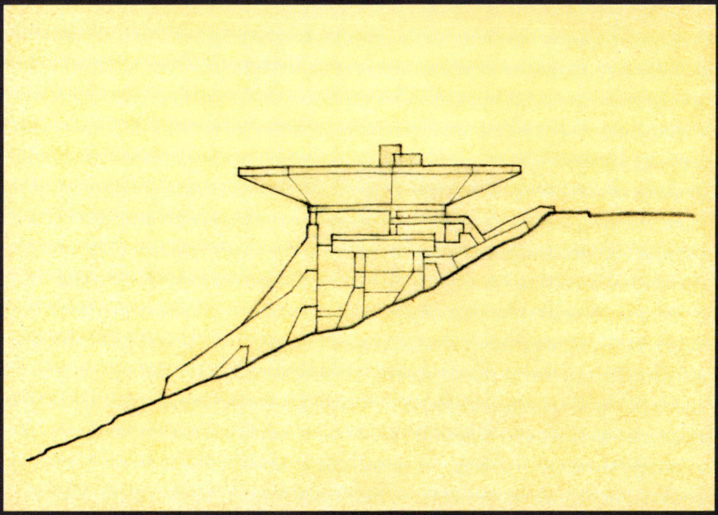

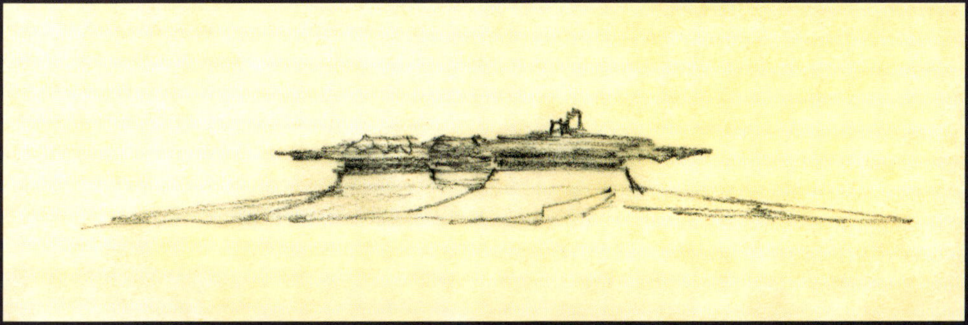

I

THE IDEA

Abstract thoughts and images that flow past the conscious window of the mind

Evoked from the unconscious by innate urges and varied stimuli

The spark that ignites that which is within

ORIGIN

BEGINNING . . . .
The birth and evolution of an idea

In each of us, who we are and what we can do starts with our first moment of being / Driven by a web of ancestral forces brought to bear / Abilities, talents, traits and sensitivities / Select genes from parents, grandparents, and a host of great-grandparents / All in place before we pass into the experiential world

How and what we perceive and retain in this world depends on our unique hereditary characteristics. The experiential world is our cognitive or conscious life, for each person a unique combination of influences – *People, Places, Events, and Images*. We all begin with a tabula rasa, a conscious mind that is clean and ready for absorption.

People along life's journey, those glowing individuals who stand out as bright pillars – parents, relatives, and mentors – stay with us always. They tap us on the shoulder to point the way, turning us a few degrees to course.

Places that are evocative, from natural environments to significant human constructs – each with its own distinctive spirit, its genius loci, embrace us and give us an intimate sense of belonging.

Events clearly lodged in our memories, each has its respective influence on our path. Some are positive, pleasurable experiences which contribute to our evolution, while others are negative, providing developmental lessons to balance reality.

Images retained from life, both conscious and subliminal, become the language of one's future – a coded intuitive mechanism that triggers our response to what we experience and is a key to our direction, calling, or destiny.

To illustrate these hereditary and experiential influences on a personal level, I recall numerous sources from my childhood that remain vivid and still stir excitement in me – things such as caves, arrowheads, ruins and the natural environment. My mother introduced us to the wonders of nature, taking my brother and me on walks in the Connecticut woods, pointing out plants and animals, telling us that flowers were "temples of God."

When one reflects deeply on his own experiences in the world, the origin of influences and events rises to the surface. The three most prominent recurring childhood images for me are:

An Ancient Dolmen

About once or twice a year during my early childhood our family would go for a Sunday drive and solemnly arrive at a giant stone dolmen. This monument was located in the small village of North Salem, New York. My father would get out of the car and slowly walk up to within 25 feet of the stone and stand there in a reverent manner with his hands clasped in front of him – as if he were in church. To a child this stone was enormous in scale, and very impressive. Taking my father's lead, I stood there quietly and observed it with keen interest. The formation consists of one huge stone sitting on top of smaller point stones so that it appears to be floating above the ground. As I look back now, it was an earth-sky image with a tension or energy between the ground and the stone. Some sources have referred to it as the largest dolmen in North America with a cap-stone weighing approximately 90 tons. My father's connection to this monument goes back to his own childhood. He was born in Connecticut about four miles from its location; I can imagine his parents visiting there Sundays, driving a horse and buggy.

Stone Walls

When I was about seven or eight, my father built a long tapered stone wall in our back yard. He brought home boulders, split them and lovingly laid up a beautiful wall. As a descendant of masons, he was very interested in stone work, the focus of our excursions through the countryside. He would point out their construction, the way the stones were laid, the space between them, the depth of the space, whether their faces were split or left natural, and very particularly, how they connected to the ground and their surroundings. Did they look as if they had grown from the earth? Were they earth connected? Although to a small boy this sounded confusing, it would all make sense later.

Earth connected stone walls / steps built by Dan Snow

Peter Mauss

Lean-to Construction

In 1950, at age nine, I built, with two other boys, a lean-to construction out of concrete blocks, steel bed rails, flat boards, and tar paper. The open side faced south, the sloping back was cut into a low bank and the floor was two steps below grade in the front. I was surprised to find that over the years I have unconsciously incorporated these same elements into my architectural designs. Things such as: orienting the building to the sun, growing the structure out of the earth, the use of flat planar forms in combination with concrete bases, and in some cases, steel frames. These are best exemplified in the Hawk Hill House (p. 238), but are also very prominent in the Geils House (p. 134), and the Roberts House (p. 140).

Later, while attending college in Illinois, I found myself intrigued by the power of the horizon: the earth's edge, often emphasized by a single tree on the plain, or silo structures on the distant horizon, or an approaching thunder cloud low over the flat landscape.

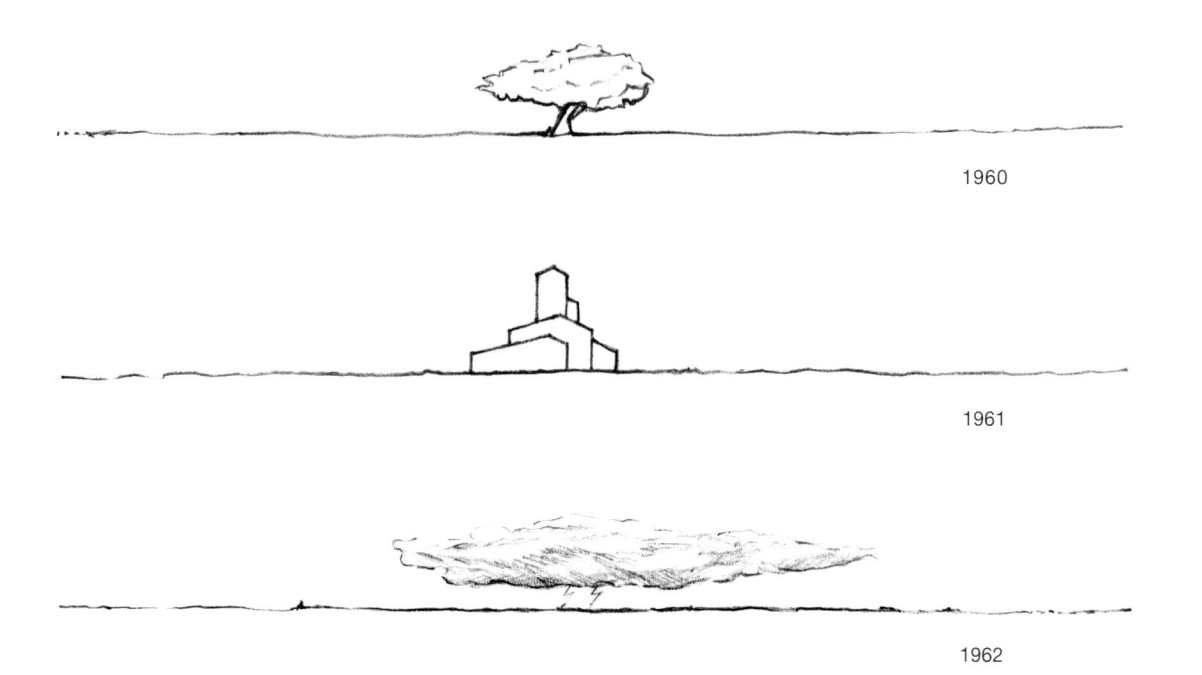

1960

1961

1962

Toward the end of my college years a friend, Art Sinsabaugh, the head of the photography department at the University of Illinois, captured on wide format film the poetic beauty of that horizontal landscape, reinforcing my response to the horizon.

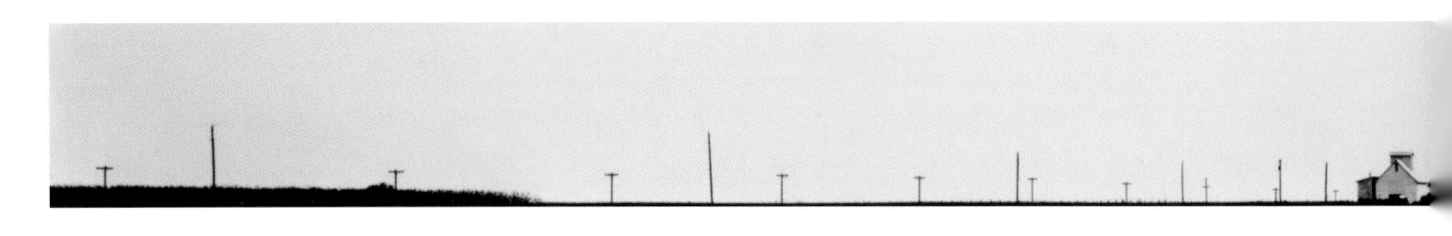

ART SINSABAUGH   Midwest Landscape   #97

ART SINSABAUGH   Midwest Landscape   #33

Seeds planted in the psyche, the unconscious, emerge years later, triggered by accidental exposure to key information and recurrent images that eventually surface to the conscious realm.

© Katherine Ann Sinsabaugh and Elizabeth Sinsabaugh de la Cova

1964

© Katherine Ann Sinsabaugh and Elizabeth Sinsabaugh de la Cova

1964

ORIGIN

. . . . . AWARENESS . . . . .
Made evident with the realization of the past

The awareness of an idea is not the beginning; in reality one is well beyond the beginning. The cocoon lies dormant, ready to be awakened. *The answers to your life are in you*, to paraphrase Rainer M. Rilke from *Letters to a Young Poet*. This has to do with one's perception of life / reality. *To see what everyone else sees, but to think what no one else thinks* is a concept that embodies one of the most important principles for achieving creative expression – your unique vision.

The key elements that triggered a realization of my direction / vision occurred by chance in my fifth year of architecture school:

I came across a book titled *Architecture Without Architects* by Bernard Rudofsky. What most intrigued me was that many of the buildings depicted had a strong connection to the earth; they looked as if they were a part of it or grew from it. They embodied the spirit of the place. That imagery stirred me deeply, bringing up childhood memories of walls, ruins, caves and dolmens. I began to realize that most of my early college designs were *earth-connected*.

Earth connected images from *Architecture Without Architects*

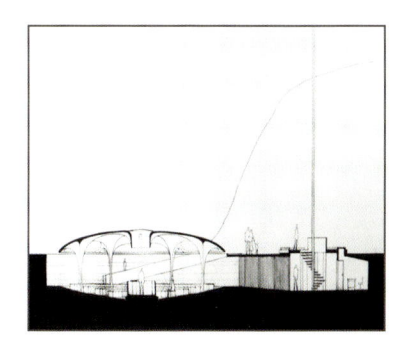

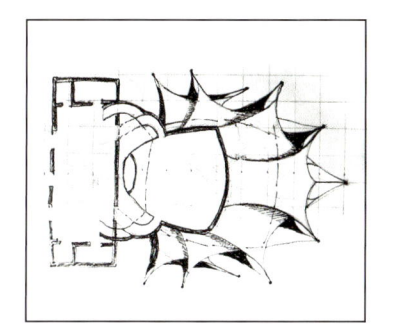

Early college designs

Key elements that triggered realization of my direction

ARCHITECTURE WITHOUT ARCHITECTS (1964)

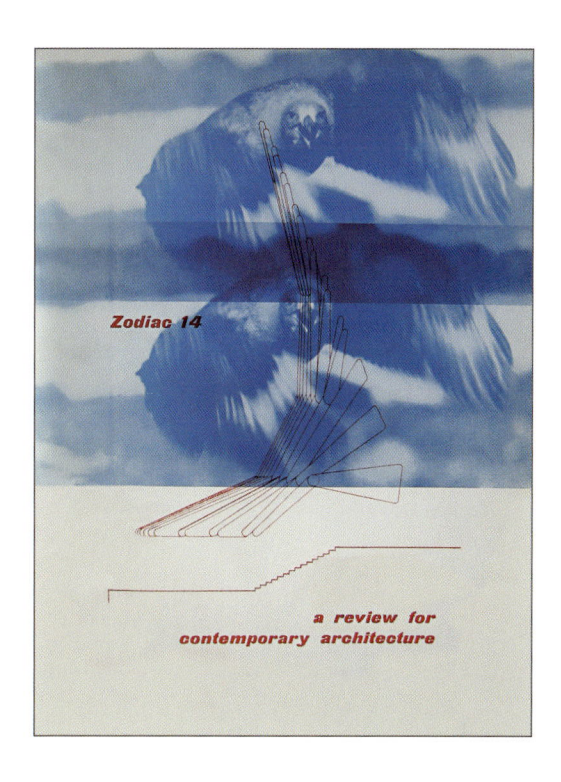

ZODIAC MAGAZINE #14 (1965)

A short time afterward, while in the college library, I happened to read an Italian architectural magazine titled *Zodiac 14*, containing an article by Segfried Giedion about Jorn Utzon, the Danish architect. This article later became part of Giedion's book, *Space, Time and Architecture*. Utzon's architectural vision and philosophy were summarized as having a ground plane or raised platform with a roof element floating above – as exemplified by the Sydney Opera House and others.

Utzon's drawing of the Sydney Opera House

Utzon's sketches

Utzon cited early historical examples in oriental structures, particularly Japanese, and also in the Mayan temples of Central America.

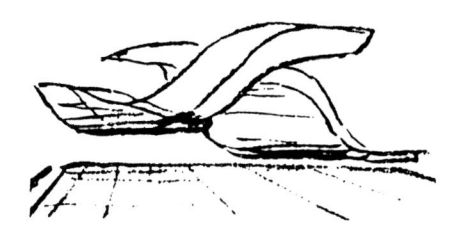

Utzon's sketches

This reinforced my own thinking and direction. I then realized that pieces of my creative path fit with my childhood experiences (those objects and images that fascinated me) and my earlier architectural designs. My vision was there, although still vague and undefined in all its manifestations.

The course in architecture was already set
Influenced by internal and external forces
Utilizing talents and abilities
Giving form to thought
Seeking meaningful ideas with a vision

We hunt for the things that have importance to us in almost everything we encounter
We develop a heightened awareness of the ideas and images that excite us
Over time we begin to define our personal and aesthetic identity
This is not just about architecture, art, photography, writing, or any creative pursuit
It is about exploring the depths of who we are

ORIGIN

.... UNIQUENESS
The distinctive characteristics of each individual

Early in childhood the seeds of who we will be have already been sown. To restate Carl Jung, "The only thing you contribute in this world is your uniqueness or individuality – all the rest is rehashed information." James Hillman, in his book, *The Soul's Code*, makes reference to what he terms the "'acorn theory,' which holds that each person bears a uniqueness that asks to be lived and that is already present before it can be lived."

We are all unique in what we find significant and record in our memories. Our recollections from infancy on through life are important clues to our direction. What draws our attention, piques our interest, intrigues us and generates enthusiasm are all indicators of what we find important. From both our innate and our experiential past, these things remain high points in our psyche. The objective is to tap into the things that make us unique: memories, interests, abilities and experiences. These are the lifeblood of our future – the things that lead to personal fulfillment.

[T]he responses we make to surroundings and events determine the characteristics that make each one of us a unique, unprecedented, and unrepeatable person. Rene Dubos [Pulitzer Prize winning microbiologist], *A God Within,* 1972, p. 5.

Every person sees the world around him differently depending on his particular sensitivities and unique perspective of reality. Dubos again states in *A God Within*, p. 21, "Each person has a unique picture of the world, largely of his own creation." What one thinks is important may not be the same for another. Each individual should come to his own place / equilibrium, based on his perception of a given focus: life, art, architecture, photography, music. To stay at the center of what you are doing you engage your own intuition, instincts and insights. This exploration has to do with going inward.

For every man truly lives, so long as he acts his nature, or in some way makes good the faculties of himself. Religio Medici.

Put aside what others may think.

Does it make sense to you?
Does it appeal to you aesthetically?
Does it contribute to your view or vision?

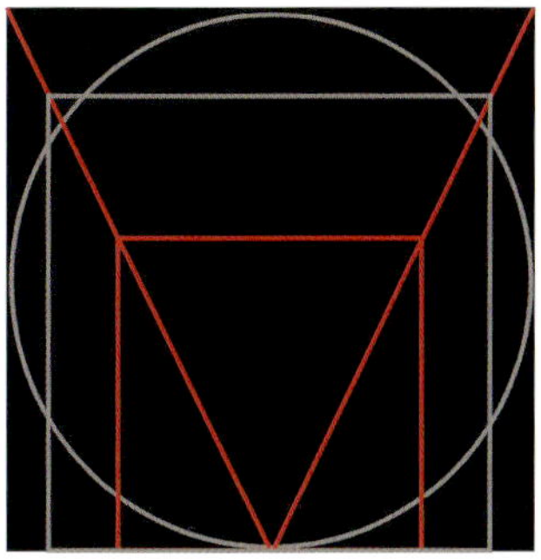

OVERVIEW

CONTINUUM . . . .
Ascertaining one's place in time and space

An *overview*, particularly creative or philosophical, orients one to a wider spectrum of the prevailing conditions, affording a more accurate perspective of reality. Overviews provide reference points to help guide one through life.

We change the emphasis from the parts to the whole with an overview. The broad perspective brings us closer to the "why" of life – the content, the meaning, the essence. We temporarily put aside the "how" – the technology, the specifics, the vehicles, and look at the effect our actions have on the world around us. Ultimately, do we contribute to fulfilling the human spirit?

One can view the world as a space-time continuum, where space is the surrounding environment and conditions. The continuum has primarily to do with time; we examine the meaningful events of history and learn from them to shape the future.[1] The continuum is the thread of history linking human evolution.

For perspective, St. Augustine describes three kinds of time in *Confessions,* ch. xx: A present of things past, a present of things present and a present of things future. The present of things past is memory; the present of things present is sight; and the present of things future is expectation.

Many people seem to have a very narrow and isolated view of life. They are primarily concerned with their own gratification, with little consideration for future generations. If we take the focus off ourselves and look at the larger context of existence, we can develop a more balanced outlook – feeling we are part of something larger that encompasses the whole of mankind.[2]

Philosophically, all a person has of life is a segment of time. The essence of our existence is what we do with that time. One can make a contribution to the human continuum, each adding his part to the whole. What we are today and in the future is derived from our past.[3]

I believe in the human continuum
The stage that was set for us

The stage we will set
For the future of human existence

Contribution is what each of us adds to the continuum, as a beautiful arrowhead is the embodiment of a human spirit past. The continuum can also have a timeless nature; some things tend to be evocative and meaningful anywhere along the path of human history. This is particularly true of certain psychically recorded imagery.

source unknown

Clovis Point arrowhead (circa 13,500 B.C.)
One of the highest levels of known human achievement at that period in time

Peter A Clayton

Giza Pyramids, Egypt (circa 2,500 B.C.)

The creative acts that produced these objects and structures are from a time when man felt more a part of nature and the earth. [4] They form an important imagery foundation along the continuum that has become an integral part of man's psyche. We can contribute in small positive ways in all we do. These efforts accumulate over time to bring about a meaningful future for mankind.

Stonehenge, England (circa 2000 B.C.)

Violet Staub DeLaszlo,
Psyche and Symbol:
A Selection of the
Writings of C. G. Jung
(1958).

Past　　　　　　　　　　1. "The psyche is not only of today. It reaches right back to pre-historic times." p. xiii.

Rene Dubos,　　　　　Pulitzer Prize 1969
So Human an Animal
(1968).

Continuum　　　　　　2. "it might be . . . important to help each individual person understand where he belongs in the cosmic order, and what gives significance to his own life." p. 184.

Mircea Eliade,
The Sacred and the
Profane: the Nature of
Religion (1959).

Past　　　　　　　　　　3. "Do what he will, he [man] is an inheritor. He cannot utterly abolish his past, since he is himself the product of his past." p. 204.

Rene Dubos,
So Human an Animal
(1968).

Nature – Man　　　　　4. "All successful individual lives, and all successful civilizations, have been supported by an orderly system of relationships linking man to nature and to society." p. 185.

OVERVIEW

. . . . SOCIETY / WORLD . . . .
Understand the prevailing operating system

It is sometimes enlightening to imagine the whole of existence as energy flowing throughout the universe to include our present microcosm. This energy, existing for billions of years, has expanded through time and space to permeate this solar system, this planet, this country, this culture, expressed now in the form of human creativity.

One can pause anywhere along this flow to analyze the system, whether it be solar, environmental, governmental, economic, social, cultural, or molecular. As an example, it would be prudent to know the economic system in which one is operating. Ours is capitalism; know the advantages and disadvantages; recognize that materialism is the dominant force which can lead to many forms of human behavior.

Some observers point out that during the early part of the twentieth century we evolved from a "character ethic" – what things are, the truth – to an "image ethic" – how things appear, not necessarily the truth. Be aware of the distinction. Understanding the prevailing operating system gives one the power to avoid its negative aspects.

An overview brings us to the point of understanding the concept of balance - balance in all we do from our personal life to the world around us. Keep in mind that the world is not external, we are an extension of it. Reality is what it is. Within that reality we must seek the balance point which works best for all the elements in our sphere of influence. Finding equilibrium in our life is essential. In the pursuit of creative endeavors, and in particular, architecture, numerous and multileveled variables are involved. Without balance, the architecture seems forced or contrived; the components do not appear as related elements of the whole. When we see ourselves within a larger system we also take into consideration the natural environment – it is the balanced organism of which we are an integral part.

Earth and man are . . . two complementary components of a system, which might be called cybernetic, since each shapes the other in a continuous act of creation. Rene Dubos, *A God Within,* p. 45.

In life, and particularly in architecture, I am concerned with ecological balance – the light touch of man's hand can enhance the fine line between nature and human constructs.

Cappadocia, Turkey – Dwellings
carved into the natural tufa rock

People have a deep psychological need for contact with nature; the planet needs the reverential care of humans. . . . I think ecopsychology could shift the whole emphasis . . . [in] showing people the prospect of greater personal fulfillment by bringing their activities into harmony with the earth. Remarks by Theodore Roszak, *The Voice of the Earth,* 1992.

Machu Picchu, Peru – Ruins,
nature reclaiming the man-made,
pulling it back into the earth

Following pages 36-37:
Simon Petra Monastery, Greece
Architecture growing out of the rock

Jeffrey Becom

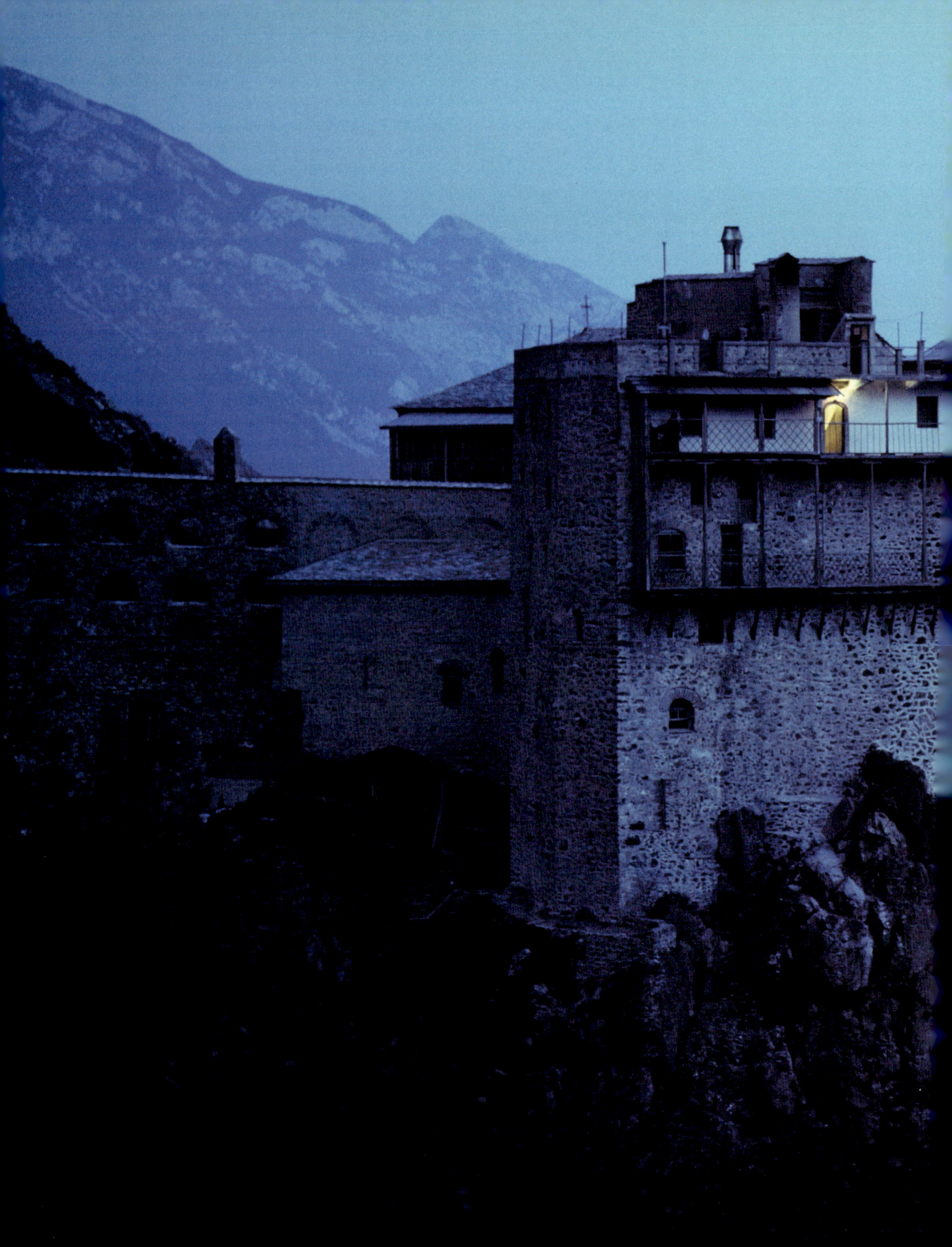

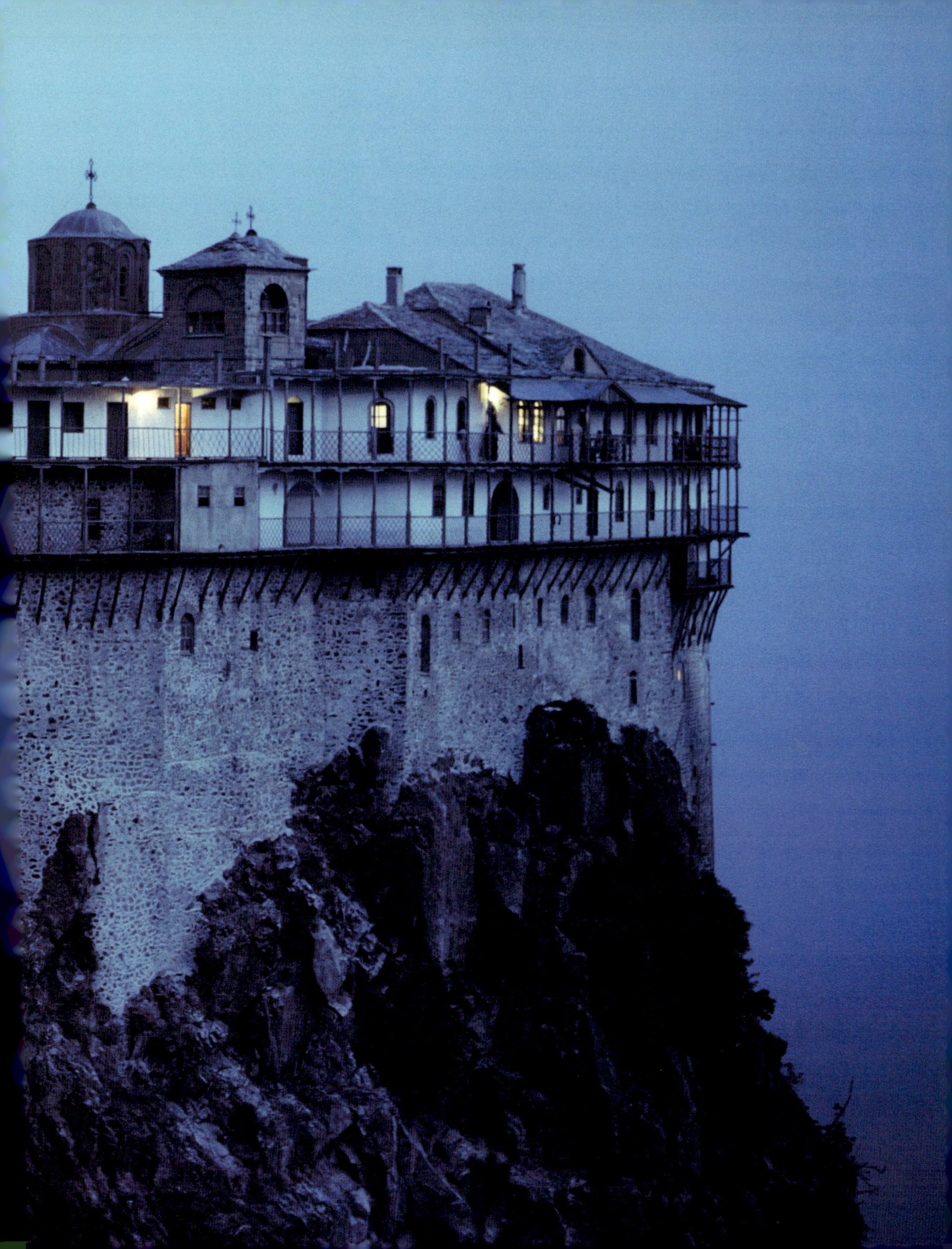

OVERVIEW

ART / ARCHITECTURE
A reflection of man's spirit and existence

Art and architecture leave testimony revealing who we are as a culture. The artistic message arrived at is both purposeful and reflective. *Purposeful*, in what we consciously want to convey; *reflective*, in what is beyond our immediate awareness, that which subliminally conveys our spirit.

Architecture is not only an irrefutable expression of its own time, but is firmly rooted in the past and projects its influence into the future.[1,2] It represents our place on the continuum. As James G. Huneker stated, "Art is an instant arrested in eternity."

I view art and architecture as very much the same thing. Architecture is an art form, which has a utilitarian function. It has been traditionally referred to as "the mother of the arts." Some have stated that art is purposely useless. On the contrary, the function of art is to evoke an image, a spirit, a memory, a feeling, a connection to the unconscious.[3] This effect can be achieved with any art form, whether architecture, photography, painting, sculpture, music, theater, dance or literature.

Although viewed as a frivolous activity by a large segment of present day society, art expresses man's need to bring forth the essence of the human spirit. It is important for us to see life from this overview. [4]

[S]tudy of the organization of the brain shows that belief and creative art are essential and universal features of all human life. . . . They are literally the most important of all the functional features that ensure human homeostasis. . . . aesthetic creation and enjoyment are fundamental features of human life. They are activities in which the brain is operating in the same way as it does in daily life, but as it were at a higher level of intensity. All human perception is a form of creative activity. J. Z. Young, *Programs of the Brain*, Oxford University Press 1978, p. 231.

Art is almost as old as human consciousness. Once man overcame the issues of basic survival, he incorporated art as an integral part of his life. He made things with love and care conveying special meaning to his objects and structures. Except for select artists, craftsmen and architects, we have lost some of our humanness by no longer making objects with *intensity and coherence* – appropriate terms from art critic Robert Hughes. The ritual of doing something creative can be sacred.

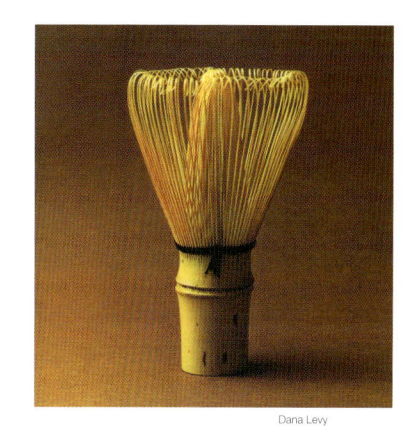

Formed and Fabricated Steel and Bronze Gates, Albert Paley

Japanese Tea Whisk

D. H. Lawrence said, "Art is, at its core, a religious experience." The advent of the Industrial Revolution, and the disbandment of the craftsmen's guilds in 1791, initiated the decline of the arts as an integral part of human existence.

Yellow Satinwood Glass Topped Table , Artist / Furniture Maker, Garry Knox Bennett

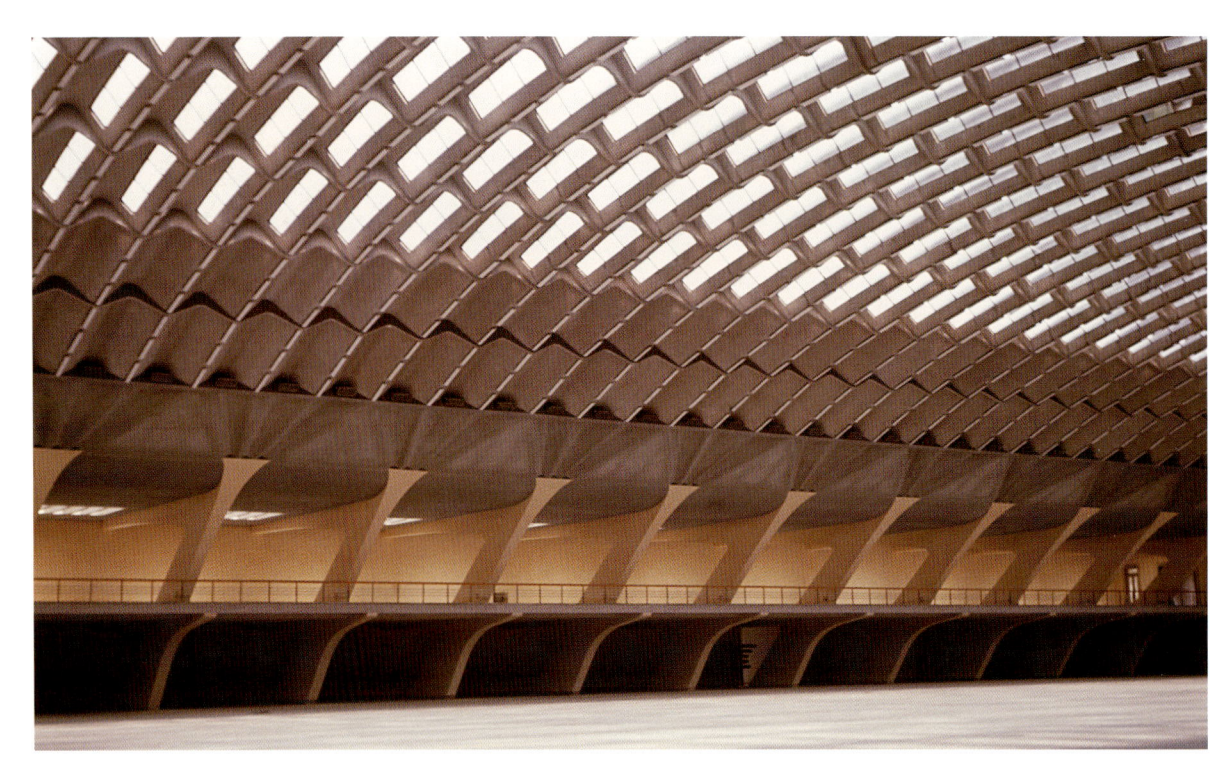

Exhibition Building, Turin, Italy, 1950 – Pier Luigi Nervi, architect

Creativity is the primary issue. To be creative means to assume nothing. Taking an overview is an essential element in being creative. You back out of a particular situation as far as you can; in the process you question all the previous assumptions you or others have made. The objective is to rethink everything in your own terms. This, in most cases, brings you to a different place from where you started.

When you step outside of yourself, you enter the realm of the universe. You go from the specific to the general and back again, all the while evaluating what you encounter and adjusting your perspective. One comes to understand he is part of a much larger whole.

In the context of the overall external environment, architecture is the most dominant element in our lives, and probably the most important. Nature once held that position, as our primordial home. We still go back to nature to revive our spirit; it is our sanctuary, our longed-for past.

Architecture, from my point of view, is man's restatement of nature – of the earth and the sky. In this, it should be uplifting to the human spirit in its form, space, and aesthetics. "Form is an expression of content" (Rene Dubos, *A God Within*, p. 12) whereas style is a manner of copying.[5] The more meaningful the form, the more lasting the architecture / art and the more a part of the continuum it will be. Through meaning one arrives at the essence of a thing / creation.

Architecture is unique in the art realm in that it is not only a thing in itself, a sculptural form in or on the landscape, but at the same time provides the capacity to set the stage for human activity and accommodate natural and man-made vistas. Architecture is an interactive and experiential art form.

I say this as I sit writing in a local cafe. It is a circular space with brick floors, wood walls, a fireplace and an operable clear domed roof admitting fresh ocean air and light. Between the top and the space below are canvas sails that provide shade, diffuse sunlight, absorb sound and create a feeling of intimacy – a wonderful space and environment in itself. It is also a place for human activity, with people coming and going, greeting one another, stopping for a short or long conversation, sitting to read the paper. The architecture and the human activity enhance each other, making for a complete experience.

Architecture is an important art form. It is an art of ever-present reality. We do not have to go to galleries and museums to exclusively see architecture; we live with it every day. It leads one to ask what influence it has on us. Winston Churchill said, "We shape our buildings, and afterwards our buildings shape us."

We are in an era of transition and multiplicity as evidenced by the present-day eclectic approach to art and architecture. This is an exciting period which can provide the clues and avenues to a meaningful architectural future.

Milwaukee Art Museum, Milwaukee, Wisconsin
Santiago Calatrava, Architect

Milwaukee Art Museum interior

Guenther Tetz

Guenther Tetz

When it comes to judging architecture and art, the criteria that has consistently held true over the ages was formulated by Marcus Vitruvius in the 1st century B.C. He wrote the first major treatise on architecture – *The Ten Books on Architecture,* which include: art, human scale, proportion, engineering, landscape design, and urban planning. These criteria still apply today. His trinity for judging architecture and art is:

Firmness — Is it structurally sound and / or technically competent?

Commodity — Does it fulfill its basic function – whether in the layout of a building or the aesthetic principles of its design?

Delight — Is it art – does it kindle the human spirit – does it create an atmosphere, touch us emotionally, stay with us afterward?

Leonardo da Vinci also drew from Virtruvius' wisdom when he created his famous drawing of the man in the circle and the square which he titled "The Vitruvian Man." Da Vinci followed Vitruvius' description of drawing the human body in a circle and a square utilizing proportions conforming to the *golden section*.

The Vitruvian Man

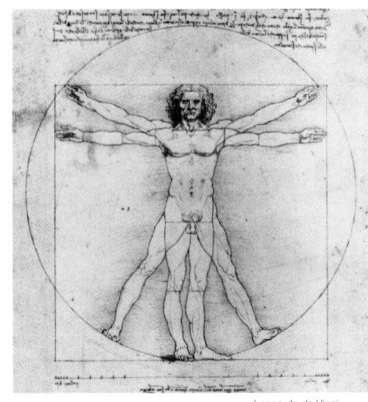

Leonardo da Vinci

One can achieve the above three criteria and still fall short of a place on the continuum. While these elements are essential, vision is the key ingredient. Occasionally a work of art or architecture may be good in itself but of short-lived acclaim. It may be a fortuitous accident, lacking direction and consistency. If original and drawn from within, it is a product of vision and has a deeper meaning – the work rings true – it becomes authentic. Without vision it lacks uniqueness and the connection to the inner self. Vision is the essence of any creative work.

Sigfried Giedion, *Space, Time and Architecture* **(1962).**

Architecture – reflection of the age

1. "Architecture . . . is so bound up with the life of a period as a whole. . . . However much a period may try to disguise itself, its real nature will still show through in its architecture. . . . In the great architectural masterpieces, as in every great work of art, the human shortcomings which every period exhibits so liberally fall away." pp. 19 - 20.

Future

2. "Architecture can reach out beyond the period of its birth. . . ." p. 20.

Artist's Role

3. "The artist, in fact, functions a great deal like an inventor or a scientific discoverer: all three seek new relations between man and his world. In the artist's case these relations are emotional instead of practical or cognitive. . . . He is a specialist who shows us in his work as if in a mirror something we have not realized for ourselves: the state of our own souls." p. 428.

Arthur Miller, *On Politics and the Art of Acting* **(2001).**

Pulitzer Prize 1949

Artist

4. "To most political people the artist is a strange bird, somehow suspect, a nuisance, a threat to morality, or a fraud. . . . But art has always been the revenge of the human spirit upon the shortsighted. . . . Artists are not particularly famous for their conformity with majority mores, but whatever is not turned into art disappears forever." p. 84.

Sigfried Giedion, *Space, Time and Architecture* **(1962).**

Style

5. When writing about architectural expression Giedion compares "constituent facts" with "transitory facts." The "constituent facts," those of meaningful symbolic imagery, have "recurrent and cumulative tendencies," whereas the "transitory facts," those of temporary superficial styles, are "almost wholly without significance to the present day." pp. 18 -19.

VISION

CENTRAL IDEA . . . .
Man between earth and sky

The earth embraces the sky / The sky embraces the earth / Separate entities but always in contact / The earth reaching up to meet the sky / As majestic mountains rise up to surpass the clouds / The sky penetrating down into the earth / Flowing into the lowest valleys and subterranean recesses / Man lives within this embrace / Between the earth and the sky / He brings the earth into the sky and the sky into the earth.

There is a unique energy in this space between earth and sky / A tension that maintains a visual equilibrium / It is this energy that interests me / My quest has been to find ways to generate and express this energy.

Sigmar Polke

A profound untapped expressiveness resides in the opposition between the earth and the aerial.
Kenneth Frampton, "Tactility", *Architecture and Body*, no. 18.

Gaston Bachelard in *The Poetics of Space*, p. 22, makes reference to – the dramatic tension between the aerial and the terrestrial – repeatedly expressed in Henri Bosco's novel *L'Antiquaire*.

The Between of Earth and Sky – Ever present in nature as a physical reality

Cloud formations over the horizontal landscape

Olaf Veltman

Tree on a hill

Its roots attach it to the earth and its branches reach out to heaven, symbolizing man's allegiance to earth and aspiration to heaven. Oliver Marc, *The Psychology of the House, 1972, p. 29.*

Left and following two pages:
Eroded rock formations with
sky related tops

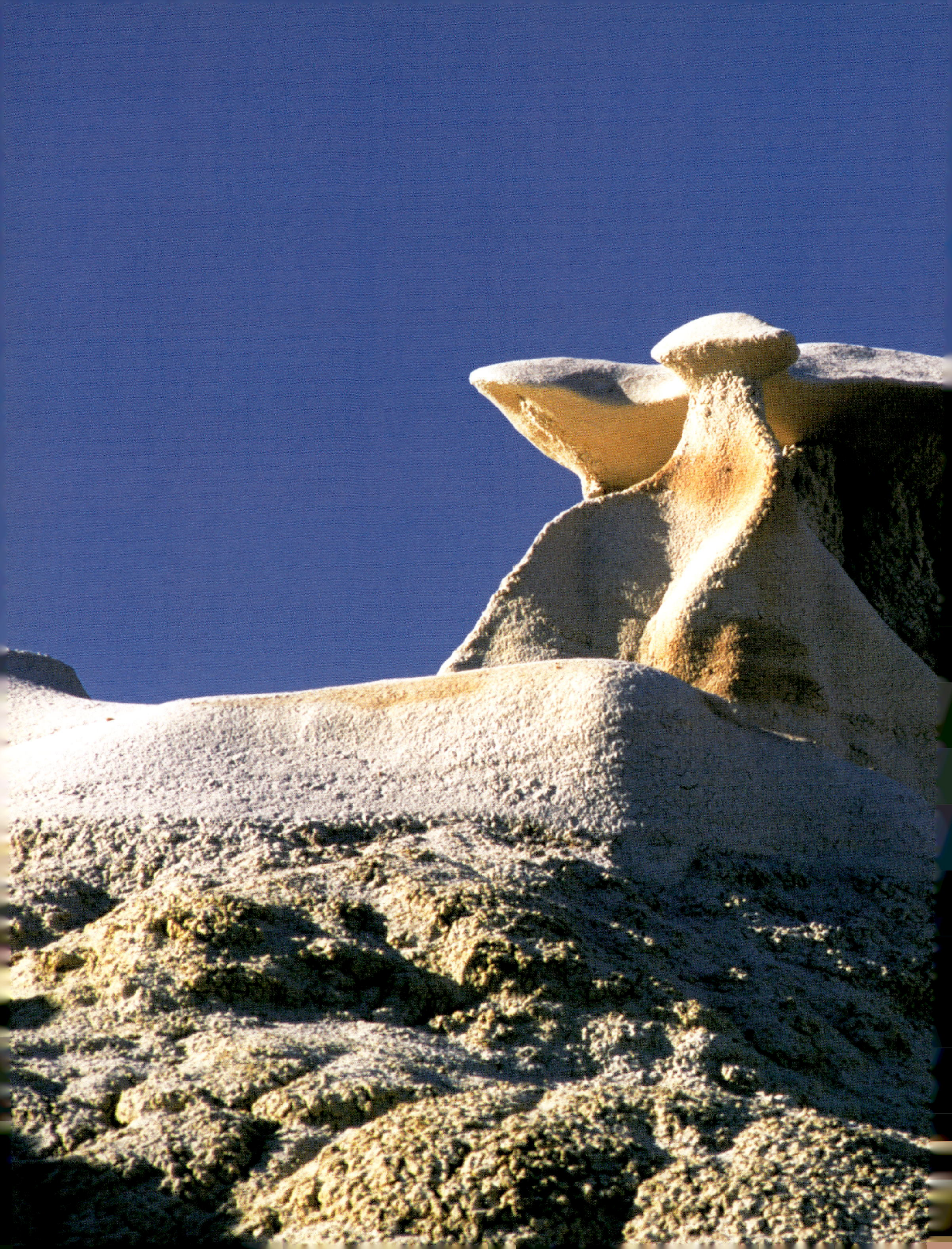

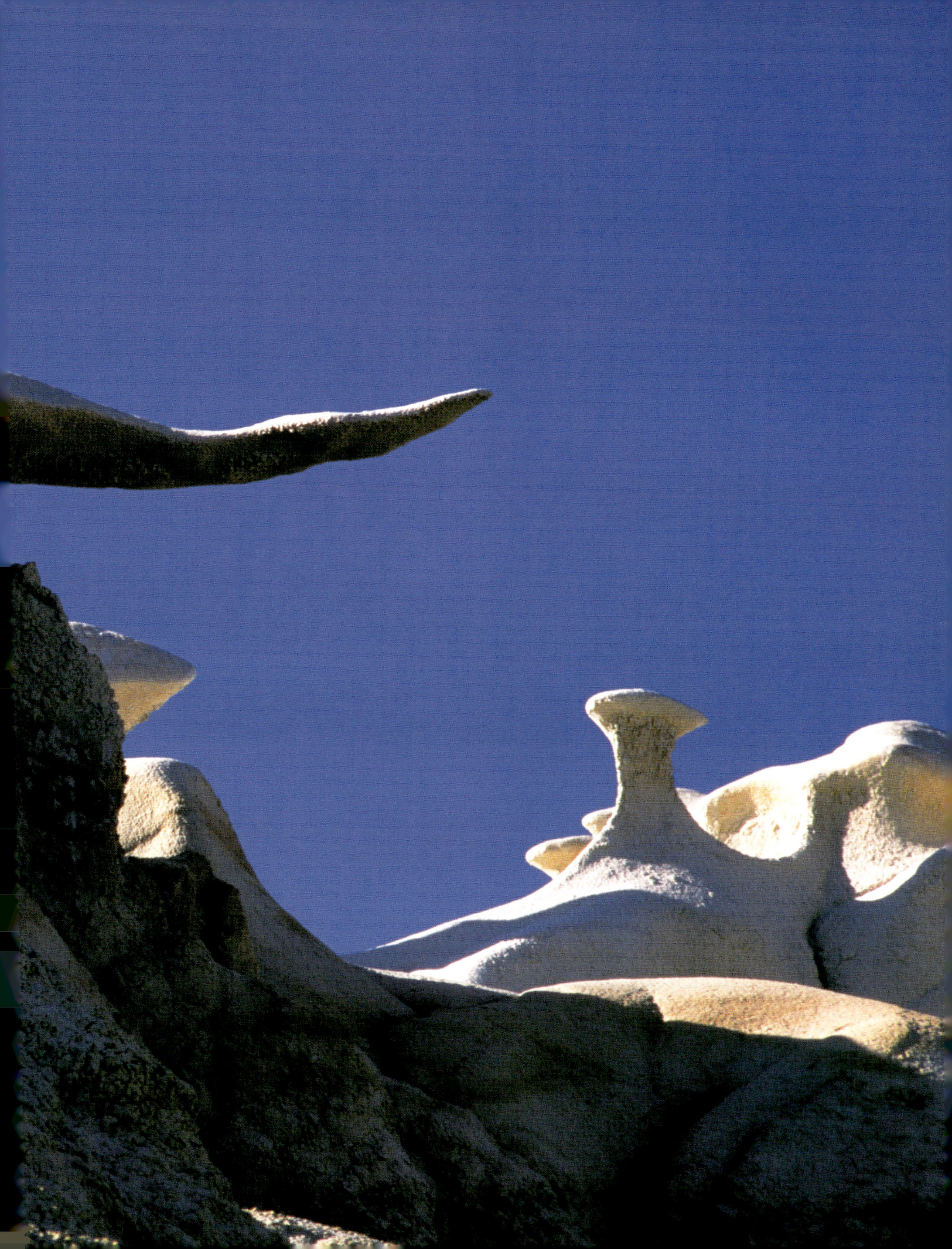

The earth and the sky are not only physical manifestations, but are also deeply rooted realities in the human psyche. With the arrival of man and his evolved consciousness these two physical elements took on a new significance.

The earth-sky connection has been with man since the beginning of human history. The oldest and most dominant experience, and all that it implies, is that of the earth beneath him and the sky above him. This is more ingrained in his psyche than any other conscious or unconscious experience.

The image of earth and sky has its roots so deeply grounded in the psyche as to give to this image the first priority. Victor Christ-Janer, *Perspecta 17,* 1980, p. 11.

When something is in nature, as with earth and sky, it just is – it exists as physical reality. When something is man-made in nature, its origin first resides in the human mind as psychic reality. "I think therefore I am" (Descartes) – *if I am therefore I can do.*

Nature's Intentionality . . . Physical reality.   Human Intentionality . . . Psychic reality. Victor Christ-Janer, *Perspecta 17,* 1980, pp. 12-13.

The Man-made in Nature – The light touch of man's hand

Cappadocia, Turkey

St. Loca, Amalfi Peninsula, Italy

Sumela Monastery, Turkey

In the realm of psychic reality, the *earth* and *sky* have potent qualities. *Earth connectedness* is rooted in the fact of gravity. The earth is our anchor point, our stable platform of reference. *Earth* brings forth thoughts and images of warmth, security, protection, and permanence; it provides us with food, water, shelter, and fuel. The earth's surface, with all its variations and wonders, is our strongest reference for beauty. It is commonly referred to as "mother," symbolizing *source*, the place of man's physical and biological origin.

Man is still of the earth, earthly. The earth is literally our mother. . . . Rene Dubos, *A God Within,* 1972, p. 38.

The earth is our base element – our foundation.

The Earth Connection – Earthscapes

Trulli House, Alberobello, Italy

Villages, Bani Murra, Yemen

Bamburgh Castle, England

The *sky* is the ever present place above us. Sky evokes feelings of mystery, vastness, and endless possibilities. It has historically been man's perceived connection to the heavens, to God, to higher powers, to the hereafter. The rhythms of our lives – daily, seasonal and lunar, are all generated by the workings of the universe, that which is beyond the sky. From the sky comes our most essential source of energy in the form of light and heat – requisite to our existence.

The sky is the vaulting path of the sun, the course of the changing moon, the wandering glitter of the stars, the year's seasons and their changes, the light and dusk of day, the gloom and glow of night, the clemency and inclemency of the weather, the drifting clouds and blue depth of the ether. Martin Heidegger, *Poetry, Language, Thought,* 1971, p. 147.

The sky is not only above, but also comes down around its edges and touches the earth. This illusory contact point where they meet is called the *horizon*.

In Gaelic, the word for horizon means "edge of sky."

The edge of the sky, the horizon, has its own unique power, which embodies the energy between earth and sky – essentially vertical. This vertical connection, the *Axis Mundi*, can also incorporate another even stronger energy. When the earth appears flat, and one is set back from an object or architecture, a new horizontal directional component appears which emphasizes the significance of the object on the land.

Objects / Architecture – on the horizon

Necropolis, Sinkiang, China

Mesa, Southwest United States

Lake Patzcuaro, Mexico

The sky is the aerial element, the unreachable, the mysterious, the unknown, the future.

The Earth Sky Connection

Celtic dolmen, Pentre Ifan, Pembroke, England

As a theoretical project, I designed a sky related roof structure over Tuzigoot Indian Ruins, Verde Valley, Arizona

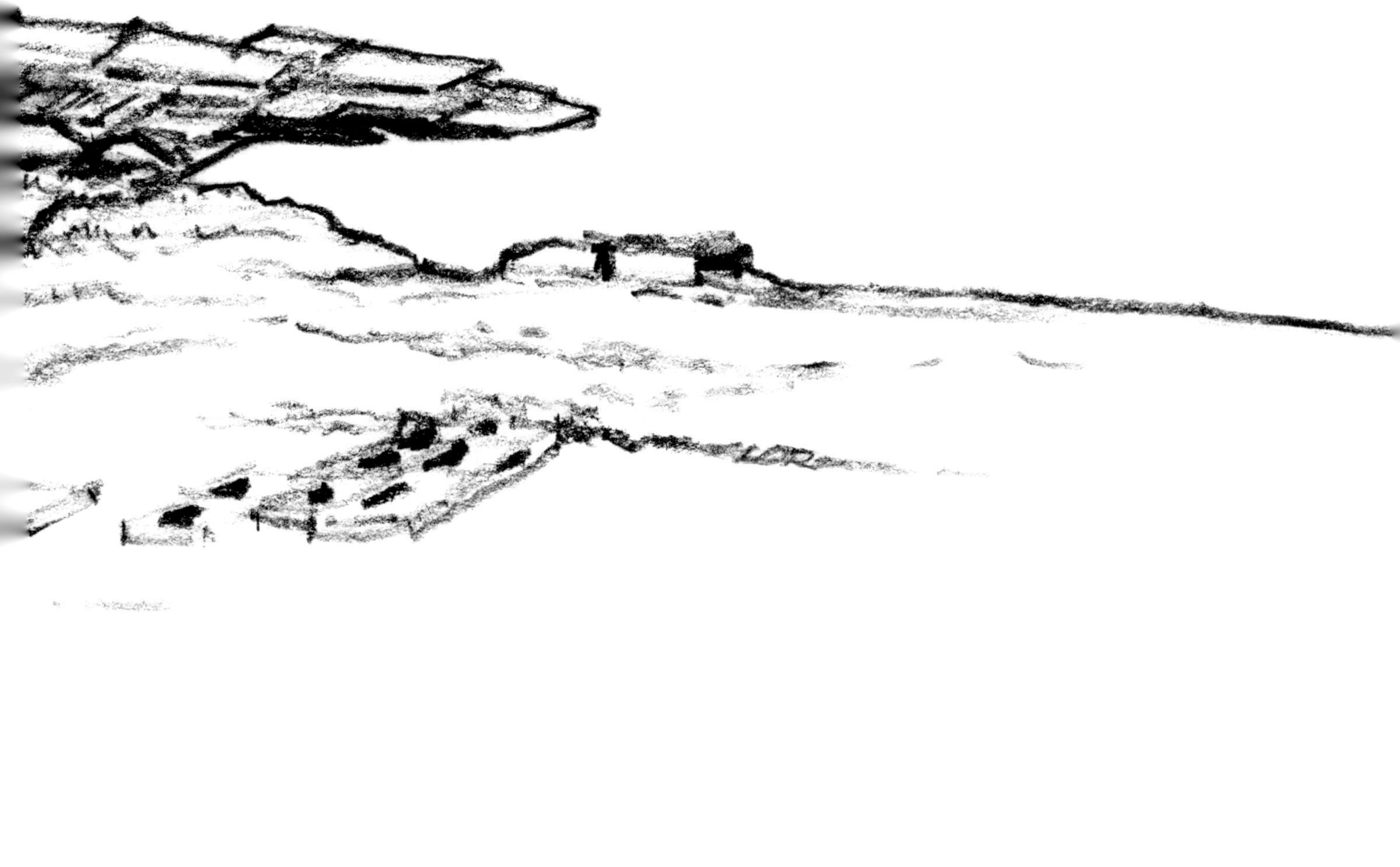

Taktshang Monastery, Bhutan

Earth and sky are two complementary elements with man between, where life, growth and evolution take place.

As a point of interest, ancient Chinese poets and philosophers depicted man *as residing in the space between heaven [sky] and earth.**

Man lives on the edge of permanence and change concurrently, a microcosm of the universe.

Change can be anchored in permanence
Permanence is symbolized by the earth
Change is symbolized by the sky
Man is connected to both
Between he lives his life
Man's past is his reference
Man's future is evolving change

This is a vision that is multileveled in its nature; it embodies not only the physical realm of earth and sky, but also the psychological, the philosophical, and consequently the symbolic. With man there is no clear line of demarcation separating these realms; they meld together into the language of the human psyche – that of images and symbols.

The premise expressed herein focuses on the timeless primordial unconscious imagery of man as he has existed, for eons, between earth and sky.

* Stephen Owen, *Readings in Chinese Literary Thought,* 1992, p. 189.

VISION

. . . . SYMBOLISM . . . .
The language of the human psyche

Man perceives symbolic meaning in life on an intuitive level. Images are more subtle, more powerful, and more dimensional than other forms of language, allowing more to be revealed.

The image is a product of human making that gives assurance to existence. Victor Christ-Janer, *Perspecta 17,* 1980, p. 10.

Imagery is unconscious representation, usually in the abstract, drawing upon experiential conditioning or our ancestral past.

Man's tendency to symbolize all his experiences and then react to the symbols as if they were actual stimuli can be traced far back in prehistory. Rene Dubos, *A God Within,* p. 60.

Symbols and Images

Ladder

Morley Baer

Skulls

Primitive Architecture

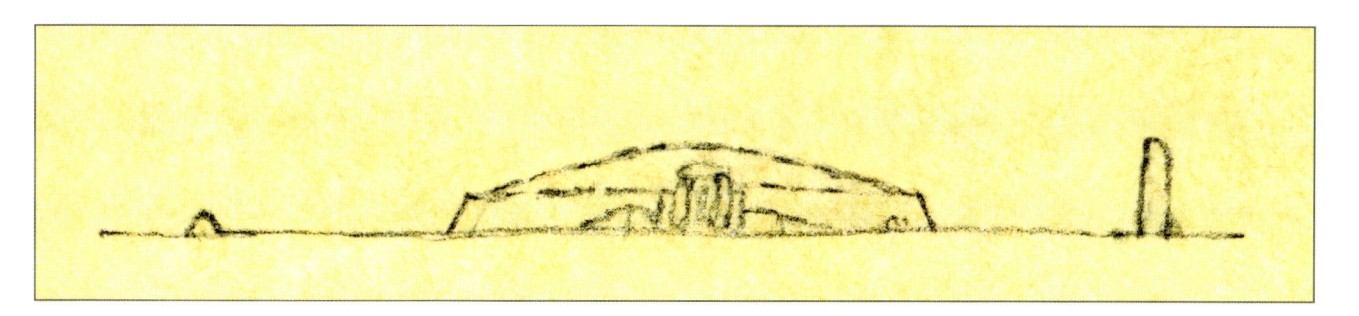

Celtic burial mound and megalith – 2000 B.C.

In death one returns to the womb of the earth, as symbolized by the entry forms of the burial mound.

The megalith is the symbolic phallus which marks a location and often accompanies a mound.

Megalith monument, Champ-Dolent, England

Dolmen entry, Bryn-Celli-Ddu, Anglesey, England

Jean Paul Gisserot

Human psyche is a realm beneath the conscious level. This is an area beyond memory and recall that may astound us with its unknown influences and powers, a psychic reservoir barely understood. Psychological studies indicate that our conscious mind is but a narrow window through which we glimpse a small part of the vast universe of the unconscious.[1] This hidden realm is the lifeblood – the source of our creativity.

There appear to be two forces at work in the unconscious. The first has to do with the absorption of information, seemingly unimportant, of things taking place on the conscious level, resurfacing later in response to various stimuli.[2] From my own earlier experience these were; the raised monumental stone, the tapered walls, and the lean-to construction. I was completely unaware of their impact, and of their future relevance.

The second force pertains to the subliminal source of our creative abilities, new and original thoughts having little or no reference to our conscious mind.[3] Guided by intuition, instinct and urges, we are able to access this vast psychic reservoir.

Both of these forces are key to the pursuit of meaningful architectural form. The former pertains to the subliminal recall of what is essential to our lineage – as part of the human continuum. The latter is where our creative powers originate and in turn are generated. The unconscious is our most essential creative tool, one we must learn to access and use.

The most direct access is to literally ask our unconscious questions such as: What does this building want to look like on the landscape? How will natural light pull one through the spaces? When writing: What am I trying to convey? The answers are often forthcoming.

It also helps to write down goals, ideas, and compile lists. When we take our ideas and put them on paper, we make them real; our psyche in turn works toward actualizing them.

**Carl Jung,
*Man and His
Symbols* (1964).**

Unconscious

1. "What we call the 'psyche' is by no means identical with our consciousness and its contents. . . . Our psyche is part of nature, and its enigma is as limitless." p. 23.

Resurfacing influences

2. "there are certain events of which we have not consciously taken note; they have remained, so to speak, below the threshold of consciousness. They have happened, but they have been absorbed subliminally, without our conscious knowledge. We can become aware of such happenings only in a moment of intuition or by a process of profound thought that leads to a later realization that they must have happened. . . ." p. 23. "when something slips out of our consciousness it does not cease to exist. . . . part of the unconscious consists of a multitude of temporarily obscured thoughts, impressions, and images that, in spite of being lost, continue to influence our conscious minds." p. 32.

Original thoughts

3. "in addition to memories from a long-distant conscious past, completely new thoughts and creative ideas can also present themselves from the unconscious – thoughts and ideas that have never been conscious before. . . . many artists, philosophers, and even scientists owe some of their best ideas to inspiration that appears suddenly from the unconscious. The ability to reach a rich vein of such material and to translate it effectively into philosophy, literature, music, or scientific discovery is one of the hallmarks of what is commonly called genius." p. 38.

Some symbols are universal, common to all peoples regardless of culture, time, and location, not to be confused with *cultural symbols* specific to heritage, tradition, and region.[4] The focus here is on those *timeless symbols* and primordial images that exist for all humans, such as earth and sky, fire, water, life, death, and sex.[5]

Symbols and images are encoded in our genes and latent in our unconscious. As driving forces in our lives, man would do well to be more consciously aware of how they influence us. This is not only the concern of philosophers and anthropologists, but something we should all be mindful of throughout life.[6]

A person, a place, a fragment of matter are the manifestations of inner forces and patterns which may remain hidden until unmasked, released, or developed by willed creative acts or fortunate circumstances. Rene Dubos, *A God Within,* p. 12.

Symbolism is manifested in all our lives in the form of visual, written, verbal, and mental imagery. The visual is expressed as art, architecture, and photography, the written as prose and poetry – as Martin Heidegger stated, "Poetry speaks in images," the verbal as conversation and storytelling, and the mental as thoughts, ideas, dreams and fantasies. Music also evokes mental images. The performing arts are a combination of many of the above.

What is proposed is the use of symbolism and imagery in creating form to which we respond on an intuitive or unconscious level. It has very little to do with our intellectual or conscious mind except to know that it is psychically familiar and right. The root of this response is timeless in nature, having relevance anywhere along the human continuum. Its origin goes back to the beginning when there was just earth and sky. With man's awakened consciousness the earth and the sky took on a particular significance. The wonder and mystery of what they embody still engender awe.

**Carl Jung,
*Man and His
Symbols* (1964).**

Cultural symbols

4 "cultural symbols . . . are those that have been used to express 'eternal truths' and are still used in many religions. They have gone through . . . conscious development, and have thus become collective images accepted by civilized societies." p. 93.

Timeless symbols

5. "'natural' symbols . . . are derived from the unconscious contents of the psyche, and they therefore represent an enormous number of variations on the essential archetypal images. In many cases they can still be traced back to their archaic roots – i.e., to the ideas and images that we meet in the most ancient records and in primitive societies." p. 93.
"'archaic remnants'. . . I call 'archetypes' or 'primordial images.'. . ." p. 67.
"They [archetypes / primordial images] are without known origin; and they reproduce themselves in any time or in any part of the world. . . ." p. 69.

Unconscious awareness

6. "Rembrandt's Philosopher with an open book (1633). The inward-looking old man provides an image of Jung's belief that each of us must explore his own unconscious. The unconscious must not be ignored; it is as natural, as limitless, and as powerful as the stars." p. 103.

Rembrandt van Rijn

Bill Schoening

63

VISION

• • • • • • • • • **PERCEPTION** • • •
The uniqueness one brings to an idea

Vision is one's *perception* of reality. Vision refers to the origination of ideas unique to one's way of seeing, thinking, and being in the world while experiencing life, observing objects, and pursuing creative endeavors. It is based primarily on unconscious intuition.

The central idea comes from vision
Vision comes from uniqueness
Uniqueness comes from experiences influenced by hereditary forces
Hereditary forces come from unconscious instincts coded into our genes

Each is the foundation for that which follows. Combined, they constitute the wholeness of a vision.

Vision can often be traced to earlier life experiences. An instance that comes to mind is the idea behind the Watts Towers in Los Angeles. When its creator, Sabatino (Sam) Rodia, was a child his mother read him the story of Marco Polo and the "land ship" he took across the deserts of central Asia to China. This vivid childhood image was a driving creative force which manifested itself in the later part of Rodia's life. The towers are not merely towers, but his interpretation of the masts of Marco Polo's land ship. Rodia picked his site because it was boat-shaped. To fulfill his vision, he worked with the only materials available to him – those from the junkyard across the tracks from his construction.

Watts Towers | Boat-shaped | Structure

Marvin Rand

As folk art, the towers are very sophisticated in their aesthetic balance and unusually inventive in their construction techniques, especially for someone with minimal artistic training. He was solely driven by his intuition and his vision.

Most of the great works of architecture and art stand out in history for the power of their creator's individual vision.

ARCHITECTURE

Jorn Utzon

Ground planes or raised platforms with roof elements floating above

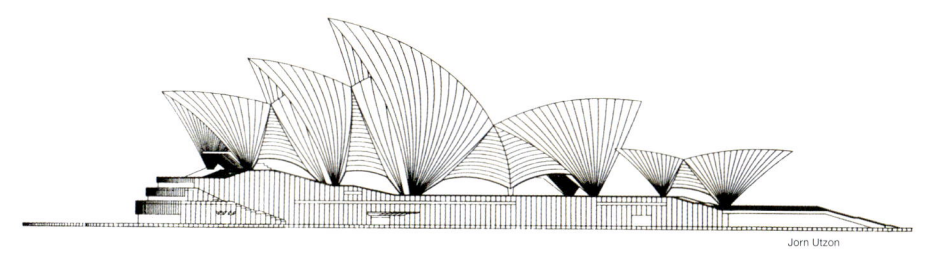

Sydney Opera House – 1957

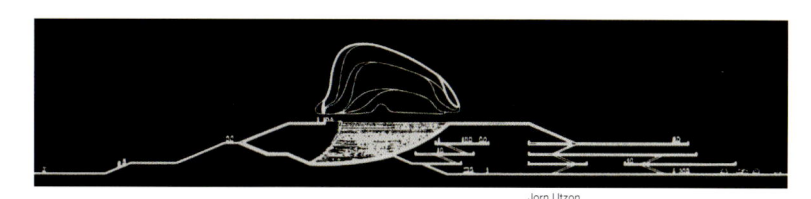

World Exhibition competition – 1959

Frank Lloyd Wright

Buildings as extensions of nature – an organic architecture

Walker Residence – 1948

Sturges Residence – 1939

Mies van der Rohe

Construction as an industrialized process

Bacardi Office Building – 1959

Seagram Building – 1958

Frank Gehry

Juxtaposition of sculptural forms

Experience Music Project, Seattle – 2000

Guggenheim Museum, Spain – 1997

ART

Michelangelo

Form as volume and mass

Head of David

Laurentian Library, Florence

Vermeer
The atmosphere of side lighting

Jan Vermeer

Jan Vermeer

Van Gogh
The world as vibrating energy

Vincent Van Gogh

Vincent Van Gogh

Christo
Objects as "revelation through concealment" (David Bourdon)

Wolfgang Volz
Pont Neuf, Paris

Michael Cullen
Reichstag, Berlin

PHOTOGRAPHY

Edward Weston

The beauty of form

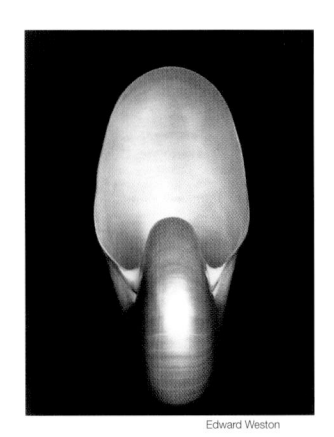

Edward Weston

Edward Weston

Edward Weston

Cartier Bresson

The decisive moment

Cartier Bresson

Cartier Bresson

Ruth Bernhard

The female nude as a cocoon or seed pod

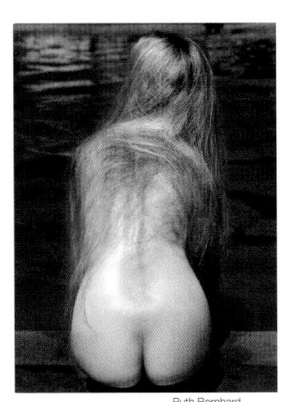

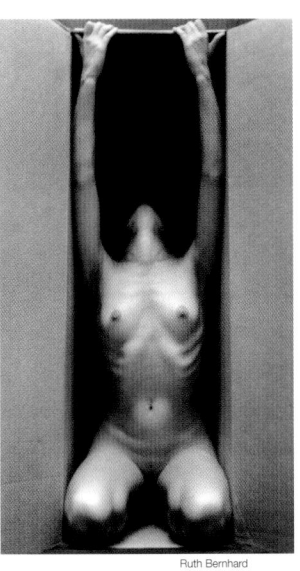

Ruth Bernhard

Ruth Bernhard

68 IDEA

Vision is akin to Michelangelo's idea that the sculpture is encased in the granite block waiting to be released by the chisel. Your vision is encased in you. It needs to be brought forth and defined.

By consciously making judgments about what is appealing to us, we define the parameters of who we are and how we view the world. Our preferences and affinities define us; our dislikes define who we are not as well as who we do not wish to be. This may seem simplistic, but it is very effective. As an exercise, go to a museum to look at art – a perfect opportunity to make judgments of likes and dislikes. By the end of the tour you will have begun to define your aesthetic personality. To further develop and record this process, put together an *aesthetic vision notebook,* to include: preferences for colors, forms, images, objects, landscapes, moods, atmospheres, and so on. The source for these samples can be magazine pictures, postcards, photographs, personal sketches or the object itself (if flat). Contrary to what one might assume, this notebook will be uniquely original. We cannot look to others for answers or comparisons since each person is comprised of a different set of variables. This exercise not only defines your general view of reality, but also gives you faith and confidence in your intuitive powers as the guiding force in pursuing your vision.

One should be looking for signs and clues as to what appeals to him. When something "clicks" with his inner being, he knows it is true and authentic. The quest is similar to being on a treasure hunt – where the hidden treasure is the inner self.

When out photographing, I am in a heightened state, my eye is searching for images of earth-connected forms and earth-sky related elements.

Even when we know generally what the main theme of our vision encompasses, we still have to explore and develop the component parts (section II – Evolution) and put them together in a comprehensible order to make our vision complete and whole (section III – Reality).

Bringing forth one's vision is a wondrous evolutionary experience in self discovery.

VISION

. . . . ARCHITECTURE
Man's symbolic restatement of nature

The earth and the sky are the dominant elements in nature, from the broad view to an intimate perspective. As both physical and psychic reality, the earth and the sky contribute to the creation of a universal imagery.

The earth, the sky, and the energy between are the elements under consideration – each one multifaceted in its scope.

EARTH

The earth, as the base element, is the natural point of departure in the creation of architecture. The first consideration is that of earth connectedness. Architecturally the objective is to visually and symbolically anchor the building to the earth so that they become one. The building grows out of the earth.[1]

The architectural expression of this vision is in essence the transition from earth to sky. The earth is expressed as surfaces or elements that rise up to embrace the sky. These elements can be manipulated to create sculptured earth forms, planes, sloping walls, or platforms. The earth makes a transition to the sky, whereas in the conventional approach the building sits on the earth as an object and is not an outgrowth or part of it.[2]

Earth – Sky connection   Conventional

Earth – Sky connection   Conventional

Earth relatedness is achieved by having a sensitivity to the spirit of that particular place, taking into consideration materials, land configurations, the physical environment, the climate, the sky, even the people and the culture, giving the architecture a visual and psychic sense of belonging to that specific location on the surface of the earth. The architect should be sensitive to these clues, as Frank Lloyd Wright was in his design of Falling Water and Charles Green in the James House.

Falling Water, Pennsylvania – 1936

James House, Carmel Highlands – 1918

The earth and the sky vary from place to place – each with characteristics unique to that locale.

Wind and swirling snow blanketing the majestic pine trees in the Sierras
Searing heat on golden sand in the Sahara
Misty fog wafting through the green forested landscape in the Scottish Highlands

The Romans referred to this unique character of a locale as "Genius Loci" or "Spirit of Place." British author Lawrence Durrell and the Swedish architectural theorist / philosopher, Christian Norberg-Schulz, wrote about the subject in detail with the respective titles: *Spirit of Place* and *Genius Loci*.

These sensitivities to the total site are the determining factors in making architecture belong – architecture in balance with place. When in balance, the earth is preserved and respected.[3]

SKY

The sky can be manifested in form or by implication. From ancient to modern man-made constructs the earth connection has been repeatedly expressed, usually with the sky implied, since the sky is always in place.

Existential philosopher Martin Heidegger in *Poetry, Language, Thought*, p. 147, makes reference to the recurrent theme "earth and sky" stating that "'on the earth' already means 'under the sky.'"

Earth expressed, sky implied – Earth connected forms piercing the sky canopy

Ancient Spanish Aqueduct, Los Remedios, Mexico

Hugh Brehme

Mont Saint Michel, France

Earth and sky expressed – Earth connected battered walls with floating roofs

The Dzong, Punakha, Bhutan

Notre-Dame-du-Haut, Ronchamp, France

Prithwish Neogy

These structures embody aesthetically pleasing and satisfying forms and images that evoke responses which have been embedded in the human psyche for eons.

ENERGY BETWEEN

The sensation of energy or tension in the zone between earth and sky enhances Vitruvius' "delight" factor (see p. 42). The energy is tangible but difficult to define. It has to do with our sense of gravity; by visually minimizing the supports one maximizes the energy.

The physical tension induced by Utzon's opposition of hovering roofs and strong earth-hugging platforms [see pages 26-27] defines the architectural space. . . . The edges of the platform and underside of the roofs mark the transition from architecture to landscape. The omission of vertical structure from Utzon's esquisses [preliminary sketches] evokes a trance-like quality of ascension and cosmic awareness. Philip Drew, *The Third Generation,*1972, p. 46.

The site of a building is a *place* that has earth beneath it and sky above it. As proposed by Christian Norbert-Schulz, this site can be thought of as a center from which to make a connection to the sky. Making this connection implies a vertical movement or energy – an *axis mundi*.

The axis mundi is . . . more than a center on earth; being a connection between the cosmic realms, it is the place where a breakthrough from one realm to the other can occur. Human life takes place on the earth under the sky, and the vertical is therefore experienced as the line of tension. Christian Norberg-Schulz, *The Concept of Dwelling,* 1985, p. 23.

Sigfried Giedion in *Space, Time and Architecture* makes reference to that – which lies at the basis of the best contemporary architecture. The radiance this emanates is generated by the respect it has given to the eternal cosmic and terrestrial conditions of a region. 1962, Introduction xxxi.

ARCHITECTURAL MAGNITUDE

An important question to consider is the role architecture should play in the visual landscape. Not every building can be a focal point. All levels of integration and emphasis are needed to achieve visual and ecological balance.

Earth connected buildings in general integrate with their environments, whether the environments are natural or man-made, they have a low visual impact on the landscape. Building with expressed sky elements may be used for emphasis or as focal points. In the end, both forms of expression can be further controlled visually depending on the use of colors, materials and forms.

**Gaston Bachelard,
The Poetics of Space
(1958).**

Earth connection

1. Bachelard, in making reference to Henri Bosco's novel, L'Antiquaire, writes "By following Henri Bosco, we shall experience a house with cosmic roots. . . . This house with cosmic roots will appear to us as a stone plant growing out of the rock up to the blue sky. . . ." p. 22.

**Kenneth Frampton,
"Intimations of Tactility,"
Architecture and Body (1988).**

Earth connection

2. "The work of Jorn Utzon exemplifies an architecture of the earth, set invariably against the 'canopy of the aerial.' It is an architecture of section predicated upon a decisive configuration to the ground, regardless of whether this profile is man-made or natural. The preferred natural forms are the mountain, the declivity, the escarpment, and the cave; their artificial equivalents are the platform, the atrium, the terrace and the cistern. These forms are occasions in which the tactile emerges into its own, for the articulation of form resides in the texture of the ground. This is an esthetic which has to be decoded by the body. In Utzon's work one invariably rises onto an acropolis, enters into an atrium, descends an escarpment, or penetrates a cave." 16. Earth.

**Martin Heidegger,
Poetry, Language, Thought (1971).**

Dwelling / Earth preservation

3. "The way in which you are and I am, the manner in which we humans are on the earth, is buan, dwelling. To be a human being means to be on the earth as a mortal. It means to dwell." p. 145
"Mortals dwell in that they save the earth." p. 148
"What we take under our care must be kept safe." p. 149
"Only if we are capable of dwelling, only then can we build." p. 158

PHILOSOPHY

WISDOM / KNOWLEDGE . . . . . .
The inherited foundations of human thought

As the intellectual platform of our existence, philosophy determines the view we have of life in the context of history. With the evolution of human consciousness, man began to comprehend himself and the world around him. His self awareness was limited by his level of understanding and mental development leading us to recognize that what we think to be truth is relative to perception. These are my perceptions.

In every era man has interpreted his universe from a different perspective. Throughout history, from primitive to present day man, each person has viewed the world and his existence from a uniquely specific intellectual vantage point. Even within the same era this varies from one geographic location to another, depending on culture, religion, race and government, as can be observed today with the clashes between Western and Eastern, Modern and Primitive worlds. We have a different perception of reality than our prehistoric ancestors. In the beginning, the world and its meaning was a mystery. Over the eons, our evolving intellectual powers and the accumulation of knowledge have brought us to a more comprehensive understanding of reality. With the advent of scientific inquiry, this process has been accelerated even more. [1,2,3]

Origins

The origin of Western thought, our way of seeing the world, began 2500 years ago with the Greeks. In principle they formulated a system of government, democracy, wherein the power comes from the people, from the bottom upward. In contrast, there are governments wherein the power comes from above in the form of dictatorships, kingdoms, and tribes; these, over the same time period, have been more prevalent in the East. Periodically, in these Eastern regions, there have been leaders who ruled with a light hand and allowed their people to excel, most notably Arabic cultures in the twelfth and thirteenth centuries, and the Chinese during parts of various dynasties.

Democracy is a form of government that lends itself to open inquiry. When the individual feels he has the power to act he is free to reinvent both himself and the things around him. Conversely, when people feel repressed and powerless, upward movement of the civilization is not sustained, particularly across the spectrum of scientific achievement.[4]

Bertrand Russell, *Wisdom of the West* **(1959).**

Nobel Prize 1951

Philosophy

1. "Science deals with known facts, philosophy with speculation." p. 6.

2. "The only way to find out what philosophy is – is to do philosophy." p. 7.

3. "The philosopher asks general questions about order in things." p. 14.

Western Civilization

4. "in some vital respects the philosophic tradition of the West differs from the speculation of the Eastern mind. There is no civilization but the Greek in which a philosophic movement goes hand in hand with a scientific tradition. It is this that gives the Greek enterprise its peculiar scope: it is this dual tradition that has shaped the civilization of the West." p. 310.

The early Greek democratic form of government was interrupted and suppressed for over 1800 years, starting with the rise of the Roman Empire and following in the period after its collapse. This latter era is generally referred to as the "dark ages," a time when the power came from above. It was not until the Renaissance that Da Vinci, Michelangelo, Galileo and others challenged the establishment with their individuality and inventiveness – bringing about the birth of a new age.

By the eighteenth century, philosophic, scientific, and aesthetic inquiry became accessible to all who could read – the educated class. The first encyclopedia of accumulated knowledge was published. These developments led to a movement known as the *Enlightenment,* characterized by an inventive spirit, a belief in progress and an optimistic view of the world. This period was referred to as *the age of reason*, a time of upheaval and revolution on all fronts: government, industry, science, philosophy, literature, art and music. Once again people felt they had the power to be in control of their lives. The *age of reason* was the beginning of the present day intellectual perspective we, in the West, have of the world and of ourselves. Numerous movements in the arts and sciences ensued.

Although most people embraced the *Enlightenment* movement, some rejected it as dehumanizing and against the natural order of things, placing more faith in science and technology and less in intuition. These concerns led to the movements known as *irrationalism*, *emotionalism* and later, *romanticism*, the most popular countermovement of the nineteenth century. The prime force of *romanticism* as a philosophy was that of man returning to nature and a belief that nature was more powerful than intellect alone and that feelings and intuition were more important than logic.[5]

Rene Dubos stated, Truth is not just intellectual, but requires the whole being.

As man moved into the twentieth century, *romanticism* evolved into *relativism*, and was soon followed by *existentialism*, the philosophy that has the most relevance to our present age. It encompasses a more complete view of life – the positive side as well as the shadow side.[6]

At some point each of us must find our own way, form our own philosophy from endless choices and directions. We are faced with many possibilities in life.[7] In most instances, if we take action and move forward, answers present themselves – answers that are reflective of our individuality. We must explore inward to find our course. Ultimately we take only what is relevant to us, what makes sense to our way of thinking. Making choices requires us to have, among other things, the indispensable qualities of character, integrity, and honesty.

Rene Dubos,　　　　　　Pulitzer Prize 1969
So Human an Animal
(1968).

Enlightenment　　　　5. "Beginning with the Enlightenment in the eighteenth century, scientific rationalism increasingly gained ground as the unifying faith of mankind. During the past few decades, however, it too has begun to lose its force because its intellectual and practical limitations are becoming evident." p. 182.

Fredrick Nietzsche

Relativism　　　　　　6. "Truth has never yet hung on the arm of an absolute."

Jean Paul Sartre

Existentialism　　　　7. "Man first of all exists, encounters himself, surges up in the world – and defines himself afterward."

PHILOSOPHY

. . . . . LIFE / MEANING . . . . . .
Life with purpose has meaning

Purpose is at the heart of our existence. It is the self in us that wants to be realized. Purpose in life requires engaging our uniqueness. We commit to a continual process of interior exploration rather than to arrive at a finite answer. With this pursuit we move deeper into our essential self. [1]

This idea of purpose may seem far afield from architecture, but it could not be more relevant. Purpose is the core reason to pursue anything, something we feel we must do, compelled by an inner drive. In my life, this force is architecture, which allows me to be creative on many levels.

We continually explore the parameters of our essence, moving closer and closer to our center. Finding direction and purpose is an internal process, not a random search in the external world. This search has many names: *calling, path, destiny*. [2] If we focus our awareness, the clues lie within. It is a matter of asking ourselves the appropriate questions and having faith in our intuition. [3]

There are no definitive answers regarding what constitutes purpose and meaning in life. In fact, there are multiple purposes related to the various aspects of one's life, ranging from the personal, the interpersonal, the environmental, and on to the cosmic, rippling in ever widening circles from the self to the universe.

Two psychologists / philosophers who offer intriguing answers, although with different perspectives, are Viktor Frankl and Abraham Maslow. Frankl emphasizes self-transcendence, moving beyond the self by committing to one's unique task as it relates to his life and circumstances. Maslow advocates self-actualization by bringing forth the self in creative acts, which in turn leads to self-transcendence. These two thinkers are similar in their views; in the end, it is a matter for each individual to find his own philosophical direction.

Each person must seek his unique purpose, which can be anything, depending on what freedoms, opportunities and limitations his life affords. If a man finds himself in restrictive circumstances, such as a prison camp or war, as Frankl experienced, he can still have purpose. It may be as basic as to stay alive, to merely survive for the ones he

Ray Stannard Baker as David Grayson, *Great Possessions* **(1917).**

Pulitzer Prize 1940

Life / Meaning

0. "I do not know, truly, what we are here for upon this wonderful and beautiful earth, this incalculably interesting earth, unless it is to crowd into a few short years – when all is said, terribly short years! - every possible fine experience and adventure: unless it is to live our lives to the uttermost: unless it is to seize upon every fresh impression, develop every latent capacity: to grow as much as ever we have it in our power to grow. What else can there be? If there is no life beyond this one, we have lived here to the uttermost. We've had what we've had! But if there is more life, and still more life, beyond this one, and above and under this one, and around and through this one, we shall be well prepared for that, whatever it may be." p. 206.

Viktor E. Frankl, *Man's Search for Meaning* **(1946/1984).**

Uniqueness

1. "Uniqueness and singleness which distinguishes each individual and gives a meaning to his existence has a bearing on creative work as much as it does on human love." p. 87.

Calling

2. "One should not search for an abstract meaning of life. Everyone has his own specific vocation or mission in life; everyone must carry out a concrete assignment that demands fulfillment." p. 113.

Nicola Abbagnano, *Critical Existentialism* **(1969).**

Self realization

3. "The world does look like a totality of meaningless events, a kaleidoscopic spectacle deprived of consistency and gravity to the man who has not chosen his task - to the man who has not found himself. But to the man who is deeply committed to self-realization, the world appears as an integrated unity which must furnish the indispensable instruments of realization. . . ." pp. 22-23.

loves and who love him; or it may be to fulfill a personal goal in the future, perhaps one of creativity and self realization. Even during the passive or respite periods of our lives, our purpose can be to enjoy nature, beauty, art and music. [4]

Purpose carries us through all the various aspects of life. It becomes the central core of our being, not to be deterred or distracted by the highs of joy, excitement and happiness or by the lows of pain, suffering and disappointment. [5]

Meaning in life has to do with fulfillment in our endeavors. It is what feels intuitively right – to be on course with our inner self. This can be achieved with love, passion, and commitment to a chosen purpose.

A person need have only one good idea to pursue for a lifetime, an idea that comes from within. It can be simple or sophisticated. Watts Towers is a case in point, a man with a simple idea and intense purpose.

Renowned Austrian sculptor and artist Walter Pichler said, I have been exploring one idea my whole life.

Life presents us with many challenges; in meeting them, *attitude is everything*. We must be positive and optimize the circumstances of each situation. Having a positive attitude does not imply that life does not have hardships and suffering, but rather, hardships and suffering are essential components for making the life experience complete. [6, 7]

One can have everything and have nothing

One can have nothing and have everything

**Viktor E. Frankl,
*Man's Search for
Meaning* (1946/1984)**

Attitude

4. "everything can be taken from a man but one thing: the last of the human freedoms – to choose one's attitude in any given set of circumstances, to choose one's own way." p. 75.

Fredrick Nietzsche

Suffering

5. "He who has a why to live for can bear with almost any how."

**Viktor E. Frankl,
*Man's Search for
Meaning* (1946/1984).**

Suffering

6. "We must never forget that we may also find meaning in life even when confronted with a hopeless situation, when facing a fate that cannot be changed. For what then matters is to bear witness to the uniquely human potential at its best, which is to transform a personal tragedy into a triumph, to turn one's predicament into a human achievement." p. 116.
"suffering ceases to be suffering at the moment it finds a meaning . . . man's main concern is not to gain pleasure or to avoid pain but rather to see a meaning in his life." p. 117.

**Rene Dubos,
So Human an Animal
(1968).**

Struggle

7. "To live is to struggle. A successful life is not one without ordeals, failures, and tragedies, but one during which the person has made an adequate number of effective responses to the constant challenges of his physical and social environment." pp. 161-162.

PHILOSOPHY

■ ■ ■ ■ ■ ■ ■ ■ ■ ■ **EXISTENCE**

Only a segment of time

If we could find the answers to how the universe works – what would it do for us? Would it give us peace? Would all the elements of life fit together? Nothing would change except our view of it. One still has only a segment of time to exist. Within this limited span we must find our own peace, security, fulfillment, beauty and love, all in the context of some risk. Life guarantees us nothing except death. [1, 2]

There are occasional periods during this segment of time when we experience a feeling of spiritual elation, a kind of deep expanding fulfillment, when we are touched by the overwhelming beauty of nature, of love, of a fine meal. A similar elation accompanies the joy of self realization found in such acts as creating art, music, architecture, or of making a scientific discovery. [3]

The shadow side of our existence should also be considered.[4] With our present way of life jeopardized by the degradation of the environment and the threat of destruction from radical extremists, there has been a tendency for man to lose his sense of history and continuity, sometimes to the extent of questioning the point of existence.

Even with the possible threat of civilization / mankind coming to an end, it does not mean we cannot attain psychological peace in the present. What we have is existential reality. That is all we have ever had and in all probability will ever have. We live or exist, from moment to moment until we do not. Life can end at any time without warning long before civilization / humankind comes to an end. It is pointless to live under a cloud of fear and anxiety. To date *existentialism* is the philosophy that best encompasses the multiple facets of life. [5] The positive and the negative have been considered with an openness for any eventuality. [6] We have arrived at this point through many evolving perspectives of ourselves.

There are as many definitions of *existentialism* as there are thinkers and philosophers. We all see existence from a different point of view. Historically the French existentialists, Jean Paul Sartre and Albert Camus, are sometimes thought to pursue the negative; the Italians, Antonio Aliotta and Nicola Abbagnano, the positive: and the Germans, George Hegel and Martin Heidegger, the more centrum perspective of existence, weighted slightly toward the positive. Of all the existential philosophers, Heidegger in my view is

Nicola Abbagnano,
Critical Existentialism
(1969).

Possibilities

1. "Man, it is true, is constituted only by possibilities and has nothing more solid nor stable to hold onto." p. 51

Risk / Faith

2. "Nothing can offer him an infallible guarantee: error is possible and everything is at his own risk. . . . reasonable faith is all that can constitute his dignity and his value as a man." p. 5

William Barrett,
Irrational Man
(1958).

Philosophy

3. "'Know Thyself' is the command Socrates issued to philosophers at the beginning (or very close to it) of all western philosophy. . . ." p. 4.

Existentialism

4. "Existential philosophy . . . attempts to grasp the image of the whole man, even where this involves bringing to consciousness all that is dark and questionable in his existence." p. 22

5. "In his Man in the Modern Age Karl Jaspers . . . sees the historical meaning of existential philosophy as a struggle to awaken in the individual the possibilities of an authentic and genuine life, in the face of the great modern drift toward a standardized mass society." p. 32.

Nicola Abbagnano,
Critical Existentialism
(1969).

Positive Existentialism

6. "A positive existentialism must satisfy two requirements: it must (1) maintain a notion of possibility in its twofold positive and negative aspects . . . (2) furnish a criterion, not infallible surely, but valid in the choice of existential possibilities." p. 48.

the most balanced and most poetic, and one of the few who ventured into the realm of architecture.

As man becomes more abstract in his thinking, [7, 8] we question whether he is losing his connection to nature and the earth. However, his abstraction or detachment is an illusion. When observing ugliness, such as urban blight, he sees it as external to himself, as he also does with the beauty in nature. In the broad sense the ugliness and the beauty are one with us, and we are one with them. They are an integral part of our existence. It is not a matter of reconnecting to nature and the earth; we are already connected, whether we acknowledge it or not. When we are stewards to the earth, we are also stewards to ourselves.

Dubos stated, We are of the earth and must protect it.

Through philosophy we are able to step back and objectively observe man with a clearer understanding of what he is doing and where he is headed.

Over time one becomes aware that most things are interconnected. This vision particularly applies to the ideas presented herein.

Our uniqueness – derived from the origin of our way of thinking

Overview of various realms – from the general to the specific

Bringing together of the individual and the world

Finding purpose and meaning in life with a central idea

Intellectual framework – philosophy – that gives relevance

Our era as it relates to man's past and his future

Exploration of these ideas broadly and specifically

Forward movement in making an idea a reality

Being mindful of the important attributes for actualization

Living with faith, intuition, commitment and wholeness

William Barrett,
Irrational Man
(1958).

Abstract Existence

7. "Collectively man, whether communist or capitalist, is still only an abstract fragment of man. We are so used to the fact that we forget it or fail to perceive that the man of present day lives on a level of abstraction altogether beyond the man of the past." p. 30.

8. "Every step forward in mechanical technique is a step in the direction of abstraction." p. 31.

ACTUALIZATION

FAITH . INTUITION . COMMITMENT .
Fulfillment requires having the courage to act

In the beginning our direction is unclear, we are carried along with the flow of *faith* and *intuition*.

Faith is quietly believing in yourself
Becoming comfortable with your intuition
Because of your uniqueness
Only you understand your vision
You cannot look to others
You are your only true critic
This demands character
Being truthful with yourself

Faith is the forward movement that allows you to proceed in finding your purpose.

The more you believe in your purpose
The more you believe in yourself
The more faith you have in your intuition
The easier things flow

All creative work involves some form of faith and intuition – faith that you can make things happen and intuition to guide you through to the desired end. Faith and intuition work together in everything you do.

When you have faith, your psyche makes a shift
Your unconscious acts to enhance your conscious mind

Faith involves belief, trust, and confidence in yourself.

Confidence is a belief in your ability to succeed at something
Confidence is a form of faith
Believing you will achieve your goals
That you will find your way on the various journeys of life

In the creative process the most difficult challenge is to see the undefined vision or image of an idea in your mind, and then proceed with the belief that you can make the idea a reality. Most times the creative gap can be bridged in seconds, other times it may take years, even decades. If one maintains an open mind to the process, positive results are almost always forthcoming.

When it happens in seconds, *intuition* is the major vehicle – an unconscious perception wherein the mind comprehends the variables and delivers the solution instantaneously.

An idea that is broader in scope usually requires a longer time to digest. It is more in the realm of realization reinforced with a current of intuition, which reveals itself days, months, or years after exposure to significant data. Ten years later you think, "Aha! I now know what the professor meant when he said, 'great art is good at any distance.'" Or it can evolve as a process, when data is collected over time, piece by piece, shifting and readjusting (as exemplified in the upcoming Evolution section of this book), eventually surfacing to conscious awareness.

Have faith in yourself
Follow the inner voice
That tells you what feels right
Trust your intuition
Intuition encompasses the forces
And experiences that make you unique
Intuition reflects your being

Commitment is a pledge to oneself to accomplish something in the future. It is a state of being impelled to a cause or purpose. Commitment requires the courage to persist in a pursuit, to stay with something and not let the mind be diverted. If one gives in to endless distractions, life can be unfulfilled. Distractions are interruptions to the flow, as opposed to respites for pleasure, adventure or to refresh the spirit.

Early in 1990 I was in my favorite bookstore in Berkeley, California, thumbing through back issues of National Geographic magazine. In a 1922 issue I found photos of unusual stone towers located in the Caucasian mountains in southern Russia. They were very similar to the towers in San Gimignano, Italy, but even older – going back to the 7th and 8th century. At that moment I knew I was going to find my way there. I had *faith* that I would do it. I started making plans to take a four to five month trip across Europe through Yugoslavia, Greece, Bulgaria, Turkey and on into Russia. Shortly thereafter, in the process of gathering material for the trip, I came across an article in the San Francisco Chronicle about a young architect who had restored a traditional Turkish house in Amasya. It was now a pension. I tucked the article away in my travel notebook.

Eight weeks later, the trip was launched from Holland, where I purchased a thirteen year old VW camper.

Before leaving the United States, I contacted the Russian embassy (then the Soviet Union) in San Francisco to obtain permission to enter Georgia at the Turkish border with my camper. The answer was a definite "No." "No cars allowed through that border." "Not on good terms with Turkey," followed by remarks about "not since the 1920s." Later, when I arrived in Turkey, I went to the Russian embassy in Ankara. Again I was given the same scenario. Still I proceeded east, stopping first to stay at the pension in Amasya. It was beautifully restored, which prompted me to stay for a few days and photograph it in some detail. In talking with the owner, I told him of my plan to go to the top of the Caucasian mountains in Russia and the difficulties I was encountering. He informed me that he had a brother-in-law in Trabzon, a city on the Black Sea, who was just starting to run tours to Russia. He provided his brother-in-law's address and phone number, but warned that he was somewhat grumpy.

After I found his back-alley tourist office, the brother-in-law instructed me to return in a week; meanwhile he would send a telegram to Moscow. Upon returning, there had been no response from Russia. His plan now was to accompany me to the border on the Black Sea and talk our way through. He would meet me on the next Tuesday at the checkpoint at 11:00 am. I agreed. As I waited at the designated spot, he did not show at 11:00, nor 12:00, nor 1:00. I planned to leave at 2:00. Three minutes to the hour, he pulled up, jumped into my camper and said "forward." At the border gate the guards stated, "no vehicles." For the next half hour we argued with them to let us through, to no avail. Suddenly, in the background, we heard the sound of a teletype machine. One guard responded and returned with his mouth open and holding a piece of paper giving us permission to pass – the answer to my Turkish companion's telegram. His tardiness had allowed the timing to fall exactly into place. The gate went up and we drove through into Georgia. In my life this is one lesson I have learned; *when things do not go as planned, keep moving forward and flow with the circumstances.*

I delivered my companion to the Grand Hotel in Batumi, a 19th century copy of Versailles and its gardens, and then proceeded on my way. I was headed for Zugdidi, the point where the road would turn east into the Caucasian Mountains. En route I picked up a hitchhiker, something I never do. His English was limited, but we were able to communicate. With the gasoline gauge going down, I asked him the location of the nearest gas station. "Gas station? No gas now, truck comes once a month" he said. I then knew one reason why the government did not want foreign vehicles in the country. My passenger informed me he knew of a "black market" gas station 30 miles in the opposite direction, so off we went. After some tough negotiations with three tall

Stalinesque characters, I was on course again with a full tank. On arriving in Zugdidi, the road to the mountains was nowhere to be found. After cruising around the town square, I found a man who offered to lead me there, saying that to find it on my own would be impossible. As it turned out, the road was no more than an alley between two old apartment buildings. It looked dubious to me. He assured me that by following the pavement between the buildings it would come to an open meadow and a dirt road. A hundred miles on that road would take me to my destination.

Once on my way a few miles, I again picked up a hitchhiker, this time a stocky woman with a slight mustache. After looking at my map, she accompanied me for twenty miles to a bridge at which she got out, indicating I should cross over it and then turn right. The wood planking on the bridge was spotty at best. Below was a deep ravine. She kept nodding to go ahead. With much faith, I drove across and proceeded up the mountain. As the road ascended it became a shelf on the face of a steeply sloping cliff. At one point, what looked to be a river of water was coursing down the rock face and eroding the road base, creating a depression approximately 18 inches deep. The depression was full of running water with a sharp drop-off on the near side and a gradual slope on the opposite edge. The rear engine VW camper would not clear that abrupt drop. I thought to myself, "I did not come this far to be stopped now." I looked around and saw appropriately sized flat rocks that would allow me to build two ramps into the water. Driving down the ramps was somewhat risky; they might collapse, causing the camper to topple over the cliff. Since the driver's side was facing the upslope, I left the door open – in the event I might have to jump out. It then crossed my mind, "what am I going to do on the trip back, when the driver's side is facing the drop-off?" As it turned out, on my return the runoff had dried up and the road had been adequately repaired.

As I approached the small town at the top of the mountain, I was surrounded by beautiful ancient stone towers scattered over the landscape. Here they were, almost half way around the world. I had reached my goal.

Within a short time after pulling up to the diminutive town square, I was greeted by a small group of community elders, who reacted to my camper as if it had just landed from outer space. They looked under it, asking how I had gotten up there without four-wheel drive. Soon there was a crowd of fifty or so people gathered, which included the local high school English teacher. She claimed I was the only English speaking person she had ever spoken to. Her English was quite good; everything she said was understandable. No one had ever seen a camper of this or any other kind before. There were many questions followed by demonstrations of the various camper components. Some said it had more conveniences than their own homes.

I was told that an American, who was with National Geographic, came up there in the early twenties to photograph the towers. I then proceeded to show them the photos I thought were his, and indicated I would like to go to those same locations. At that point the town fathers assigned me a guide named "Rocci." Rocci was 6'- 3" tall and had an English vocabulary of about 100 words. He would say, "Louis – come here – sit down – eat," in a deep voice. And the story goes on and on.

The experiences I had on the journey will stay with me for a lifetime. Without *faith, intuition, and commitment* I would never have found my way to that unusual, dramatic and remote place. These are the same motivating forces that have allowed me to start this book and follow it through to completion.

Village of Mestia, Western Caucasus, Russia

Typical Bridge

Villages in the Caucasus, Russia

ACTUALIZATION

■ ■ ■ ■ ■ ■ ■ ■ ■ ■ **WHOLENESS**
Recognizing the interconnectedness of all things

In its simplest terms, *wholeness* can be defined as a *balanced system*, or put more poetically, *harmonious equilibrium*, where the parts, entities, elements and components relate to one another and the whole in a supportive and reinforcing manner.

[A]ll living things are interwoven each with the other; the tie is sacred, and nothing, or next to nothing, is alien to aught else. Marcus Aurelius, *Meditations*, 167-180 A.D.

The system can be anything from:

A molecule	A building
A plant	A city
A human body	A natural environment
A car	To the universe

Each entity is part of a larger system, and made up of smaller systems, microcosms, complete and capable of functioning as a unit.

Wholeness exists on all levels and on all scales. This is most evident in nature which embodies wholeness in a highly evolved form. The flower is whole in itself, yet is part of the meadow, which is part of the landscape, which is part of the ecosystem and so on to the solar system and beyond.

This leads one to the idea of the interconnectedness of all things and how they influence and relate to one another. I find, when designing architecture, I am always looking for connections from one system or realm to another, even when there is no apparent similarity. In many cases, ideas and/or principles can be cross-pollinated to have a significant influence on the final outcome.

There are other levels of interconnectedness to be aware of on multiple scales. By adding or subtracting something from a *field* the whole field changes. Visually, this is evident in the composition of elements and the spaces between them when one is striving for symmetrical or asymmetrical equilibrium – wholeness. This *field* concept can apply to anything at any level, in the case of architecture, from the concept to the particulars, the execution and finally, to the finished product.

The nature of wholeness is such that we strive for the ideal. Since we can never achieve absolute perfection, the objective is to come as close as possible.

A dictionary defines wholeness as: "perfect – perfect implies the soundness and the excellence of every part, element, or quality of a thing – frequently as an unattainable or theoretical state. *Whole* suggests a completeness or perfection of a thing in its entirety . . . that nothing has been omitted or left out, everything has been considered."

When creating or designing, one works from the inside out and from the outside in concurrently (as further covered on pp. 201-204). This process is related to wholeness, where the objective is to balance the inner and outer forces at work on a system. This principle of harmonious equilibrium applies to anything one creates – whether art, music, architecture, or a mechanical device.

There is a tipping point, where, if the system is sufficiently lacking wholeness, it will break down. This occurs when the parts are working against one another, as with an engine that is overheated and seizes, or an ecosystem that is polluted beyond recovery, or a human body that has consumed unhealthy foods leading to illness and death. This can happen visually, functionally, technically or physically, on any level or combination of levels. One could conclude that if enough of the universe were out of balance, it would disintegrate.

In architecture, wholeness embodies all of the elements under consideration:

Vision	Site
Concept	Orientation
Form	Climate
Function	Materials
Construction	Context
Budget	Natural environment

Achieving wholeness in creativity involves striving for the essential character or constitution of a thing, in the case of architecture, to establish its spirit – to balance all the variables. It is important at the beginning of any creative endeavor to have in mind the concept of the *whole* as the key consideration in all that follows.

We are aware of and aim for wholeness so as to optimize our life and the world we inhabit.

THE EVOLUTION

Summoning forth that
which is within and making
it real in fragment and part

Guided by intuition and an inner
drive toward a vision emerging

Seeking a balance of forces in
search of essence

DISCOVERY

EARLY EXPRESSIONS . . . .
Indicators of a future vision

SCHOOL DESIGNS

My preference was for buildings close to the earth, simple in expression and connected to nature, especially to the movement of the sun and the play of light on form. These school designs were executed in a spontaneous, intuitive manner without a conscious awareness of the vision of earth and sky, which surfaced later.

GOLF CLUBHOUSE   Third Year   Spring, 1963

Conceptual studies

Site Plan

Simple geometric elements conforming to the land
Power in simplicity

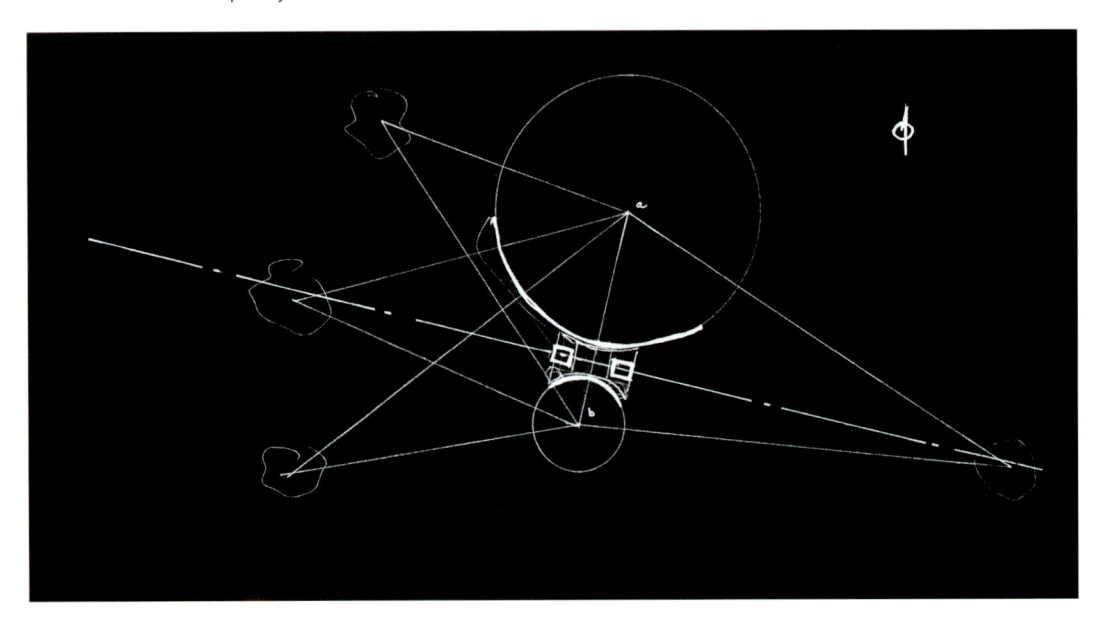

Walls low to the ground – earth connected

Oriented to the south – play of sun on forms

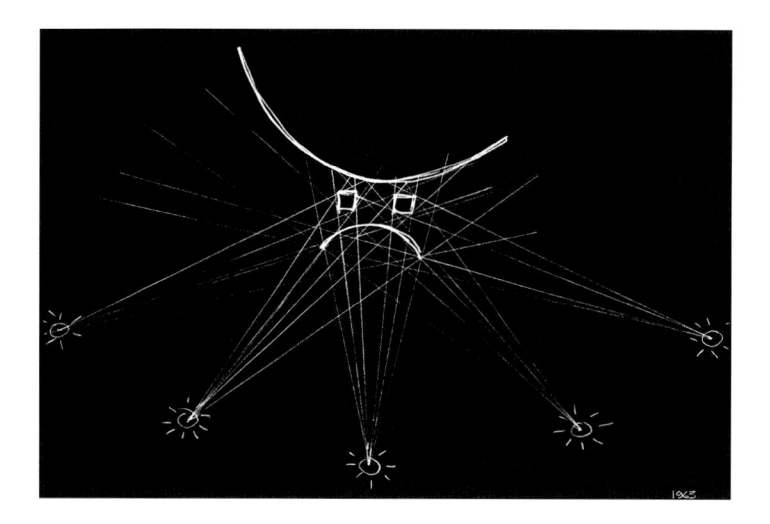

Final elevation

Floating sky related roof – low over tapering walls

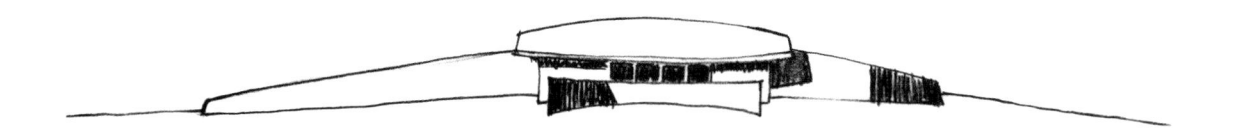

ISLAND CULTURAL INSTITUTE   Fifth Year   Fall, 1964

Site Plan

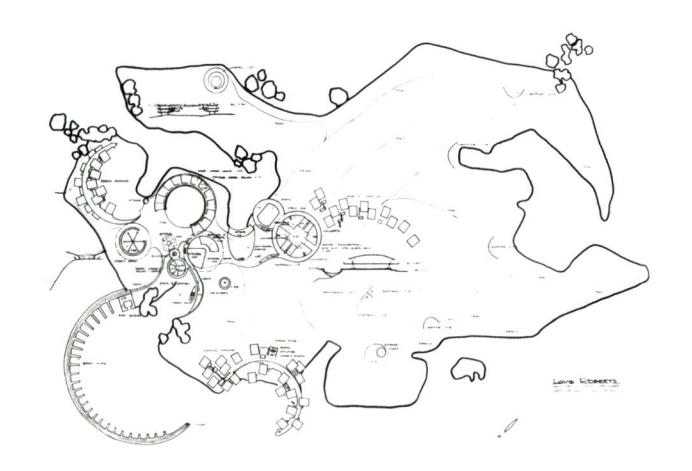

Circular and semicircular forms reflective of the island's shoreline
Buildings low and integrated into the landscape

Floating roof forms over selective circular elements
On the one hand, the unity of form, on the other, testing the limits of the circle

Multi-denominational Chapel section

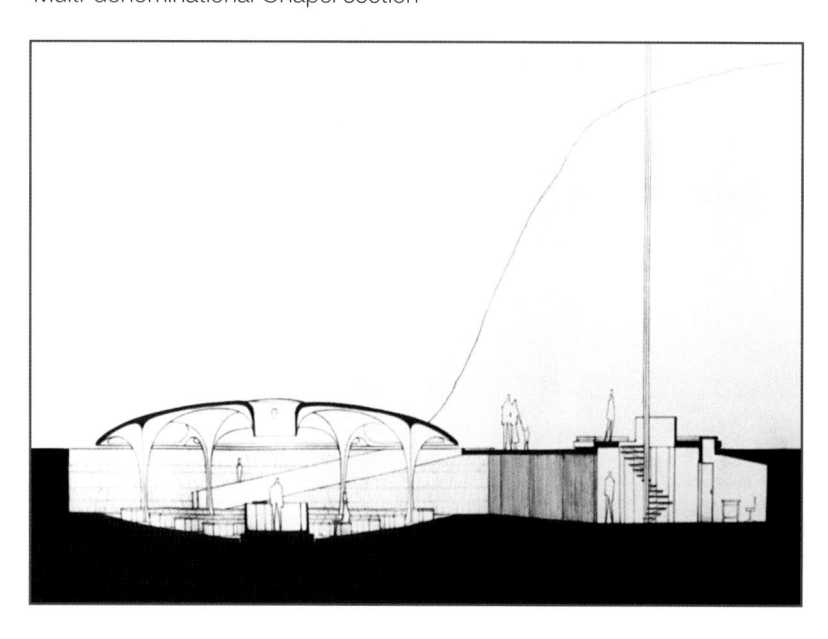

RAILROAD TERMINAL   Thesis Design Award   Spring, 1965
Champaign, Illinois

Design Concept

A building as a linear expression of movement – stepping up the raised track platform – covering the natural flow of pedestrians

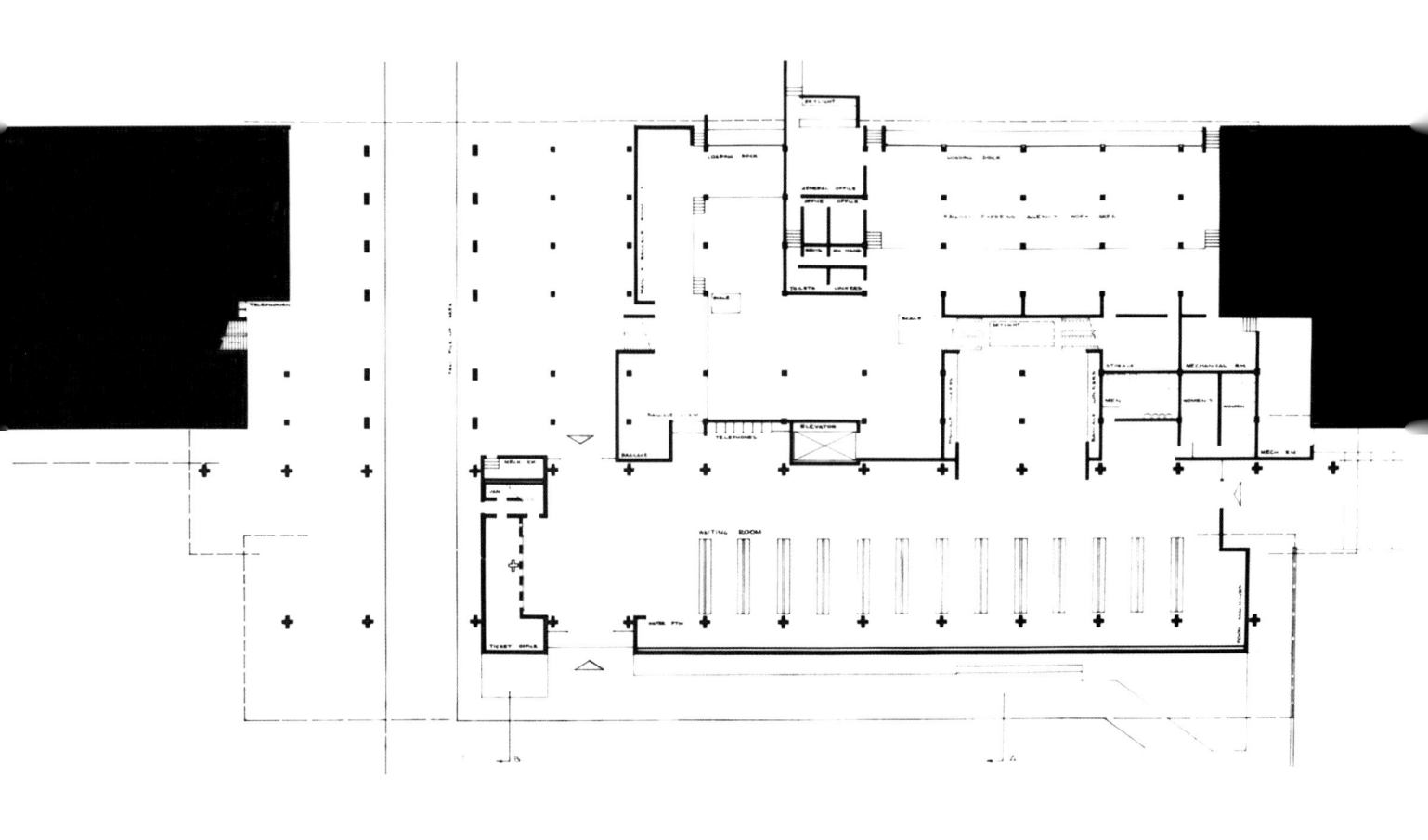

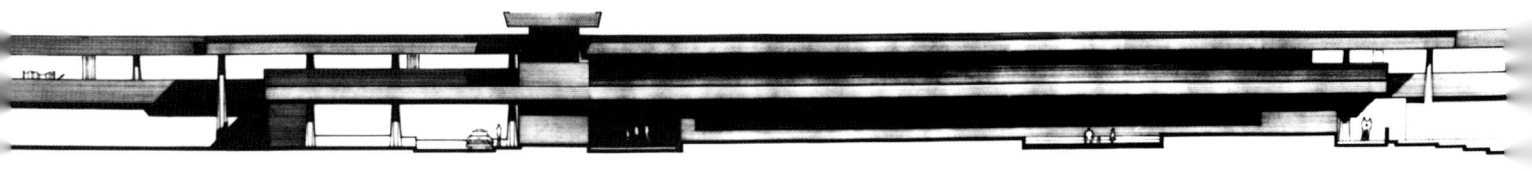

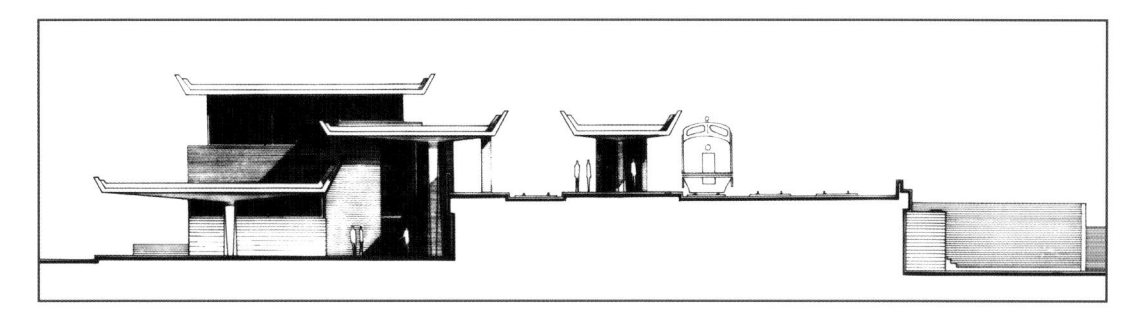

Multiple floating roof elements over contoured land form

Separate passengers from Railway Express facilities – opposite sides of platform

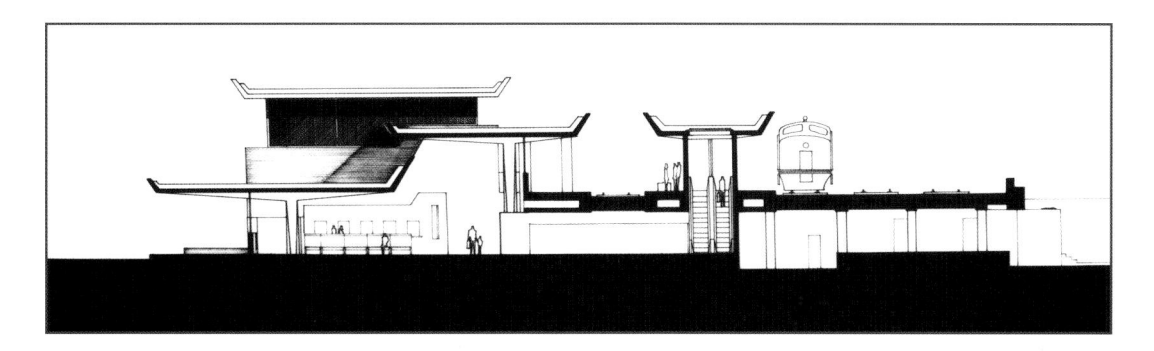

COMMUNICATION CENTER / FALLOUT SHELTER   Fall, 1965
Masters Program

Concept Sketches

A floating roof tower element over a building expressed as expanding integrated ribbed land forms – in essence earth and sky

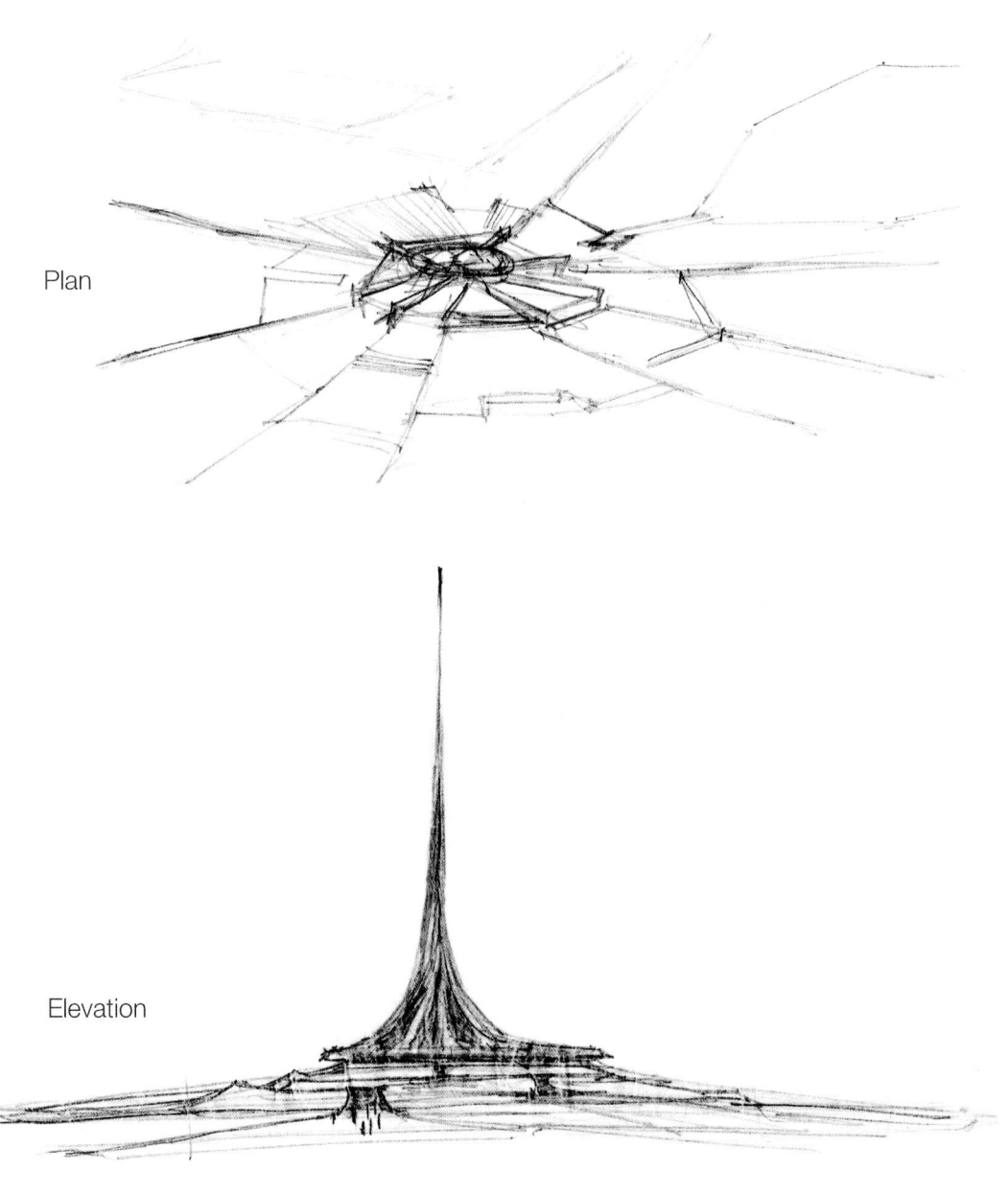

Plan

Elevation

OFFICE APPRENTICE DESIGN

COUNTY GOVERNMENT CENTER
Bel Air, Maryland

Spring, 1968

The buildings, plaza and parking are designed and configured to conform to the natural contours of the land. The lower site is landscaped to visually shield parking and allow for overviews of the surrounding unspoiled terrain.

An expression of earth connectedness

Site Plan

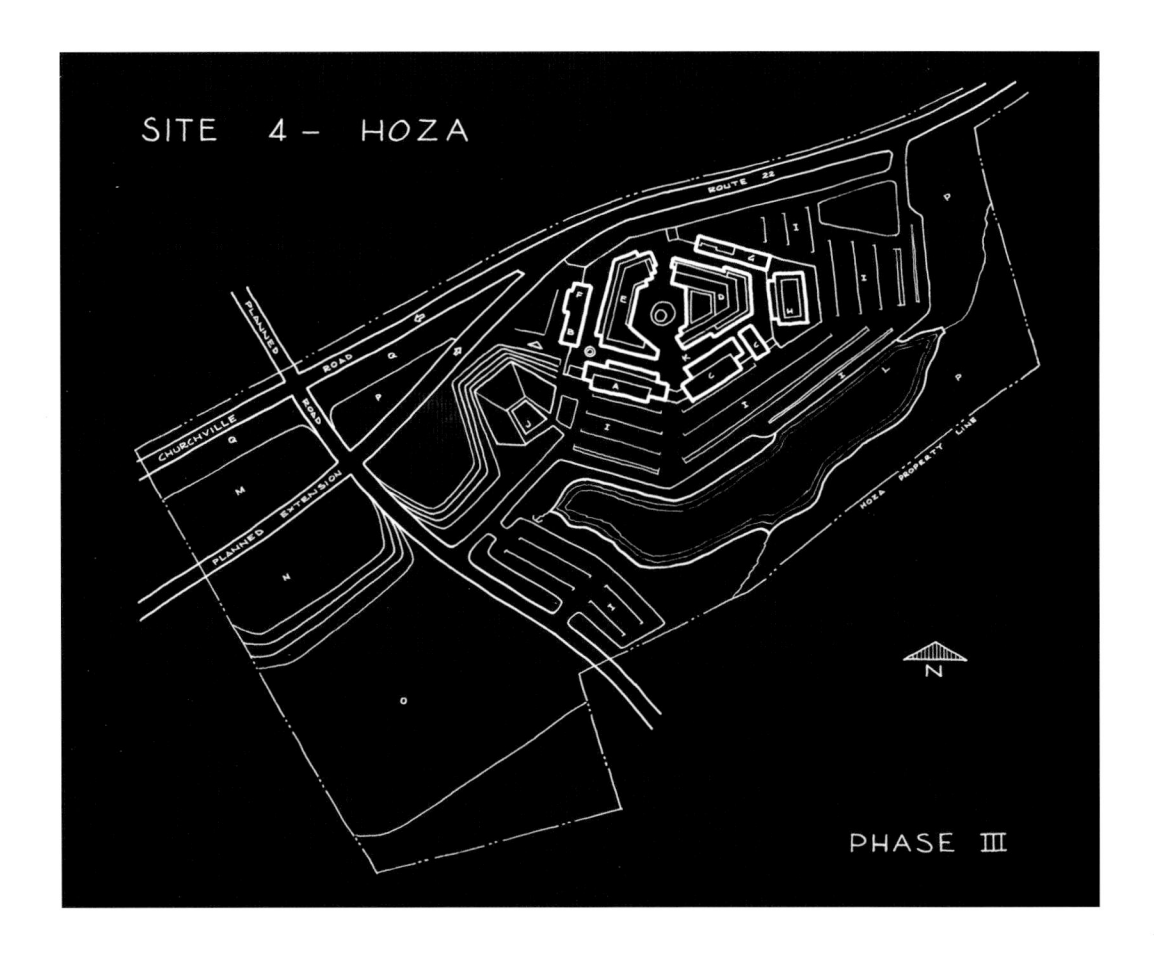

DISCOVERY

▪ ▪ ▪ ▪ ▪ GATHERING FRAGMENTS
Responding to one's intuition

**These are 3 x 5 index cards
– see page 198 for details**

Earth connected stone park building resembling the base of a tree trunk

Stone wing walls tieing the barn shed to the land contours

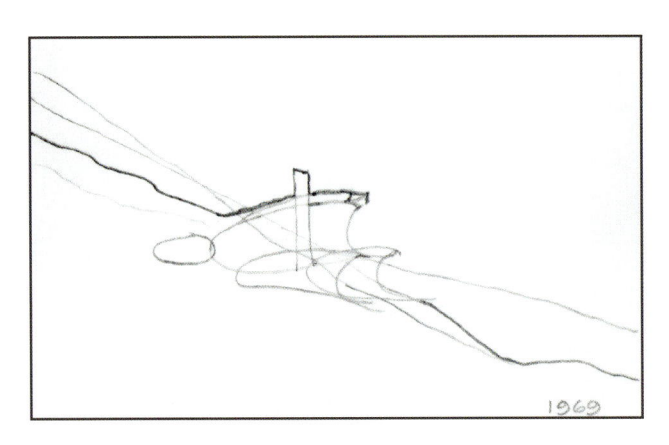

Early study of an imagined earth-integrated house built into a hillside

Gravity flow of dwelling elements down a hillside

Integrating in-ground structures to various land slopes

Dwelling built into a gentle slope with cave entry

Solar collector built into the overhang of the above house

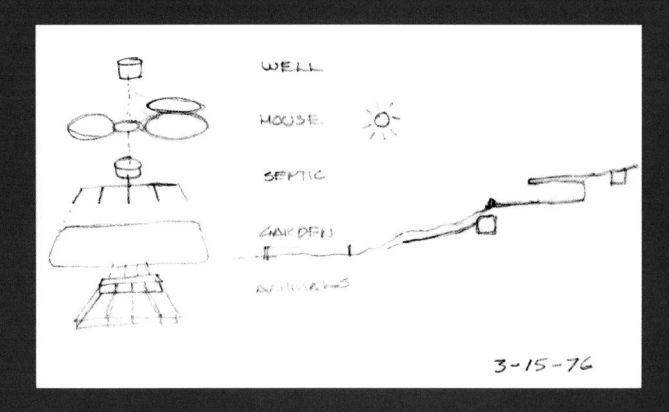

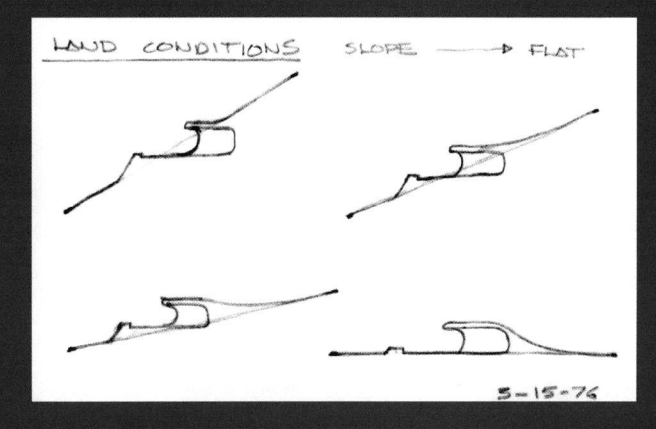

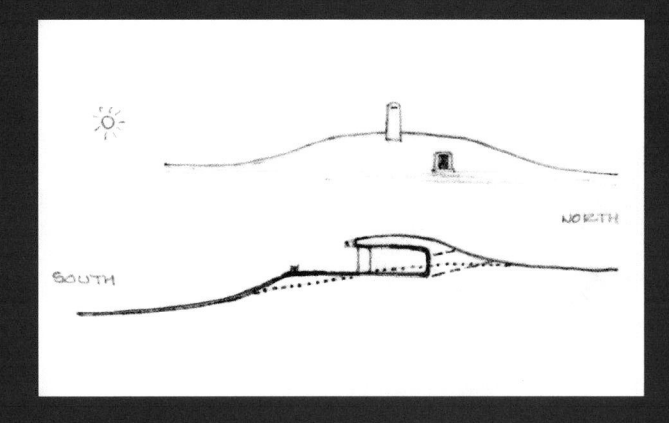

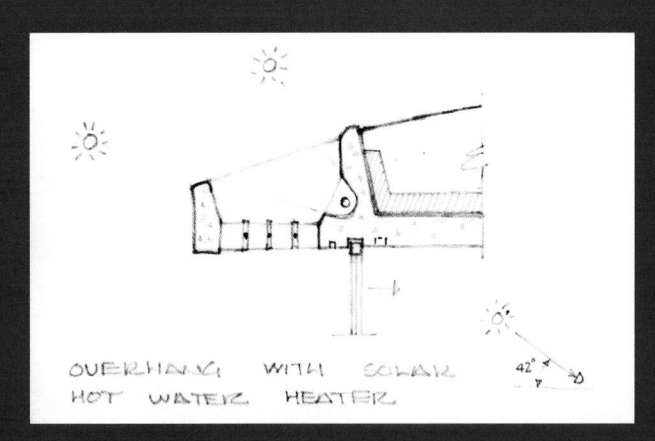

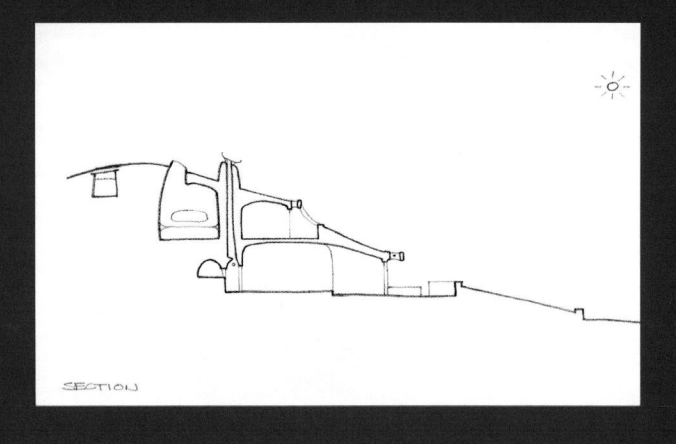

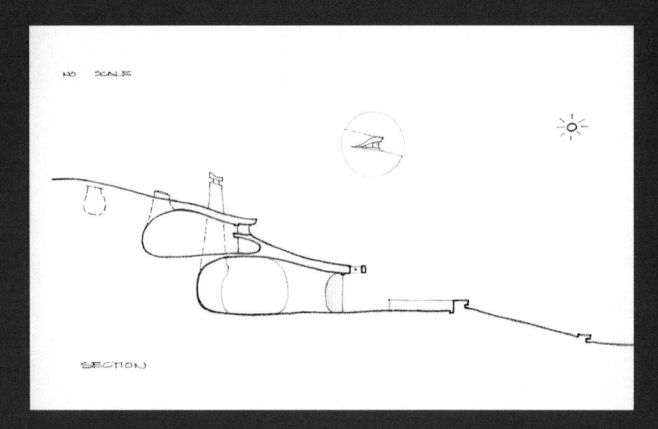

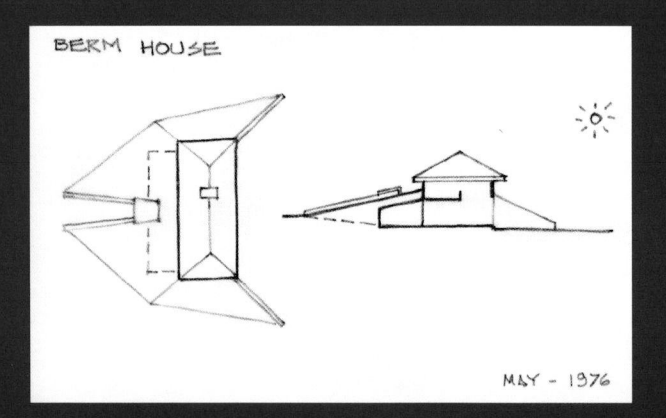

Sectional study of self-sufficient earth-integrated house

Section of free-form self-sufficient earth-integrated house

Sectional study of earth-integrated house cut into a hillside

Conventional masonry structure protected from the elements with earth berms

Earth connected well structure in southern Italy

Earth connected Saudi Arabian tent dwelling reflective of the desert sand dunes

The simplicity of passive solar sun collection

Passive evaporative cooling methods used in Saudi Arabia

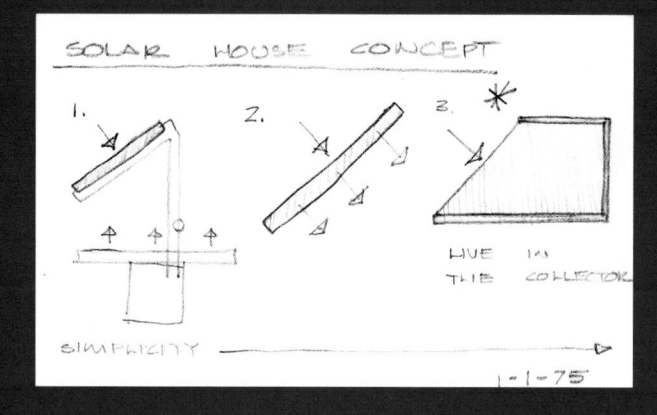

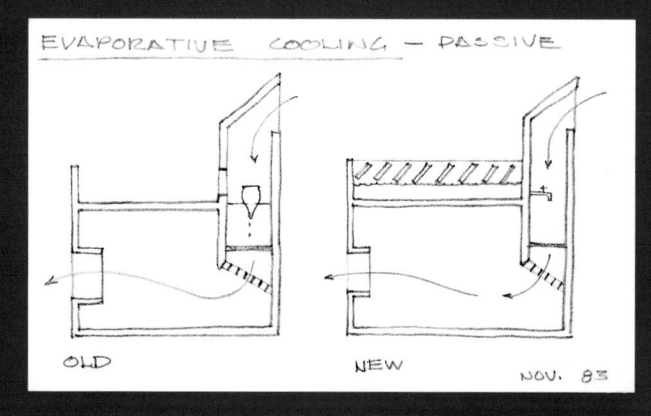

DIRECTION

SOURCES / INFLUENCES . . . . . .
Maintaining an open-minded receptiveness

NATURAL ENVIRONMENTS

FORMS IN NATURE

Architectonic stone formations – imagined buildings and cityscapes

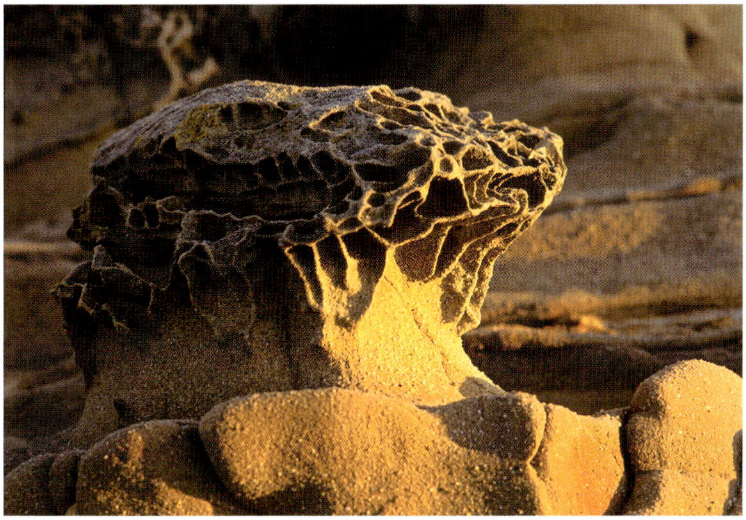
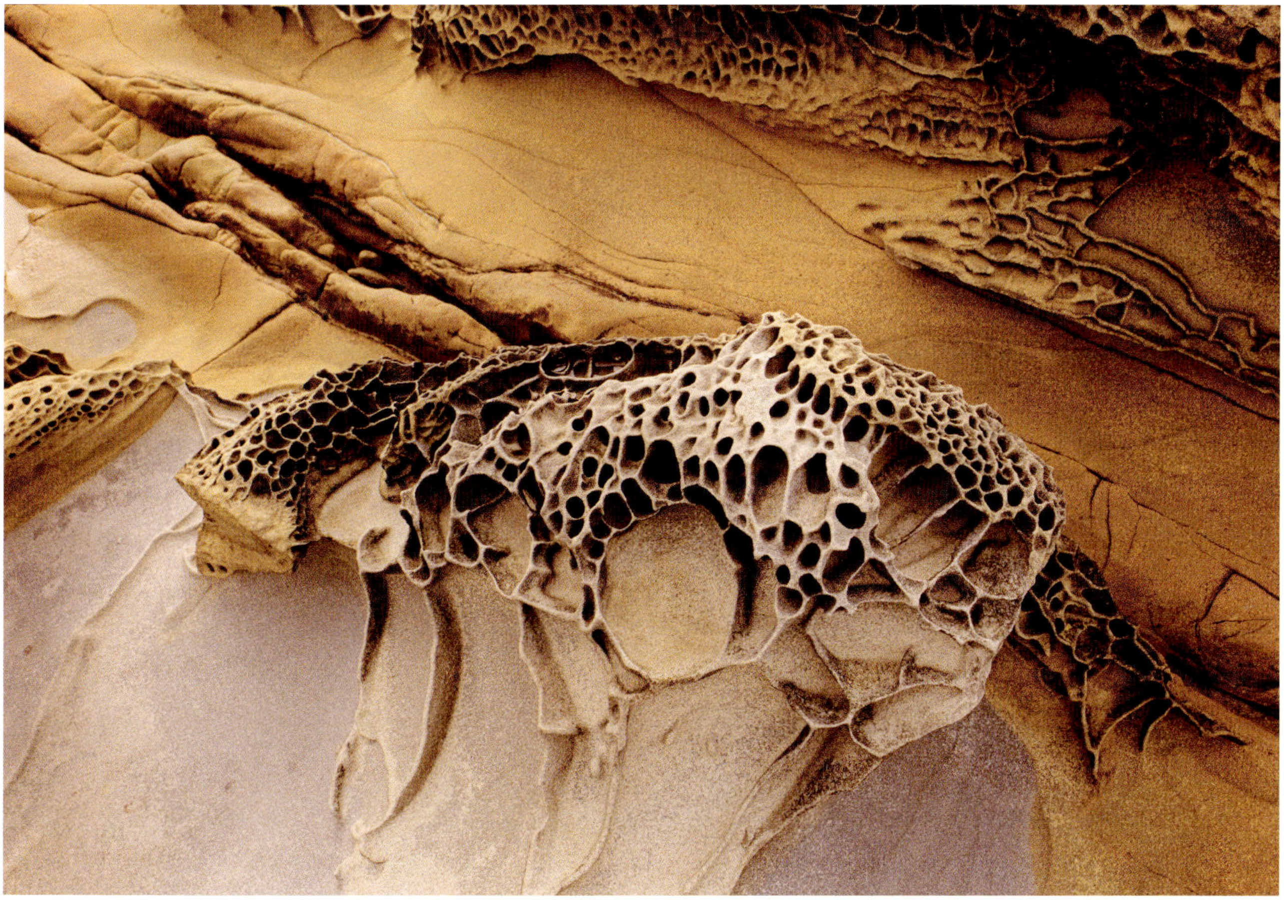

Earth connected natural rock formations

Positive and negative sculptured earthscape

112 EVOLUTION

Landscape with earth connected stone megaliths

Earth connected walls and pathways cut in the natural terrain

Eroded stone cone as an imagined highrise

Mesa as a towering building complex

Earth connected Southwest mesa at sunrise

115

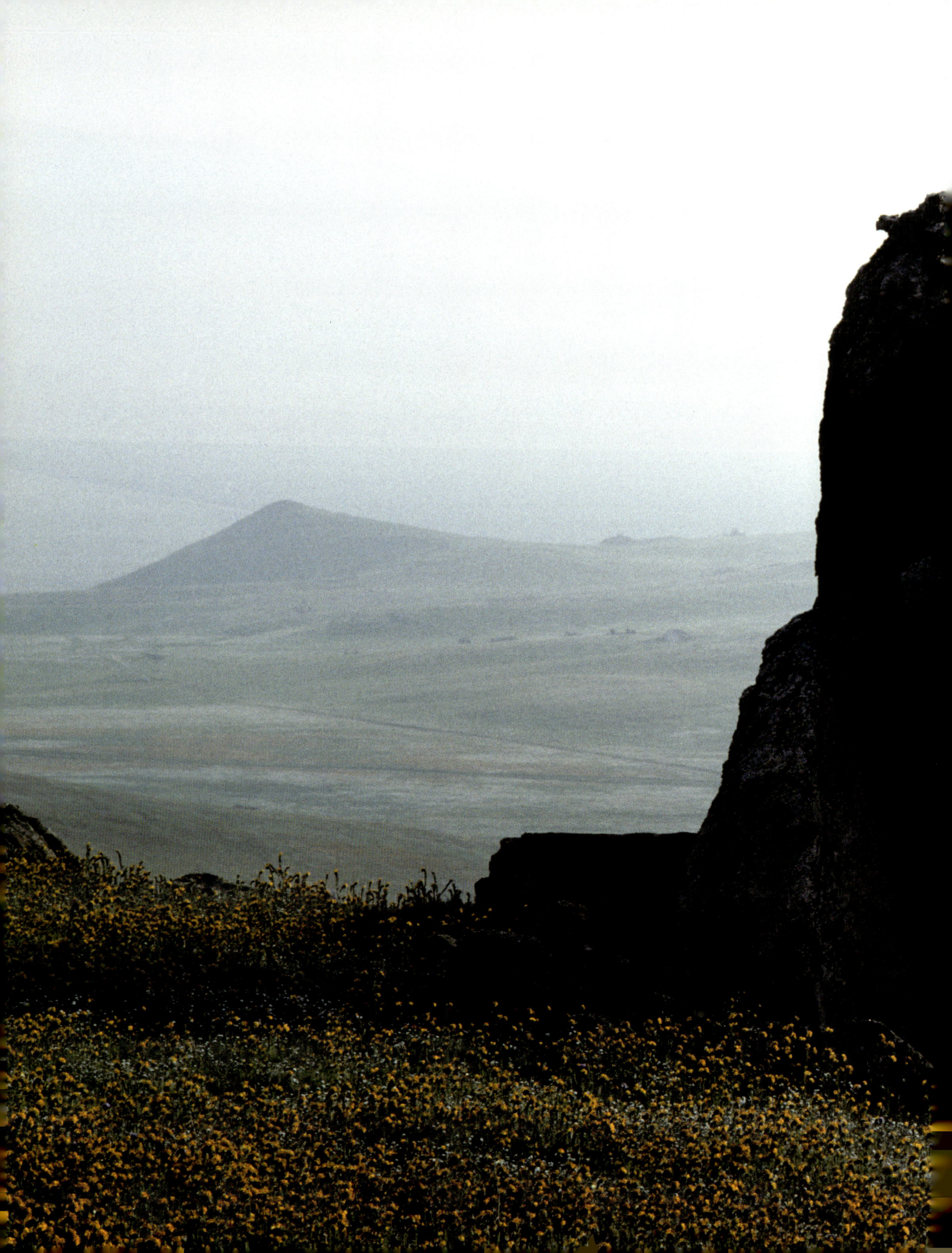

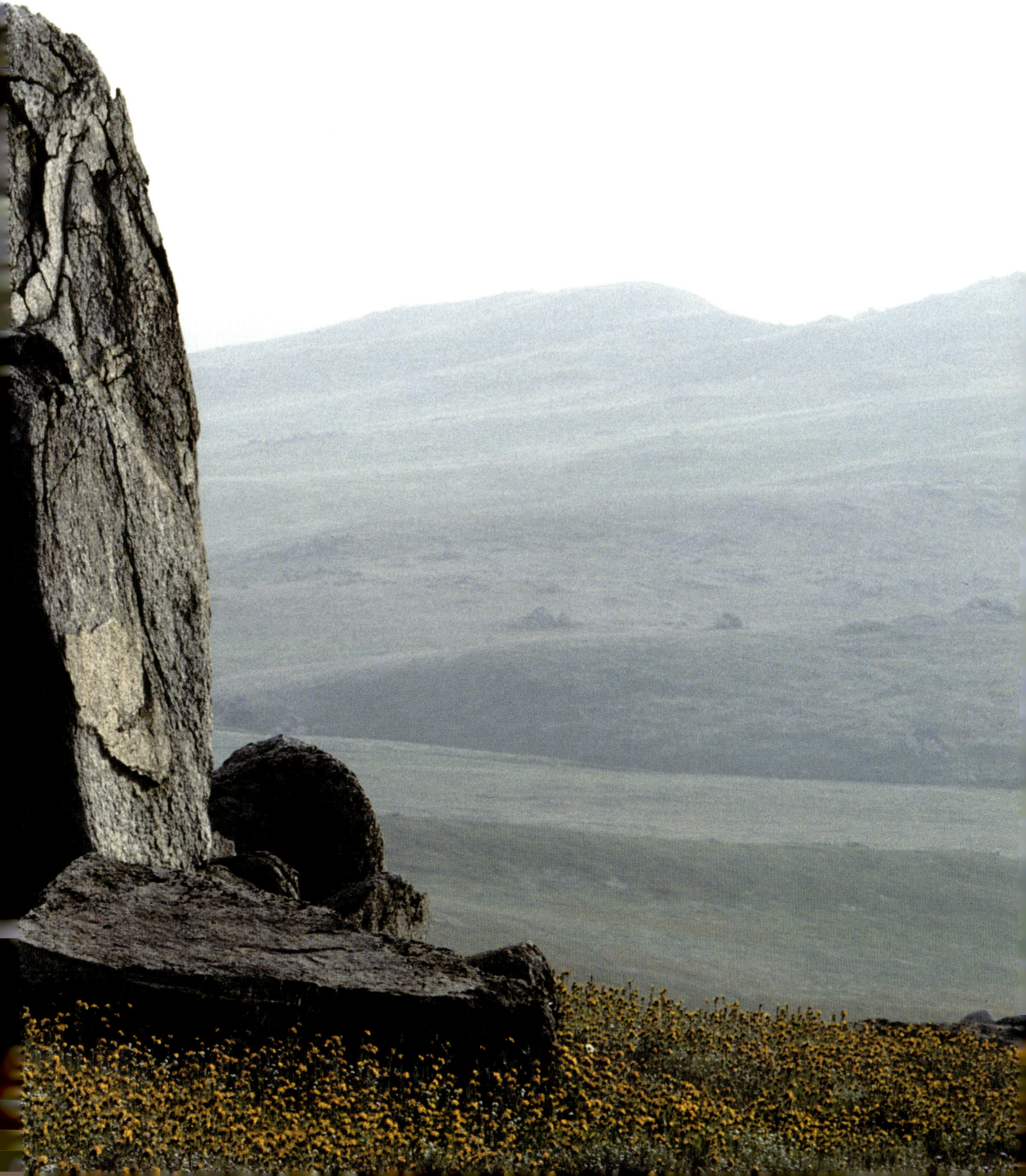

Energy between earth and sky

Previous pages 116-117:
Natural stone megalith, California foothills

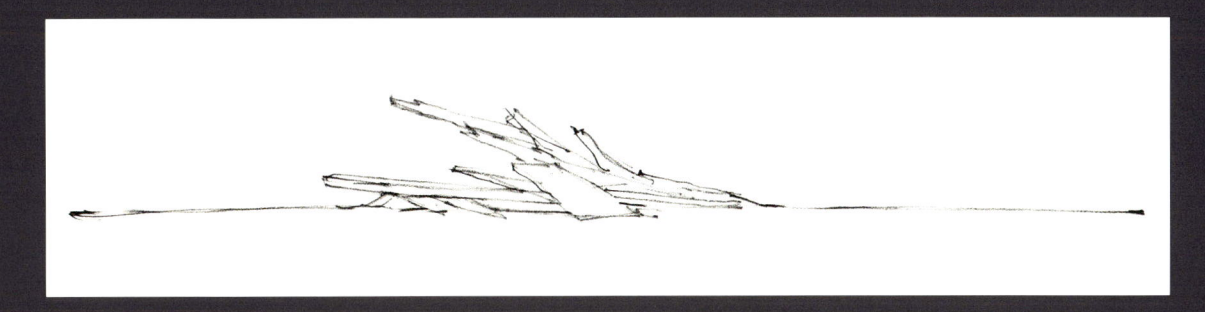

Study of planar forms on the landscape – influenced by ice jams

Painting of ice jam formations by Casper David Friedrich – dynamic play of planar forms

119

EARLY HUMAN HABITATS

Environments carved from soft tufa stone erosions

Dwelling interior with storage cubicles in the opposite tower unit

Ancient chapel interior in the vicinity of the opposite dwelling tower

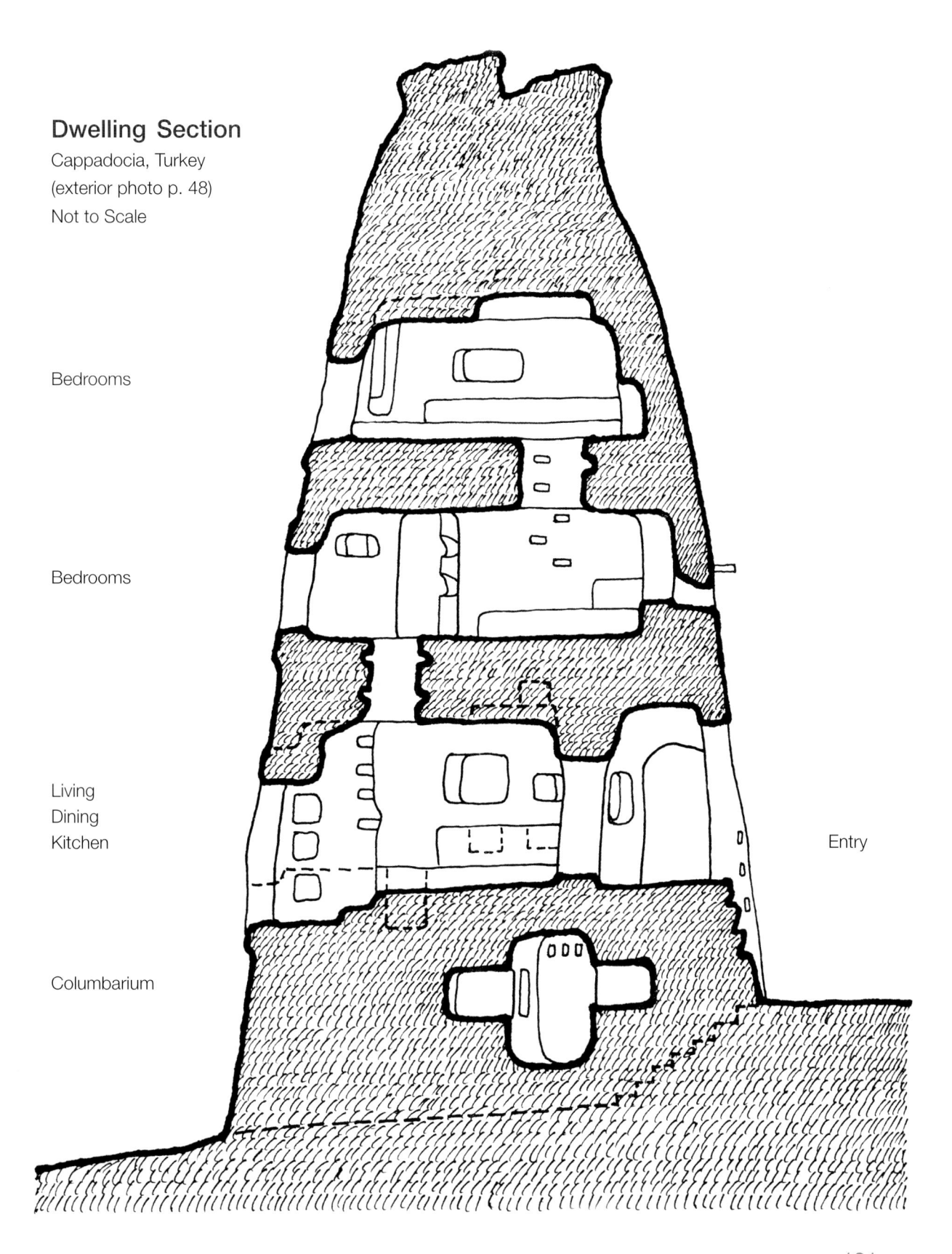

Dwelling Section
Cappadocia, Turkey
(exterior photo p. 48)
Not to Scale

Bedrooms

Bedrooms

Living
Dining
Kitchen

Entry

Columbarium

121

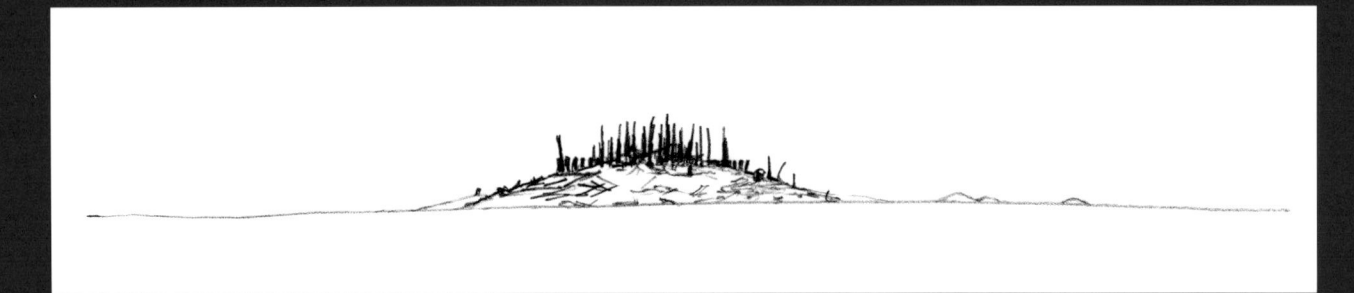

Ancient cemetery, Sinkiang, China

Earth related forms on the horizontal landscape

Ruin of Viking fortress, Carn Liath Broch, Scotland

Three standing stones with alter, Brittany, France

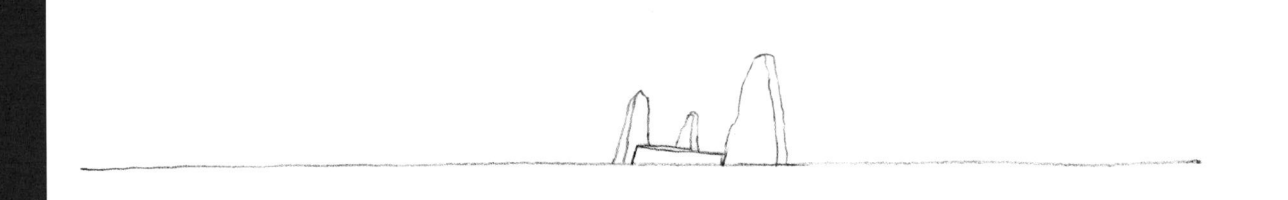

Cave entry to burial mound, Anglesey, Wales

Man-made mound, Silbury Hill, Wiltshire, England

Organic earth integrated plan of Viking village, Skara Brae, Orkney Island, Scotland

Sign from site

124 EVOLUTION

Earth connected ruins and berms at Broch of Gurness, England

Ancient Japanese cemetery with sculptured masonry earth related tombs

Following pages 126-127:
Stonehenge with earth and sky elements

125

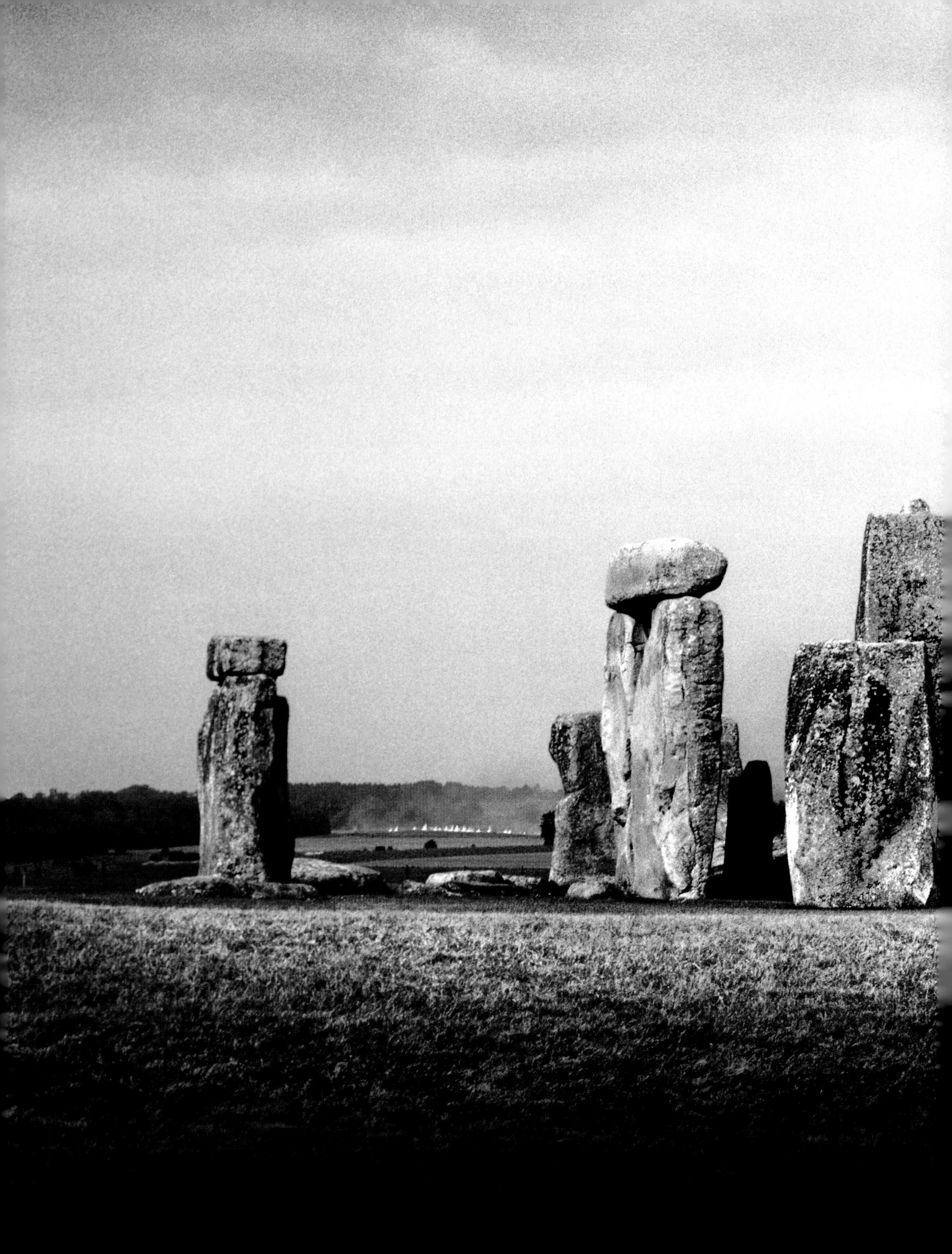

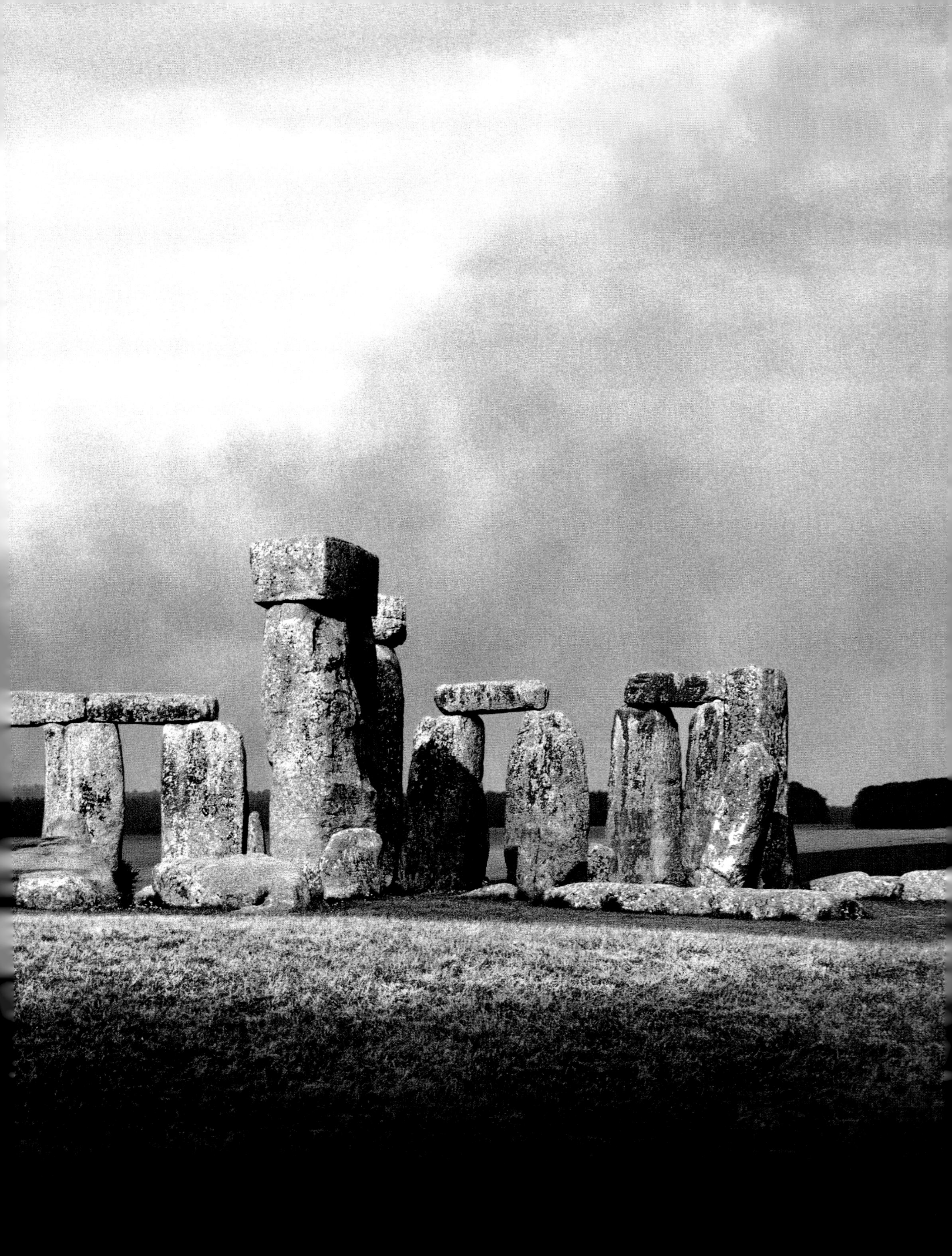

INDIGENOUS ARCHITECTURE

Earth-sky tower buildings in the Himalayan country of Bhutan

Earth connected ruins of a Byzantine church at Ani, Turkey

128 EVOLUTION

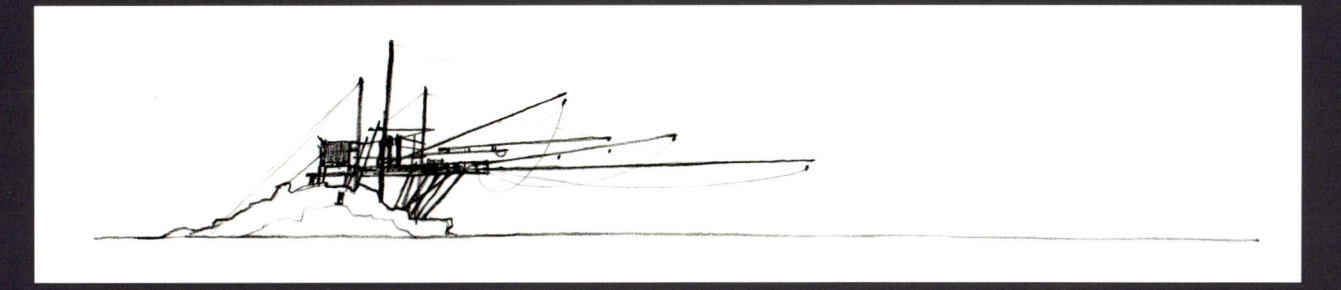

Sky related fishing structures anchored to natural rock outcropping, Pescara, Italy

Scandinavian farm built close to the earth protecting it from harsh winters

Evolution of land related structures constructed by ancient man over time

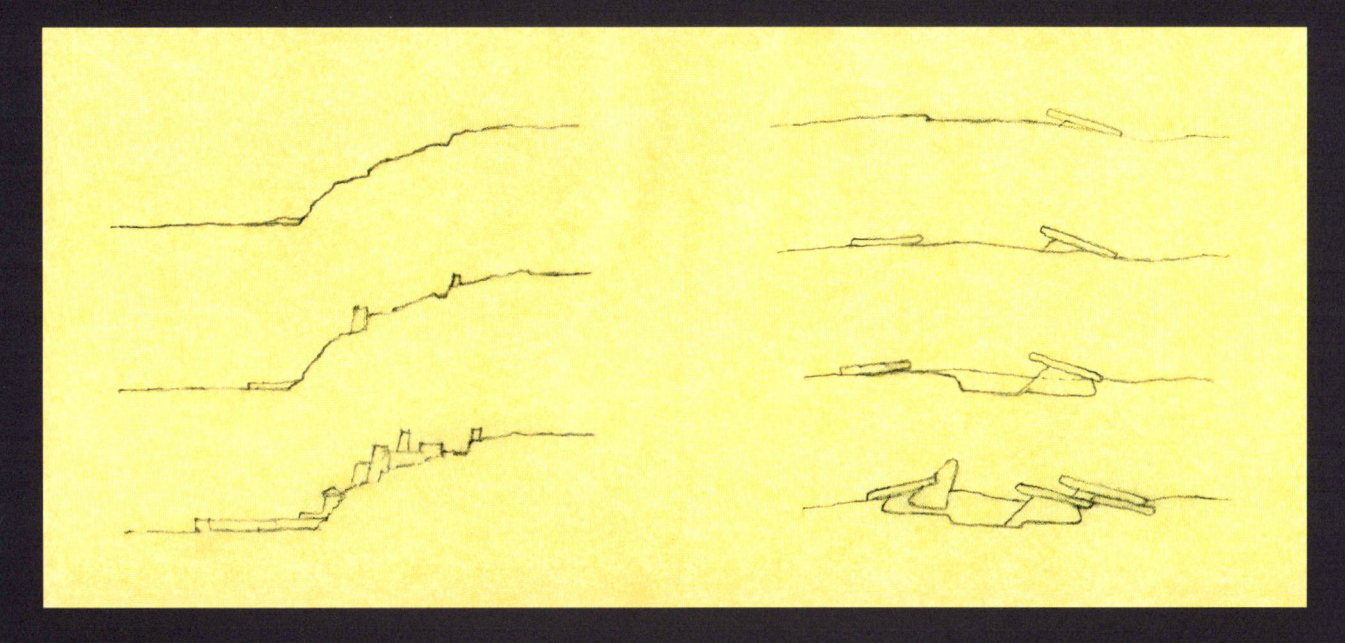

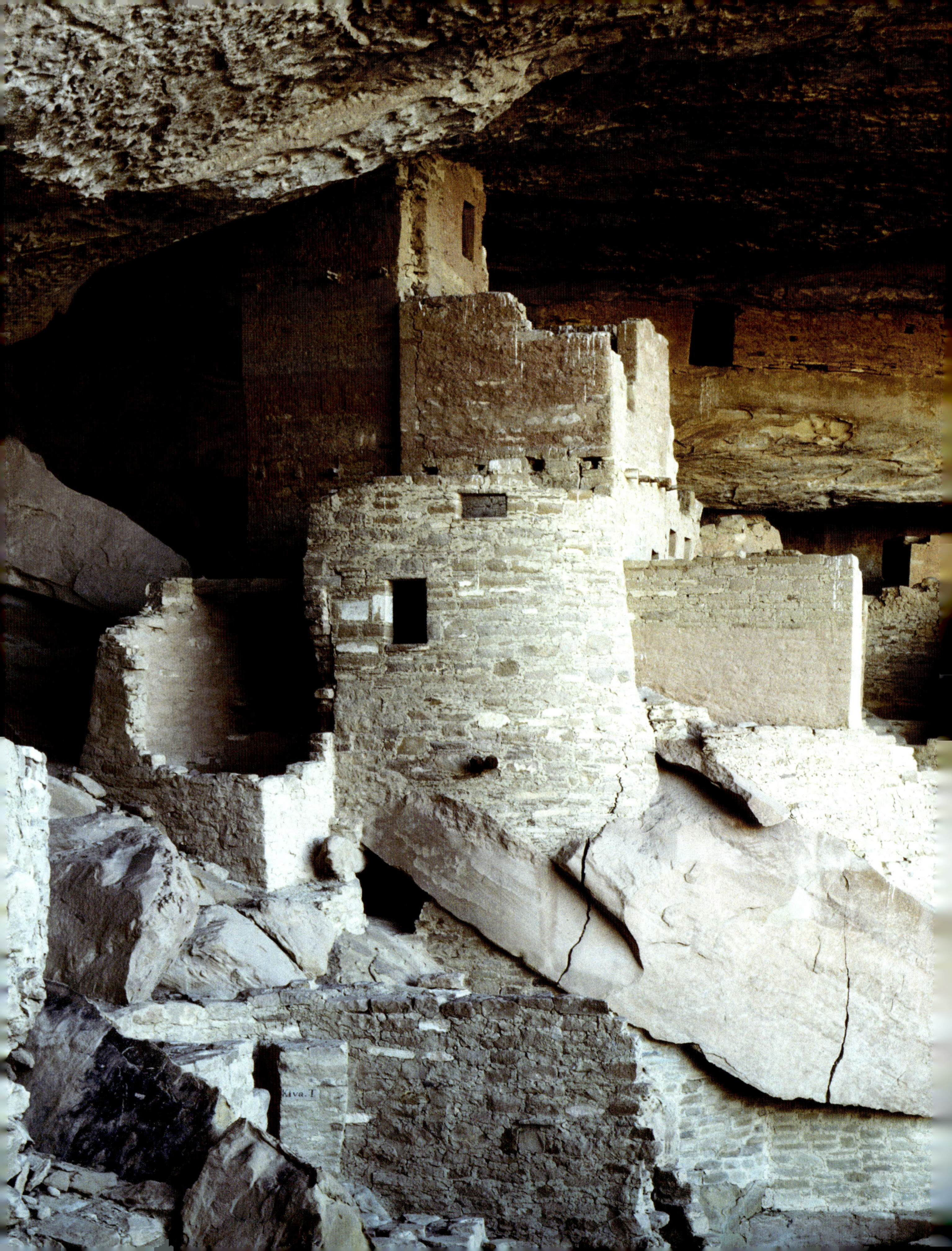
Kiva. I

Earth connected castle and fortress – Island of Saint Michael, Cornwall, England

Himalayan monastery made up of earth related building and wall elements

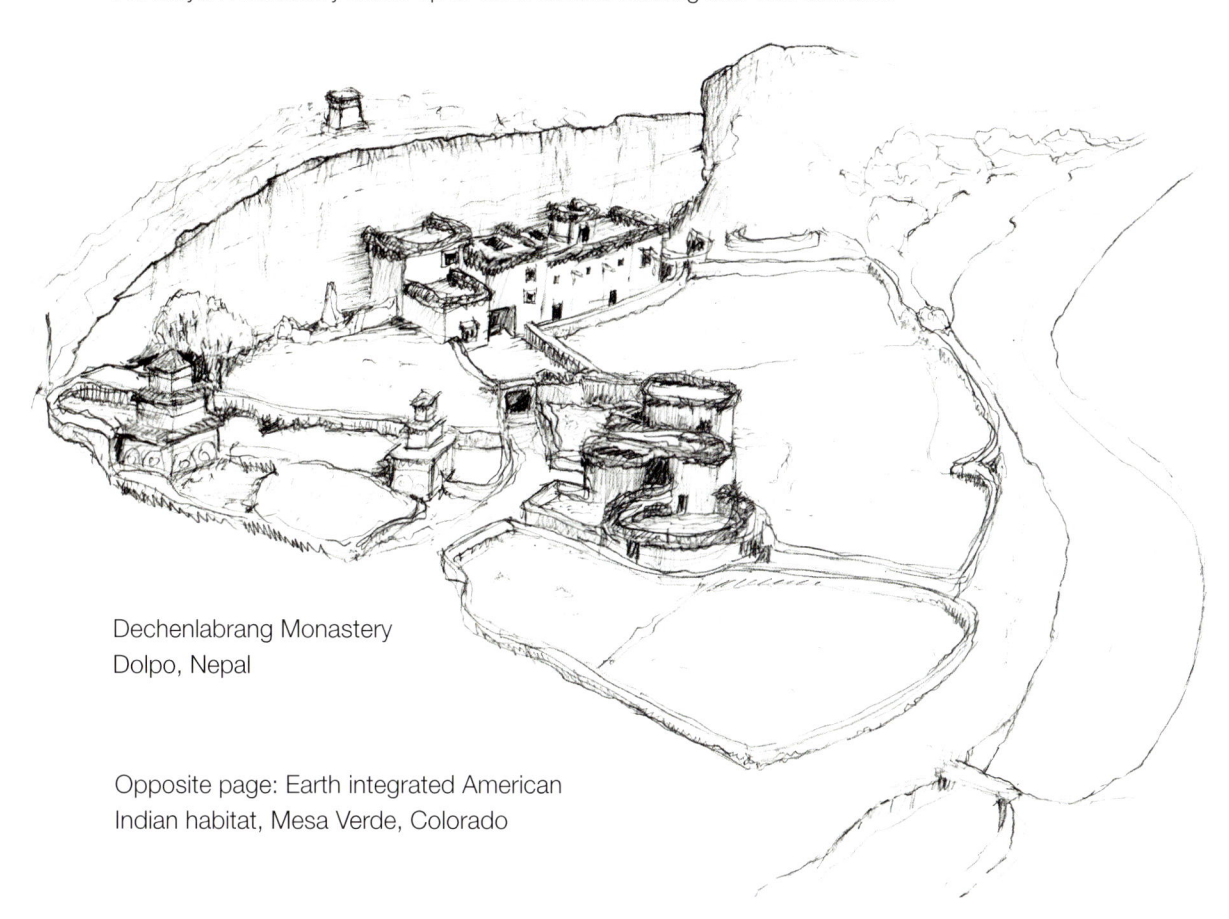

Dechenlabrang Monastery
Dolpo, Nepal

Opposite page: Earth integrated American Indian habitat, Mesa Verde, Colorado

131

CONTEMPORARY ARCHITECTURE

Earth connected Unitarian Church, E. Hartford, Connecticut, Victor Lundy, architect

Balthazar Korab

Roof forms in sympathy with the surrounding Colorado snow drifts, by Richard Loarie

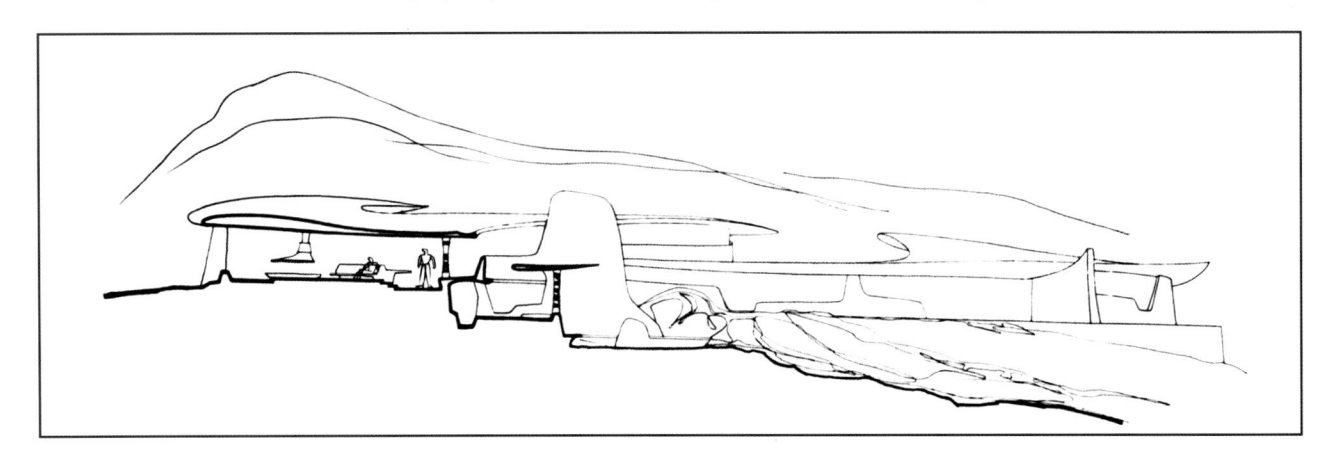

132 EVOLUTION

GENERAL THINGS / OBJECTS

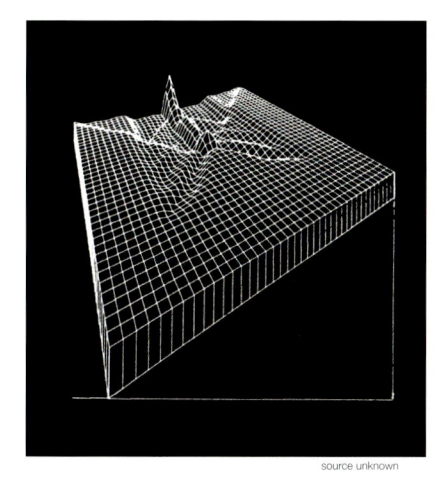

Computerized landscape

Futuristic painting by John R. Covert, 1916

Sailing ships as earth – sky related planar forms, painted by Lyonel Feininger

DIRECTION

▪ ▪ ▪ ▪ ▪ ▪ EMERGING PATH
A consistency of expression and vision

GEILS RESIDENCE　　　　2800 Square Feet Plus　　　1971
Greenwich, Connecticut

Louis O. Roberts, architect

Earth connected structure with sky related elements

Cave entry to the northwest

Earth connected stone walls

Terrace and windows oriented to the south-southwest sun, garage/utility underground

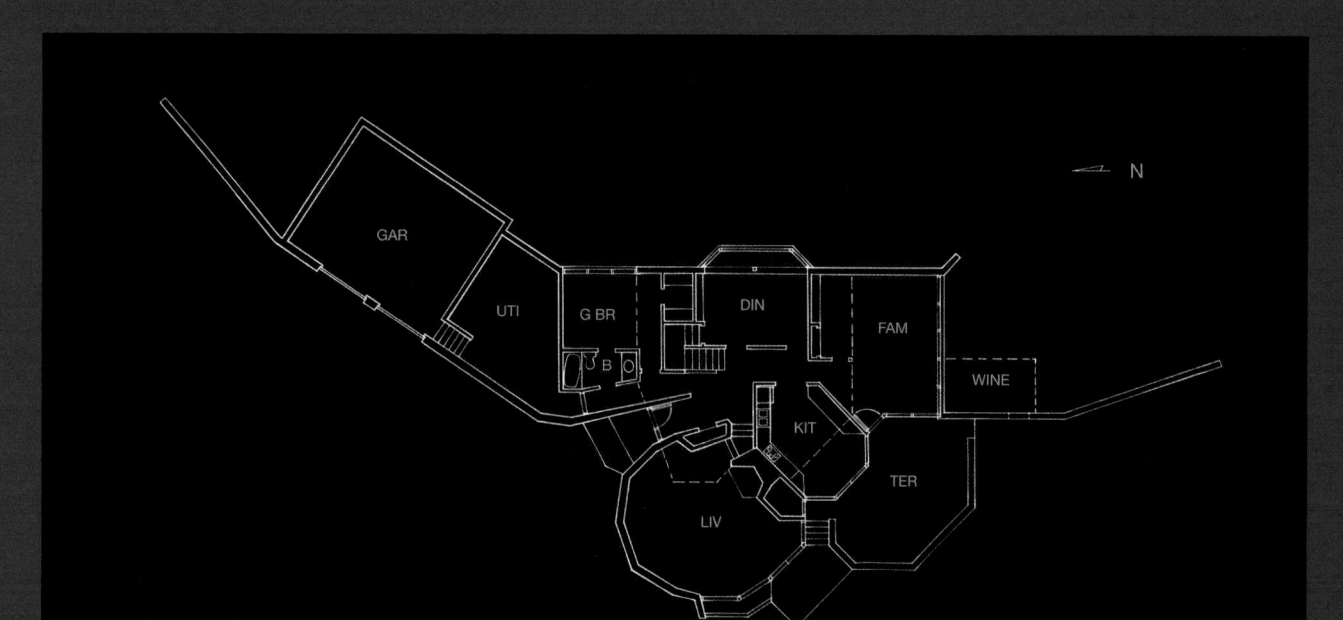

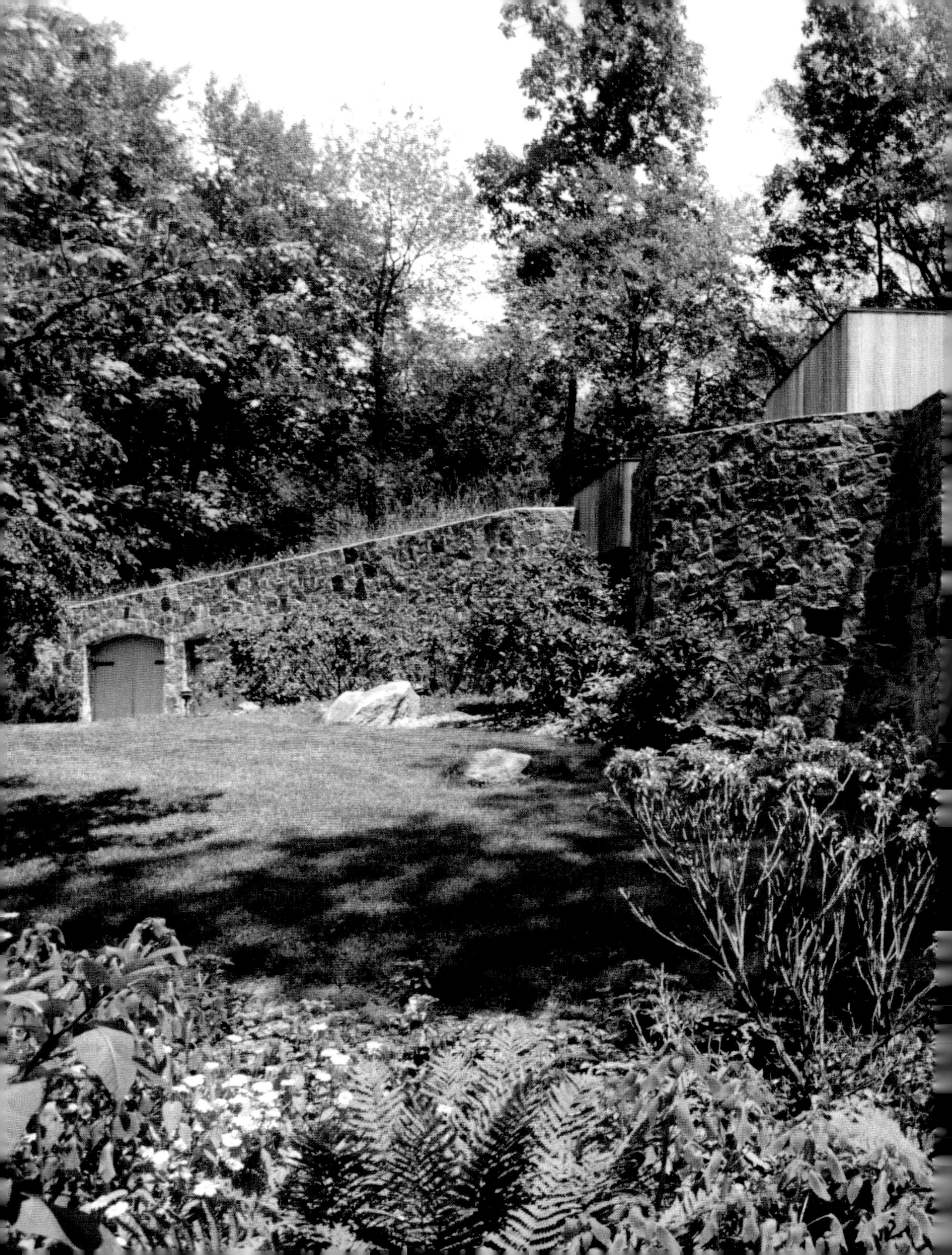

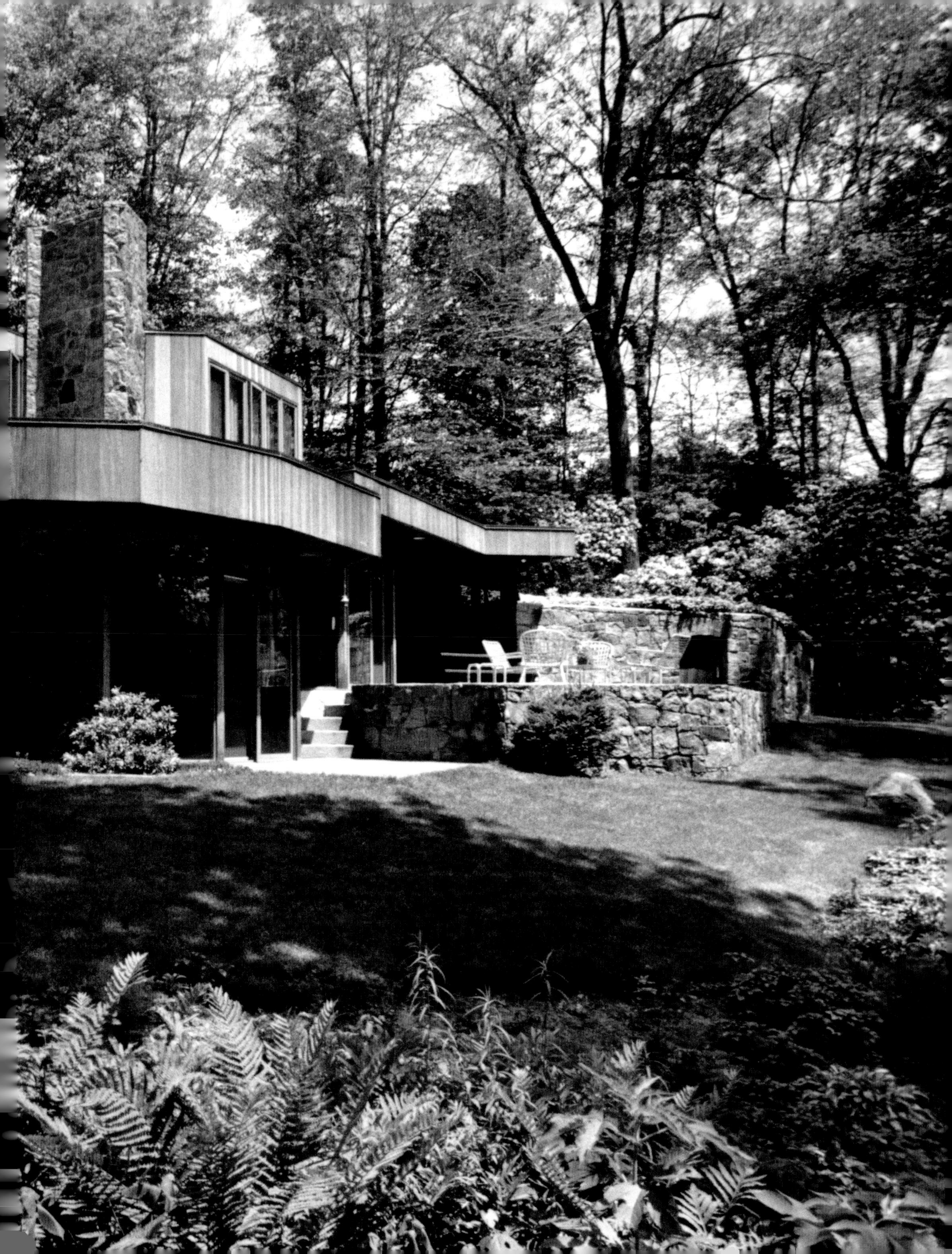

JOHNSON RESIDENCE
Hidden Valley, California

1000 Square feet

1978
Conceptual Drawing

JOHNSON RESIDENCE
NO SCALE

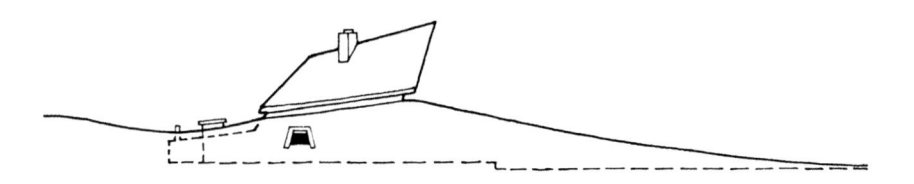

ELEVATION

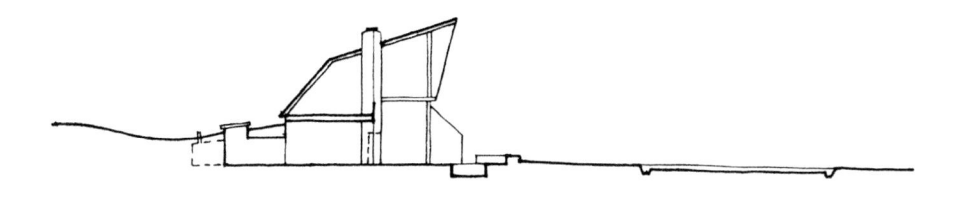

SECTION

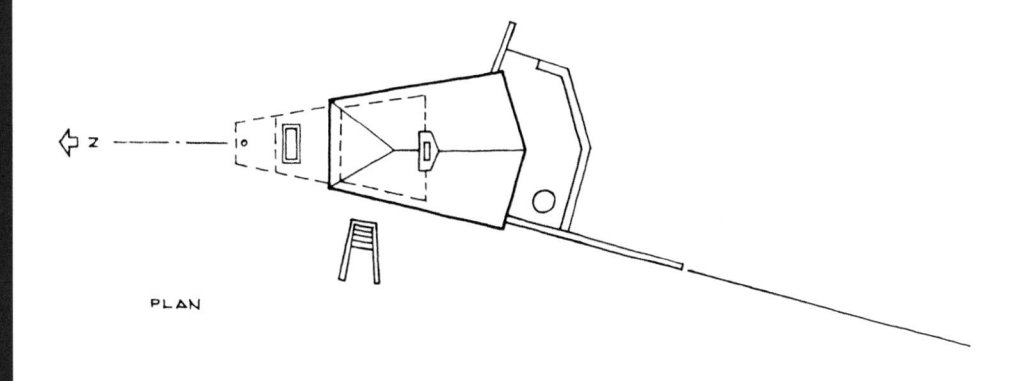

PLAN

N

1975

LOUIS O. ROBERTS — ARCHITECT

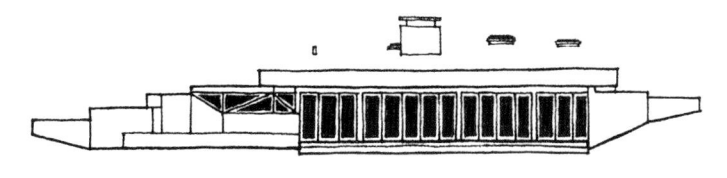

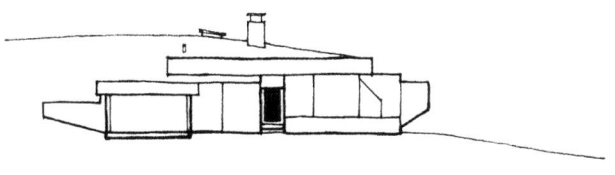

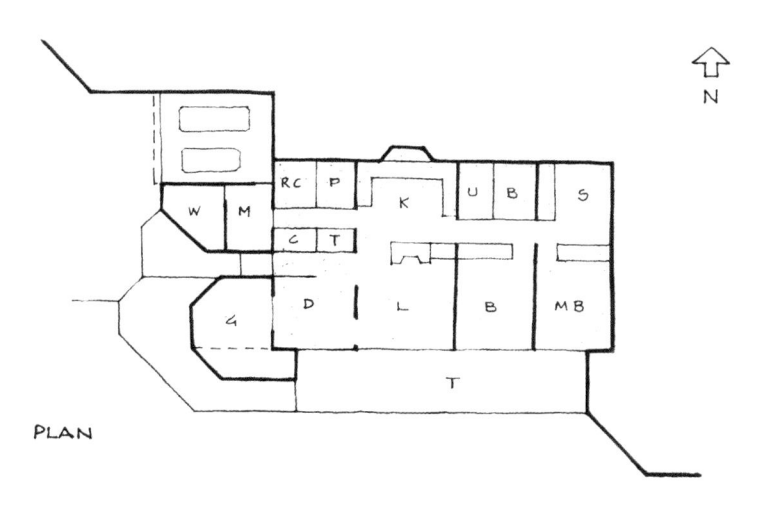

PROTOTYPE EARTH INTEGRATED HOUSE — 1981
Conceptual Drawing

ROBERTS HOUSE   2400 Square Feet   1978
Roxbury, Connecticut

Louis O. Roberts, architect

Concept: earth integrated house blending into the landscape

Organic plant Influences

Evolution of conceptual sketches

Organic plan and elevation sketches

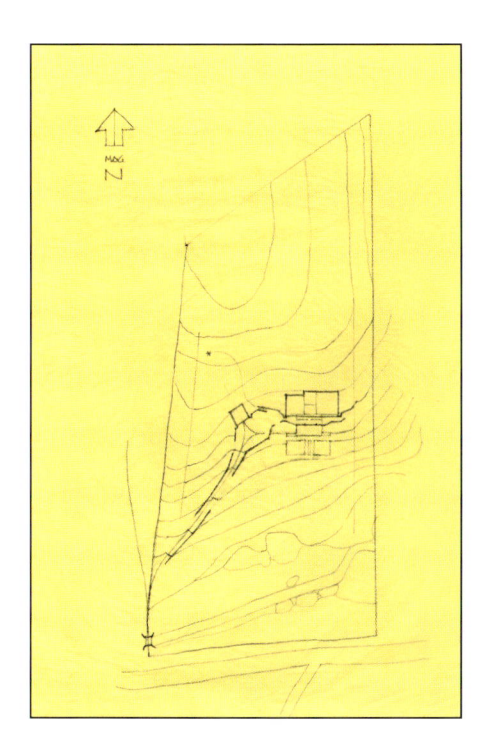

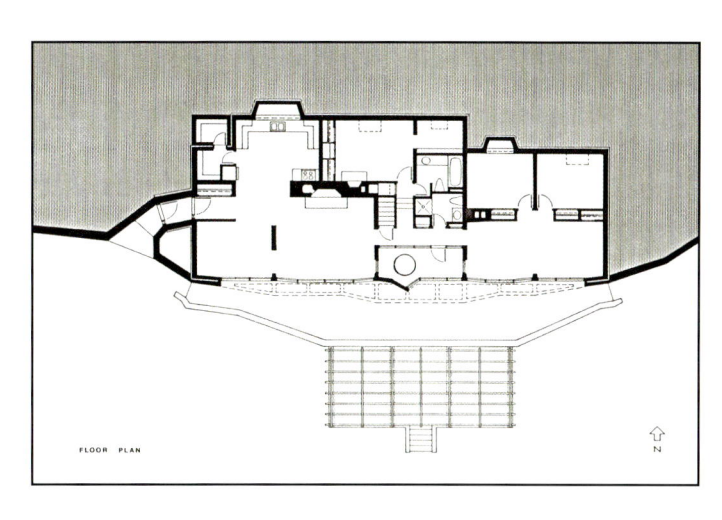

Site plan – final

Floor plan – final

West elevation

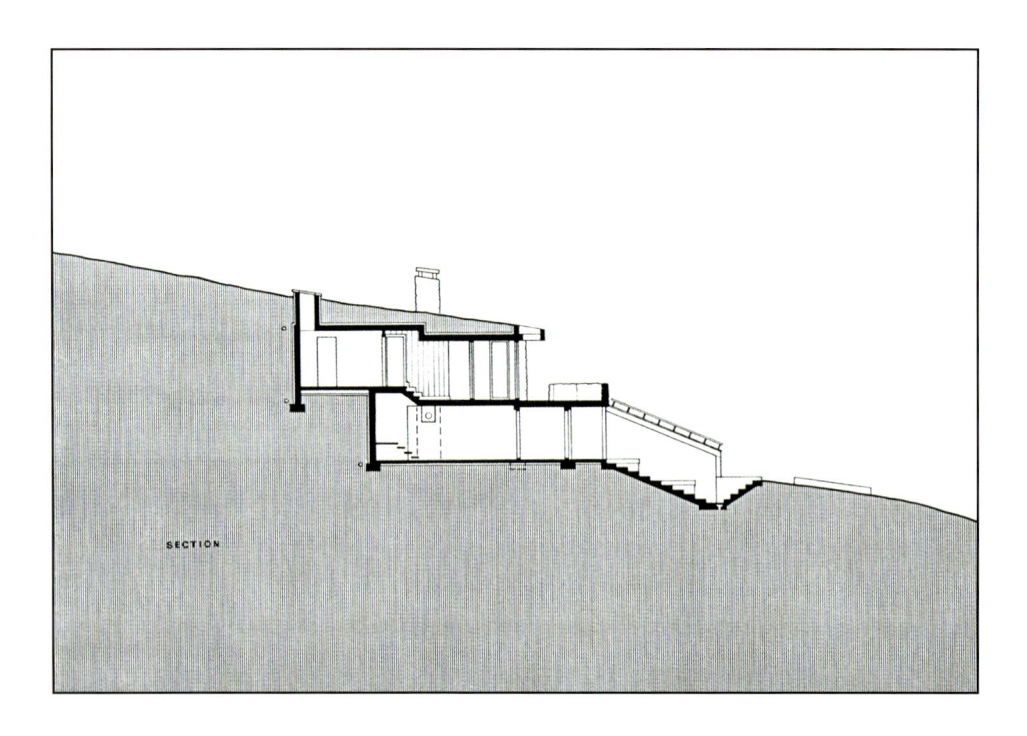

Section cut into natural slope

Living room interior with kitchen beyond

East elevation with skeletal overhang, greenhouse below

DEVELOPMENT

EXPLORING IDEAS . . . .
Investigation of diverse possibilities

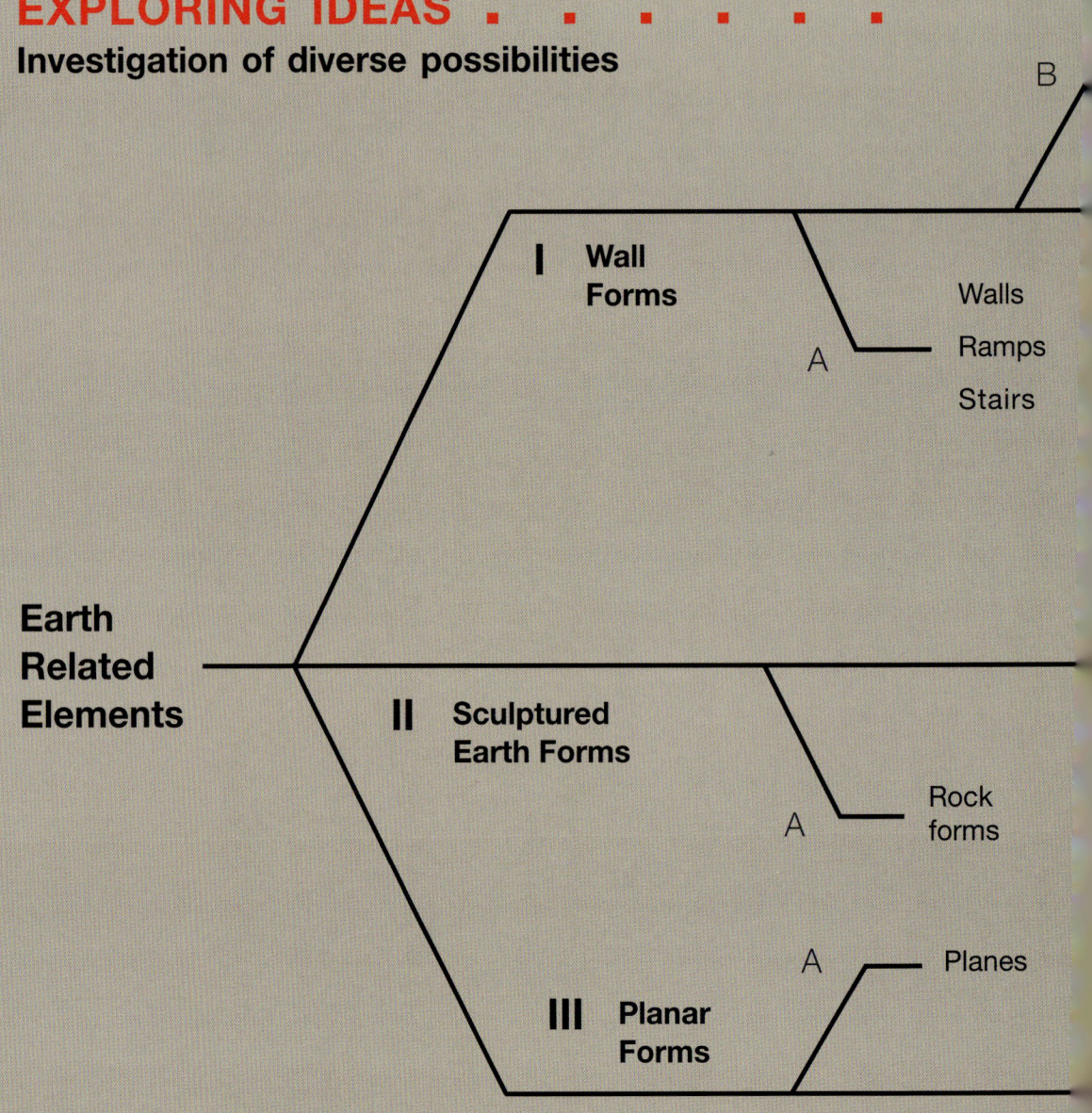

Earth Related Elements

I Wall Forms
— A — Walls, Ramps, Stairs
— B

II Sculptured Earth Forms
— A — Rock forms

III Planar Forms
— A — Planes

144 EVOLUTION

C — Shapes
Building forms
E — Ribbons
D — Extrusions

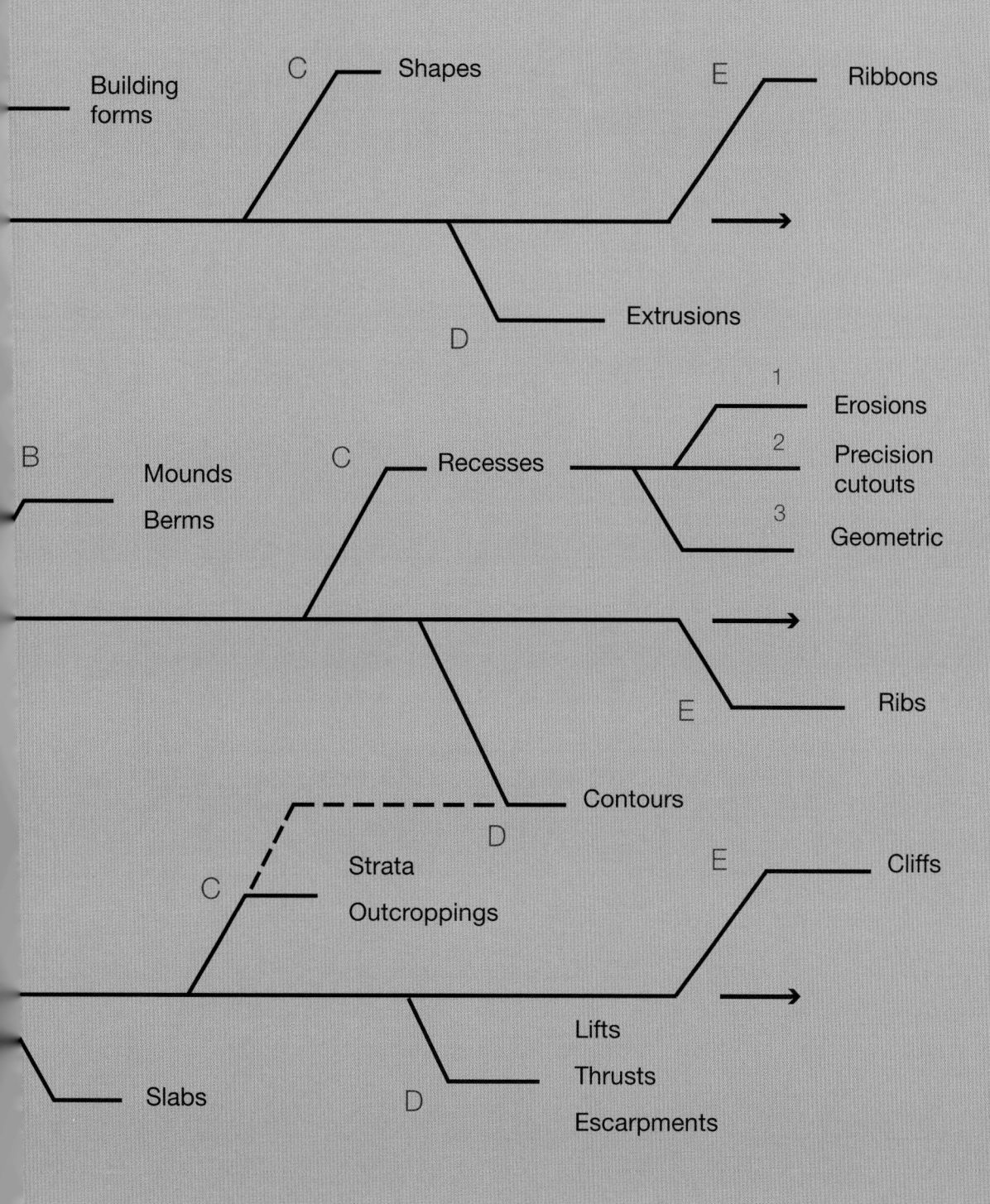

B — Mounds / Berms
C — Recesses
1 Erosions
2 Precision cutouts
3 Geometric
E — Ribs
D — Contours

C — Strata / Outcroppings
E — Cliffs
Slabs
D — Lifts / Thrusts / Escarpments

EARTH RELATED ELEMENTS   Idea Sketches

The following pages contain a sampling of drawings demonstrating my approach to the creative process – primarily in the realm of random thoughts and free association. When one puts pencil to paper something occurs allowing the unconscious to deliver more than is contained in the conscious mind.

| Wall Forms

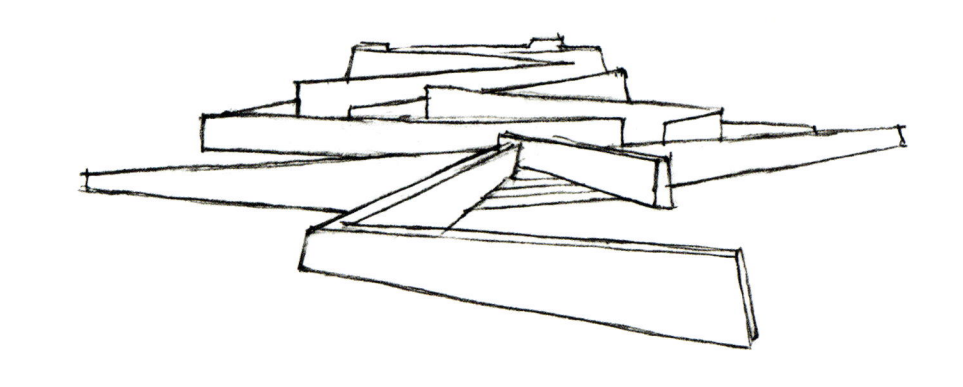

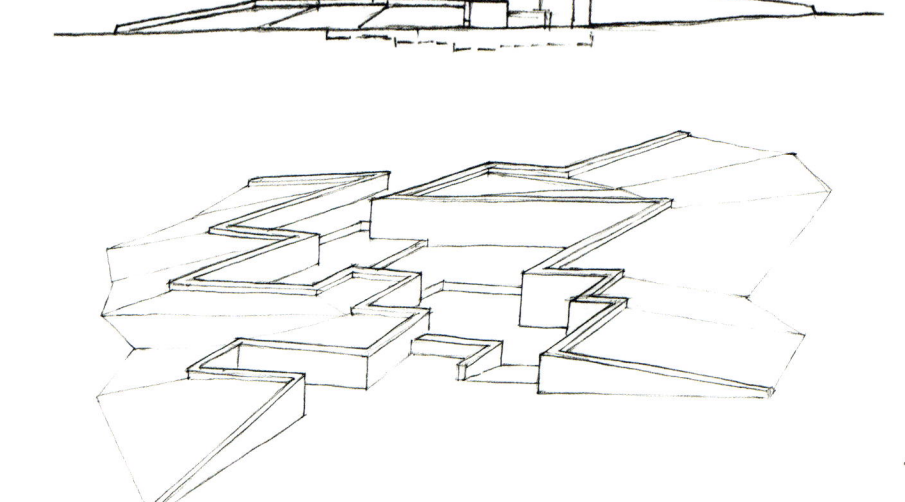

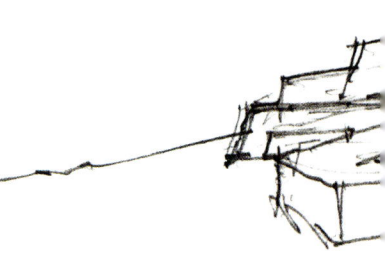

1992

A Traveler's House – opens and closes

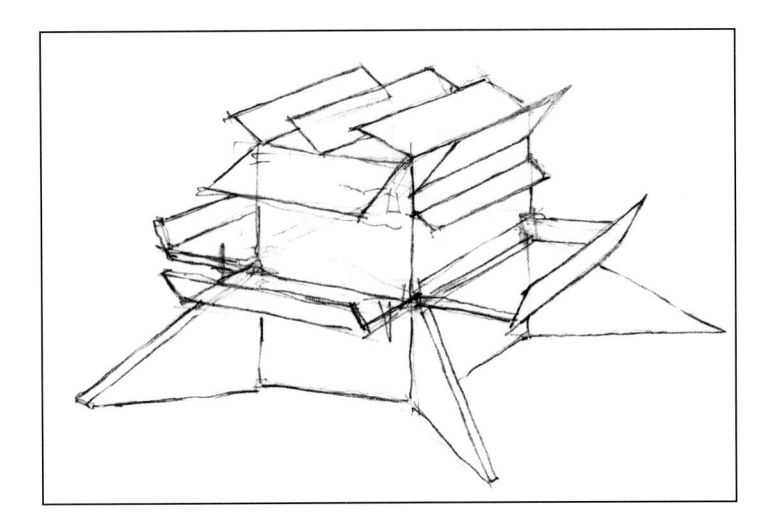

1992

Notes accompanying these study sketches:

Explore various top forms
Try more studies – as with bird wings – feathers laying one over the other

Metal panels / elements
could be *Corten* steel

Use hydraulics

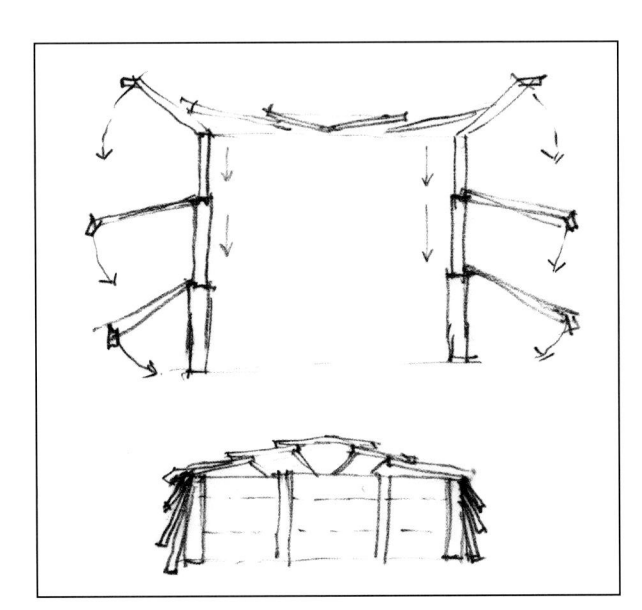

1992

148 EVOLUTION

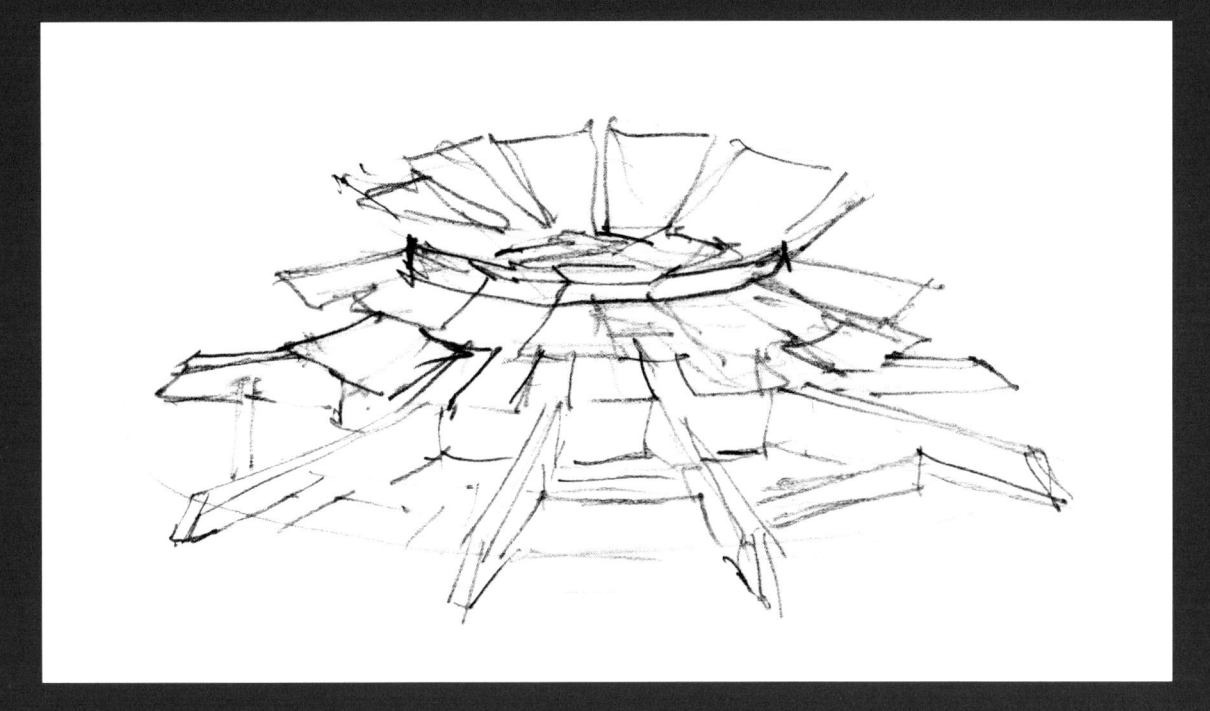

A combination of walls and planar forms   1992

A building that locks down similar to a tortoise – operated with hydraulics

149

II Sculptured Earth Forms

Earth Mound House
North Country, England

Front view sketch with inserted man-made elements

Natural earth mound   1993

150 EVOLUTION

Earth / Sky – Ribbed house / roof   1992

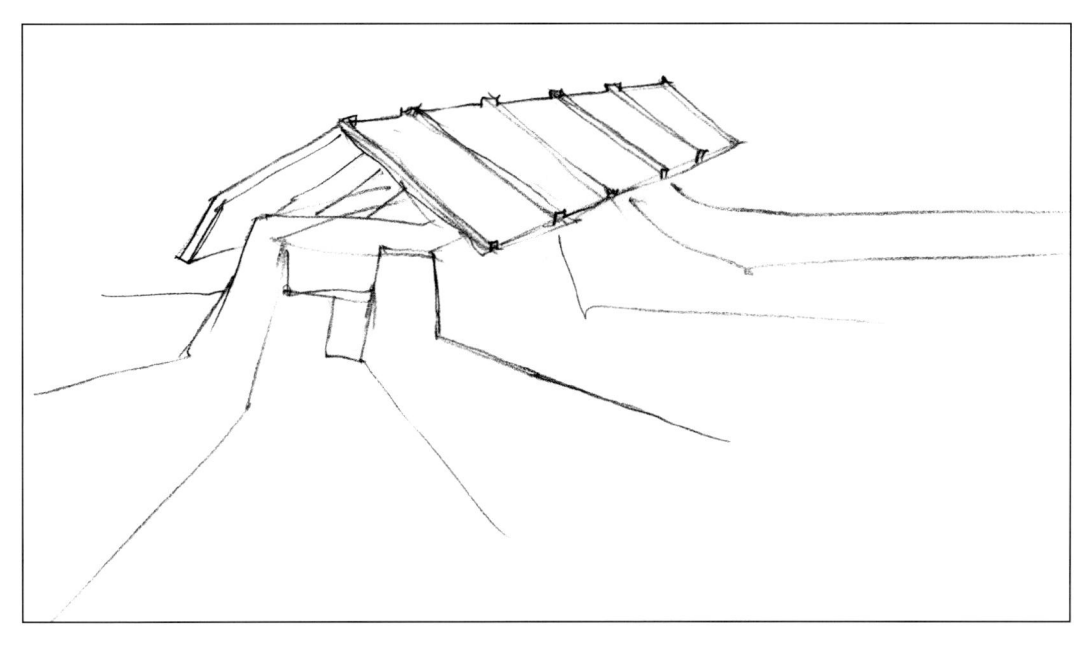

Ribbed earth / wall base

Ribbed metal roof in the form of folded planes

Tree roots inspiration

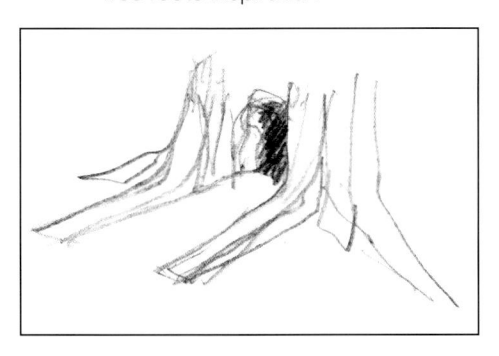

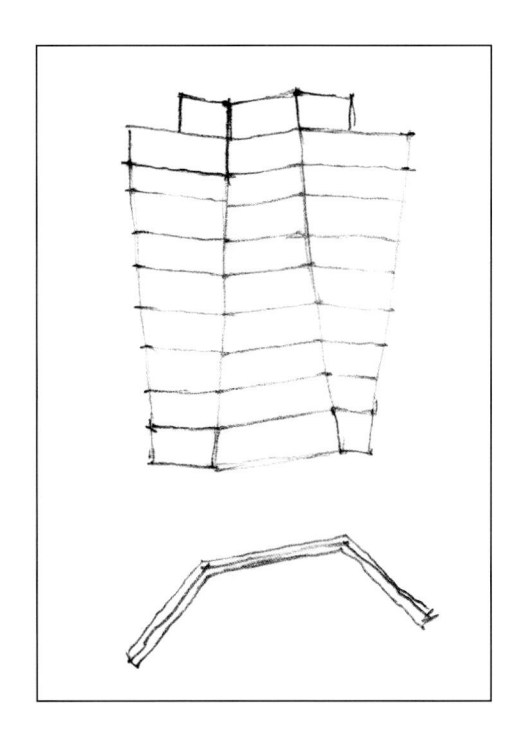

151

III Planar Forms

Idea sketch of planar mound with earth ribs					1992

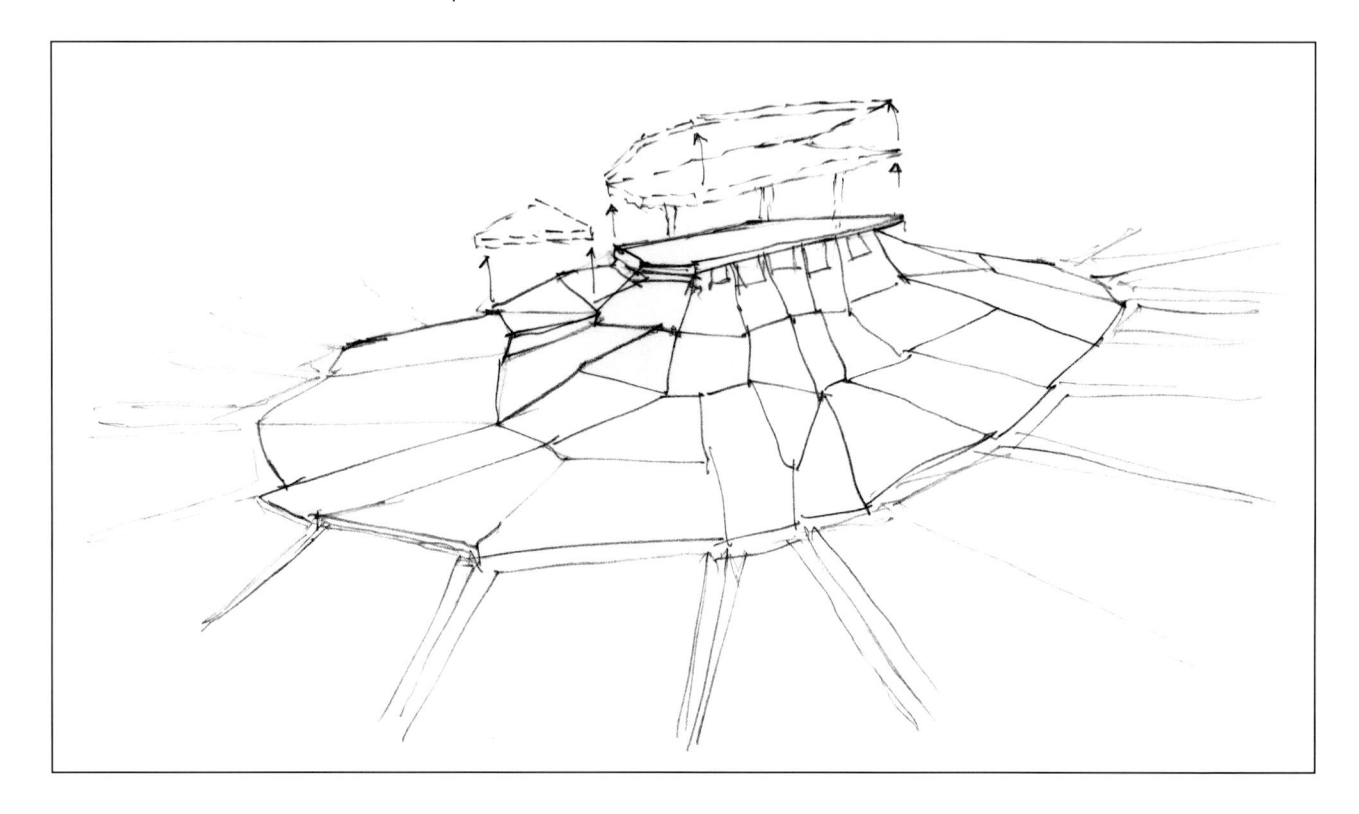

Notes accompanying above study sketch:

The building might be envisioned as planes erupting from the earth with some panels rising up above the others to become sky related elements. The top of the panels could be made of *Corten* steel – earth related. The underside could be a light color – so when in the up position and viewed from below it appears as sky related.

Do study of planes, slabs and slab volumes in model form.

Building / Museum as erupting earth planes   1997

Existing land forms translated into planar landscape   1992

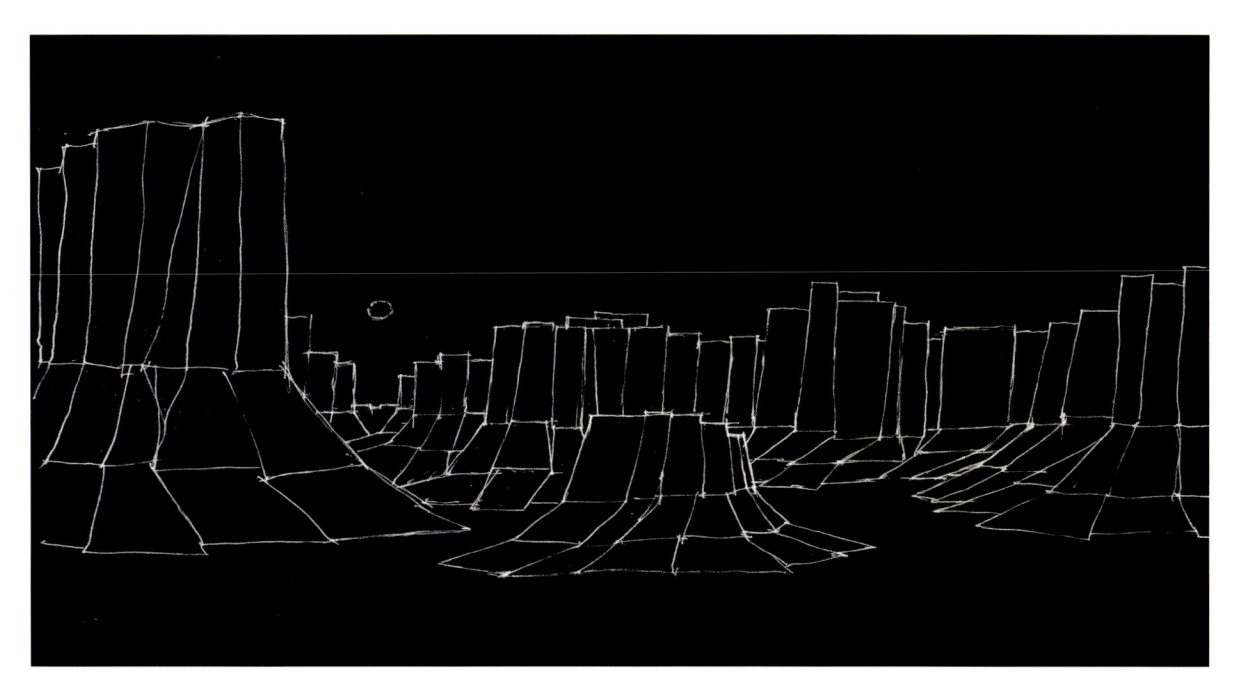

153

EXPLORING IDEAS . . . . .
Investigation of diverse possibilities

A

I Planar Forms

A — Cubes

II Geometric Forms

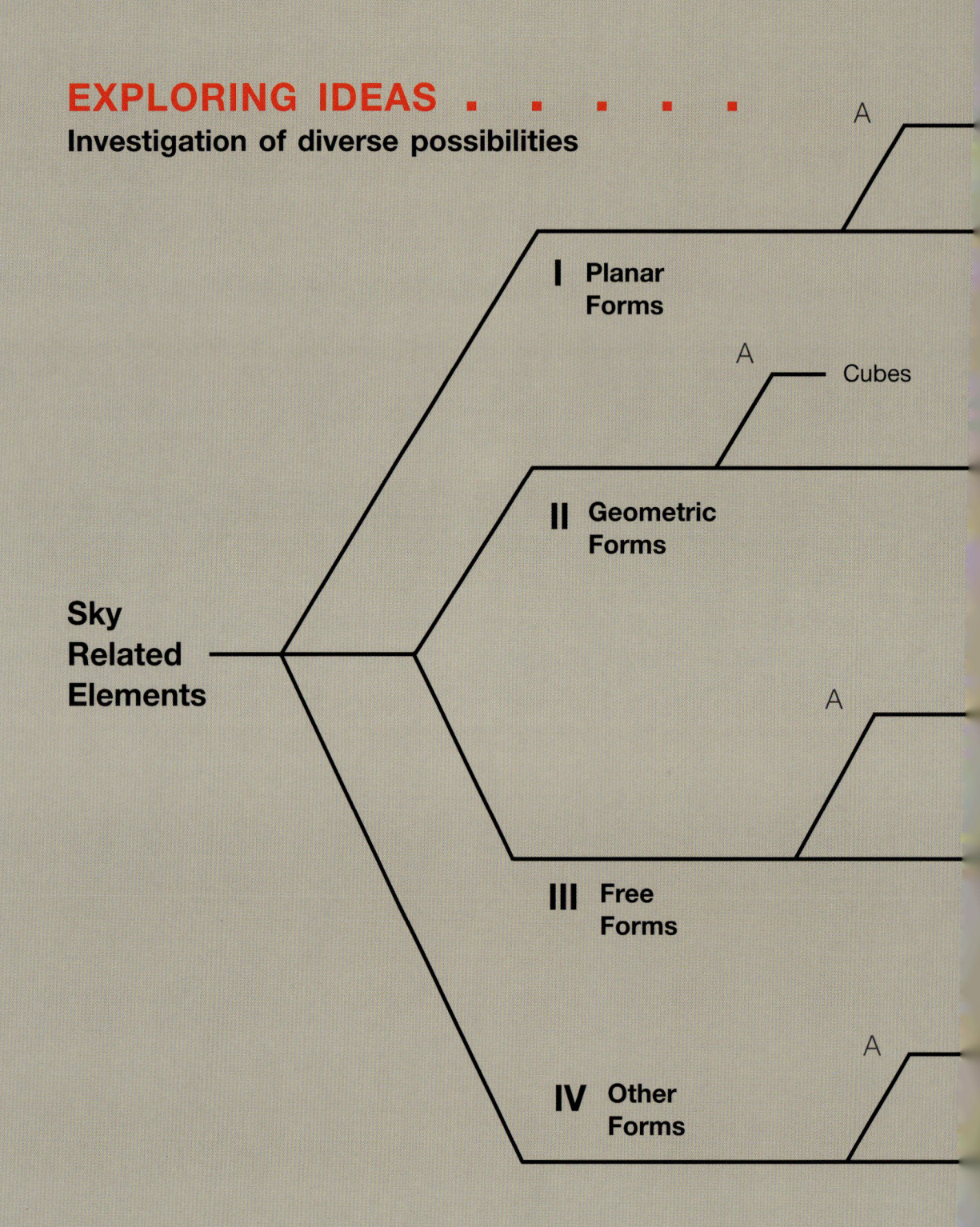

Sky Related Elements

A

III Free Forms

A

IV Other Forms

154 EVOLUTION

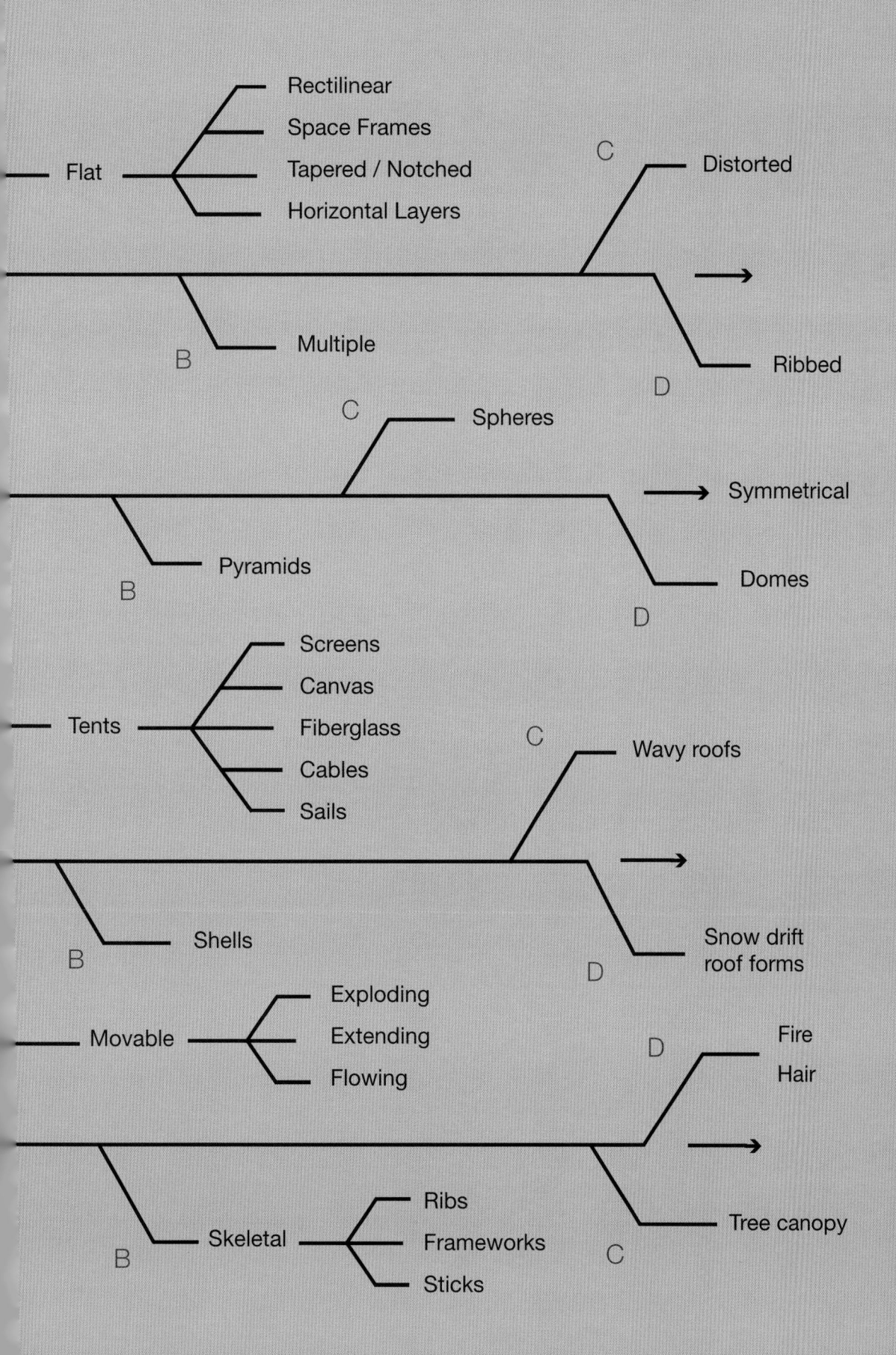

```
                    ┌─── Rectilinear
                    │
                    ├─── Space Frames                  C
── Flat ────────────┤                                  └─── Distorted
                    ├─── Tapered / Notched
                    │
                    └─── Horizontal Layers
──────────────────────────────────────────────────────────────→
              \                                     \
               \── Multiple                          \
              B                                       D ─── Ribbed

                         C
                          \─── Spheres
              \                                          → Symmetrical
               \                                        /
                \── Pyramids                           /
              B                                       D ─── Domes

                    ┌─── Screens
                    │
                    ├─── Canvas
                    │
── Tents ───────────┤─── Fiberglass         C
                    │                        \─── Wavy roofs
                    ├─── Cables
                    │
                    └─── Sails
──────────────────────────────────────────────────────────────→
              \                                        \
               \── Shells                               \── Snow drift
              B                                        D    roof forms

                    ┌─── Exploding
                    │                                              ┌─── Fire
── Movable ─────────┤─── Extending                    D            │
                    │                                  \           └─── Hair
                    └─── Flowing                        \
──────────────────────────────────────────────────────────\───────→
              \                                           \
               \                    ┌─── Ribs              \── Tree canopy
                \── Skeletal ───────┤─── Frameworks       C
              B                     └─── Sticks
```

155

SKY RELATED ELEMENTS   Idea Sketches

| Planar Forms

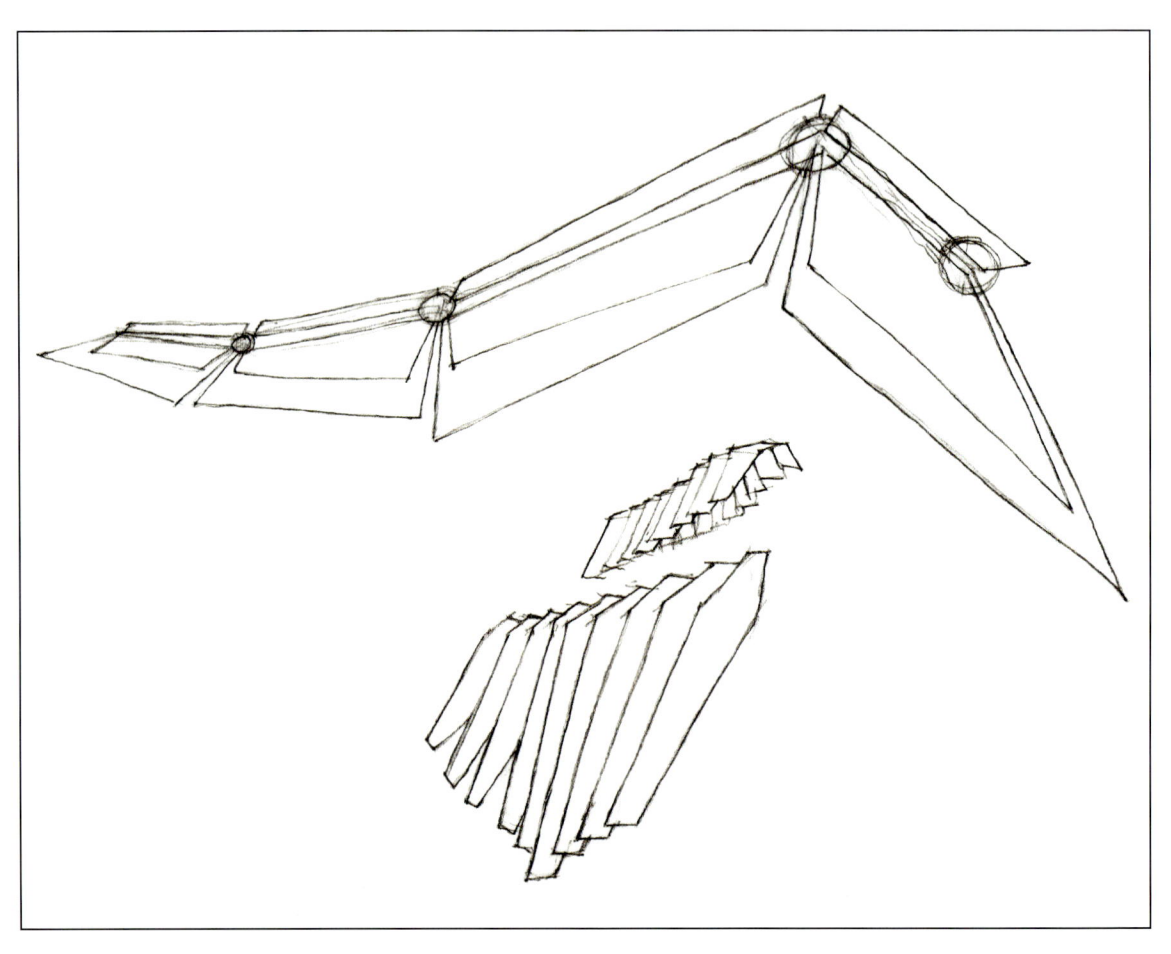

Bird wing planar elements as possible roof structure   1992

Fanning planar elements

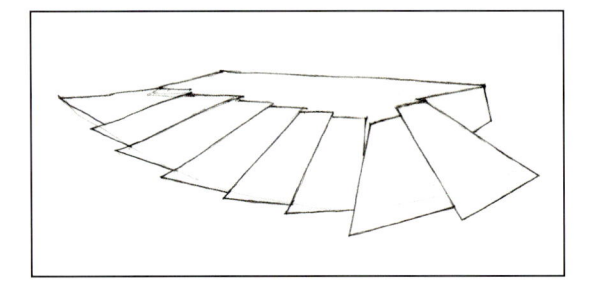

Faceted planar elements

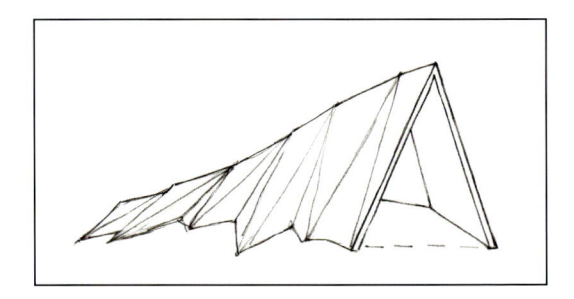

Natural setting　　　　　　　　　1992

Similar man-made environment

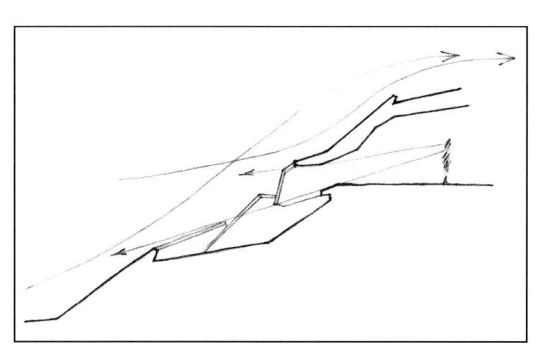

Wind deflection over planes

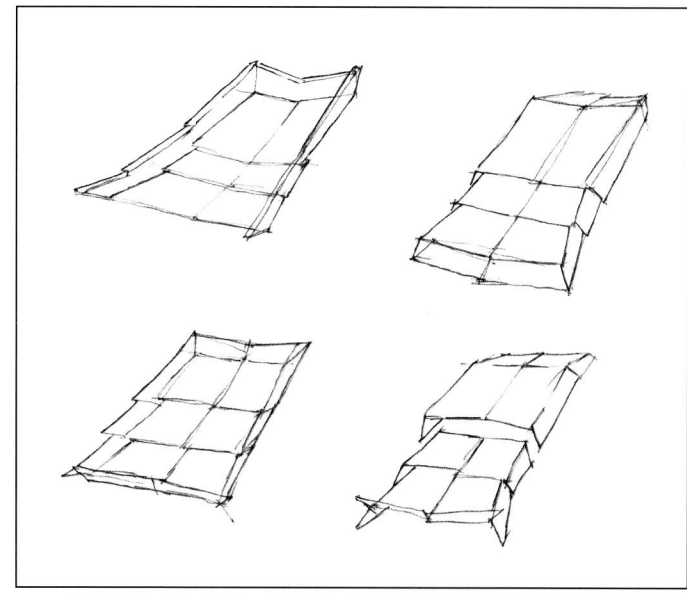

Moveable planes　　　　　　　　1992

Flexible and foldable roofs　　　　1992

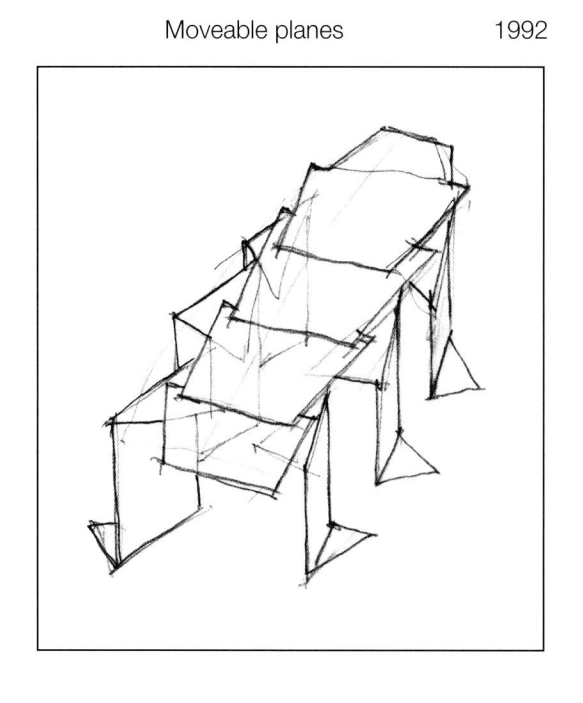

Earth-sky planar building / structure　　1992

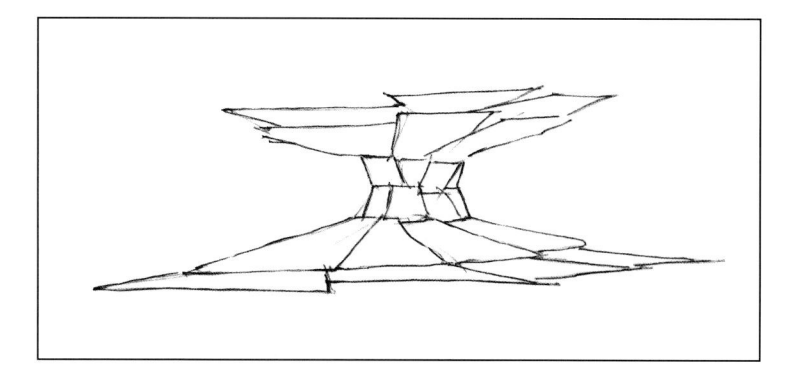

157

II Geometric Forms

1992

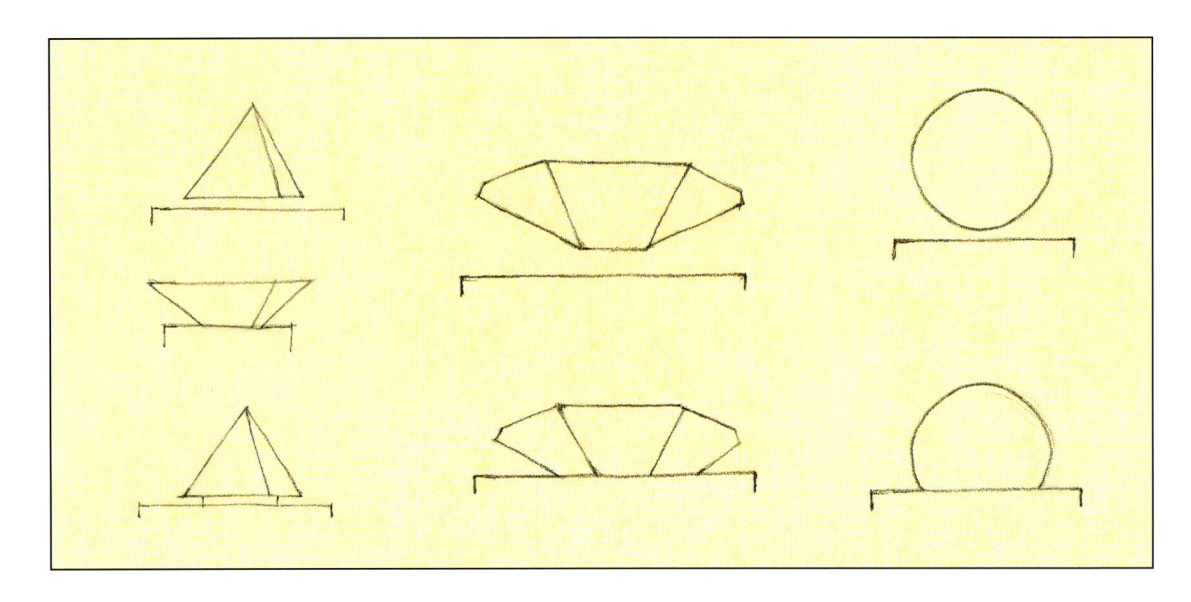

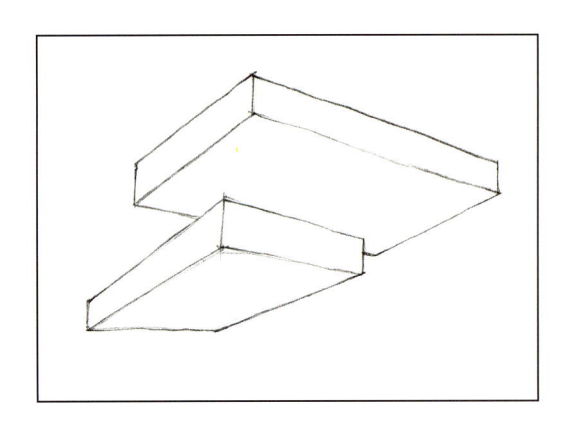

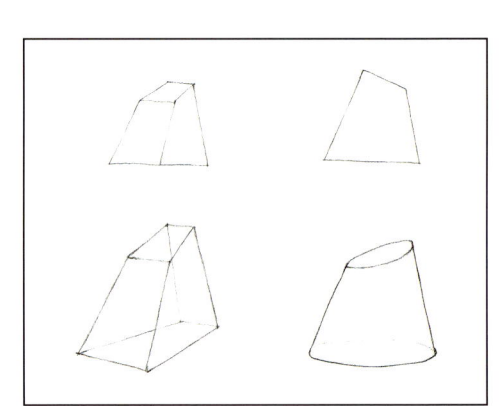

III Free Forms

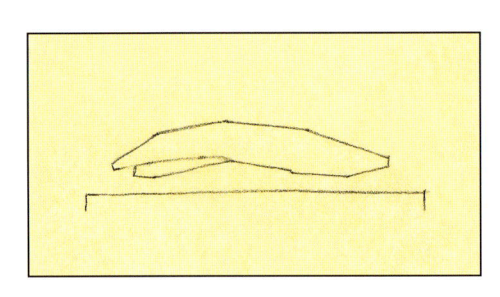

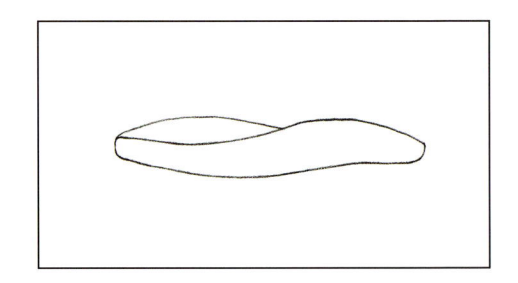

158 EVOLUTION

IV Other Forms

Various Top Possibilities:

Naturally formed sculptural top / sky element reflective of wind forces

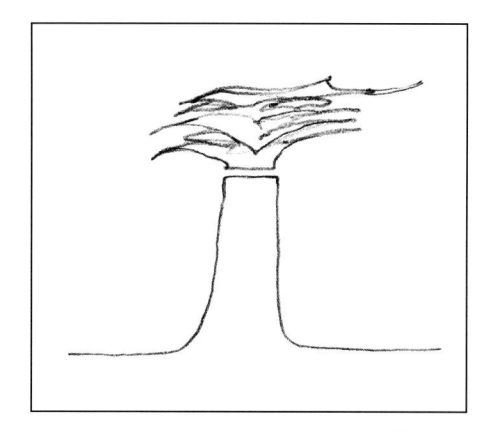

1992

Fire – controlled fire / lighted ribbons on top of the building

Hair – explore different types of synthetic hair forms – bamboo, fiberglass, fiber optics and others

1992

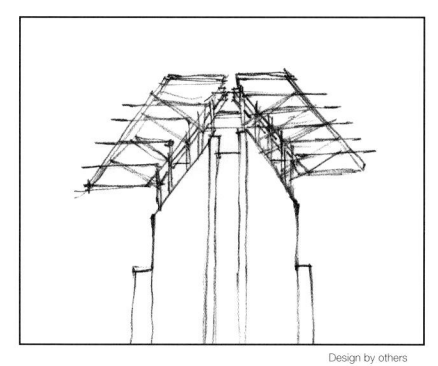

Skeletal stick structures as sky related high rise tops

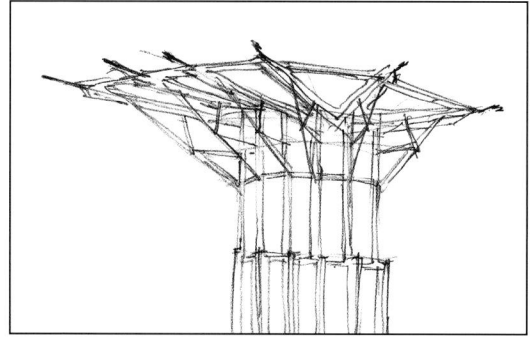

Design by others

Design by others

DEVELOPMENT

▪ ▪ ▪ ▪ ▪ ▪ STUDIES / DRAWINGS
Images that define and make ideas real

Buildings as berms with floating geometric roofs with windows between   1992

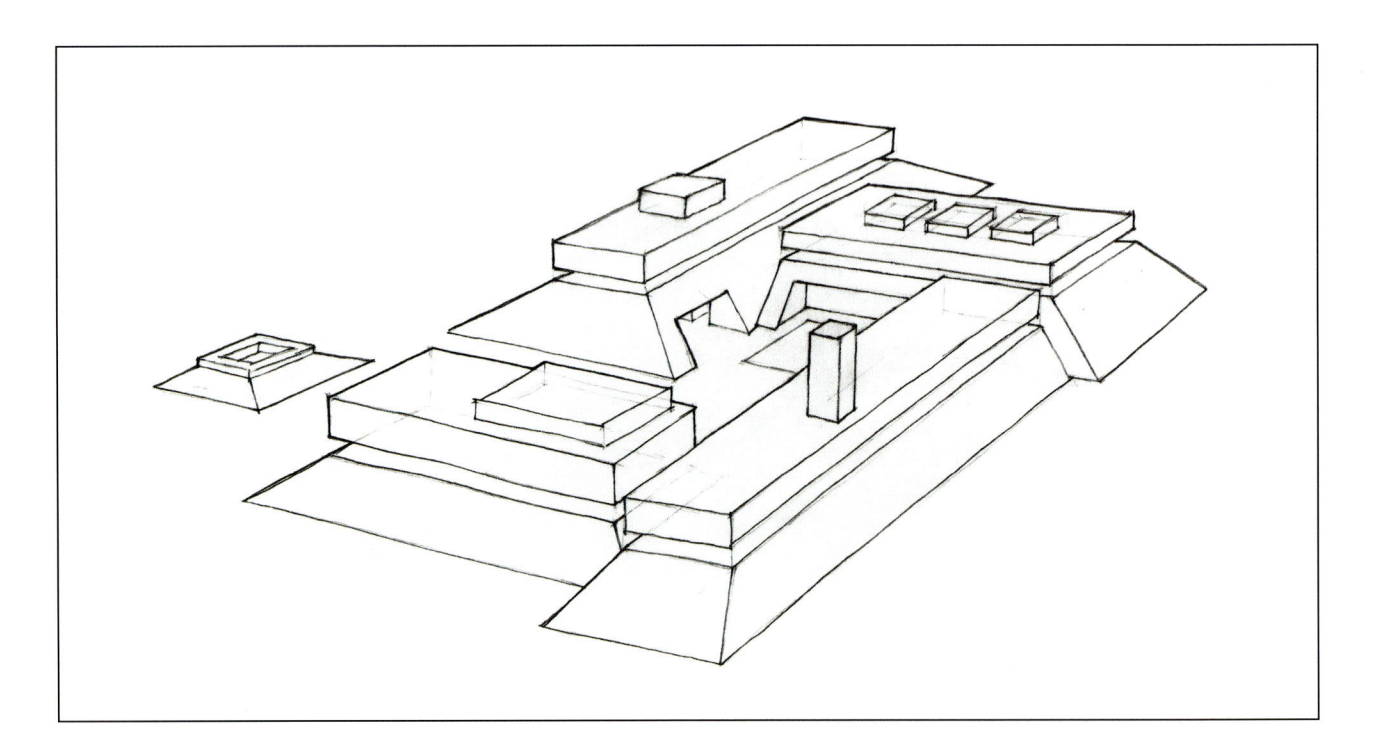

160   EVOLUTION

Evolution of Form   1992

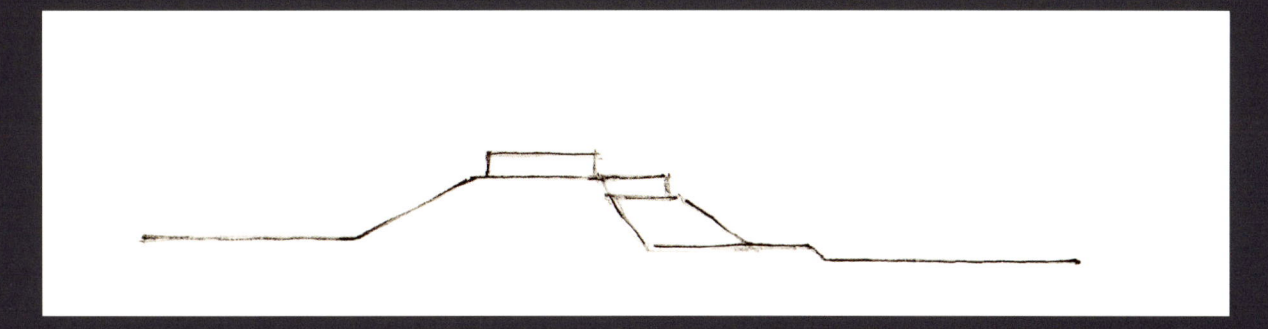

Earth related base and terraces with glass viewing element above

Inverted pyramidal roof form added to make the sky connection

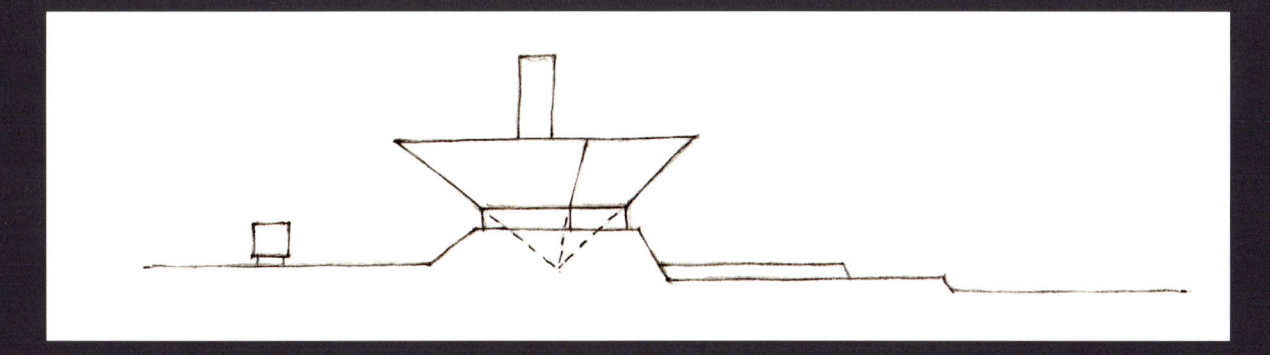

Reproportioned to be lower and wider with additional element in the background

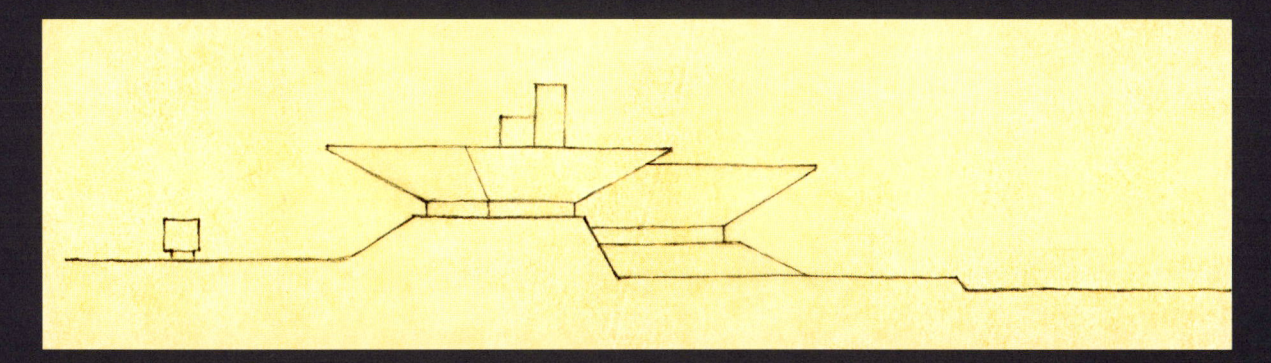

Mesa as earth connected building 1991

Winged roof over earth related planar elements with cave entry 1992

Winged roof over building as sculpted concrete forms 1992

162 EVOLUTION

Building as sky related element on a mesa 1994

Sketch of earth-sky buildings with plan below 1994

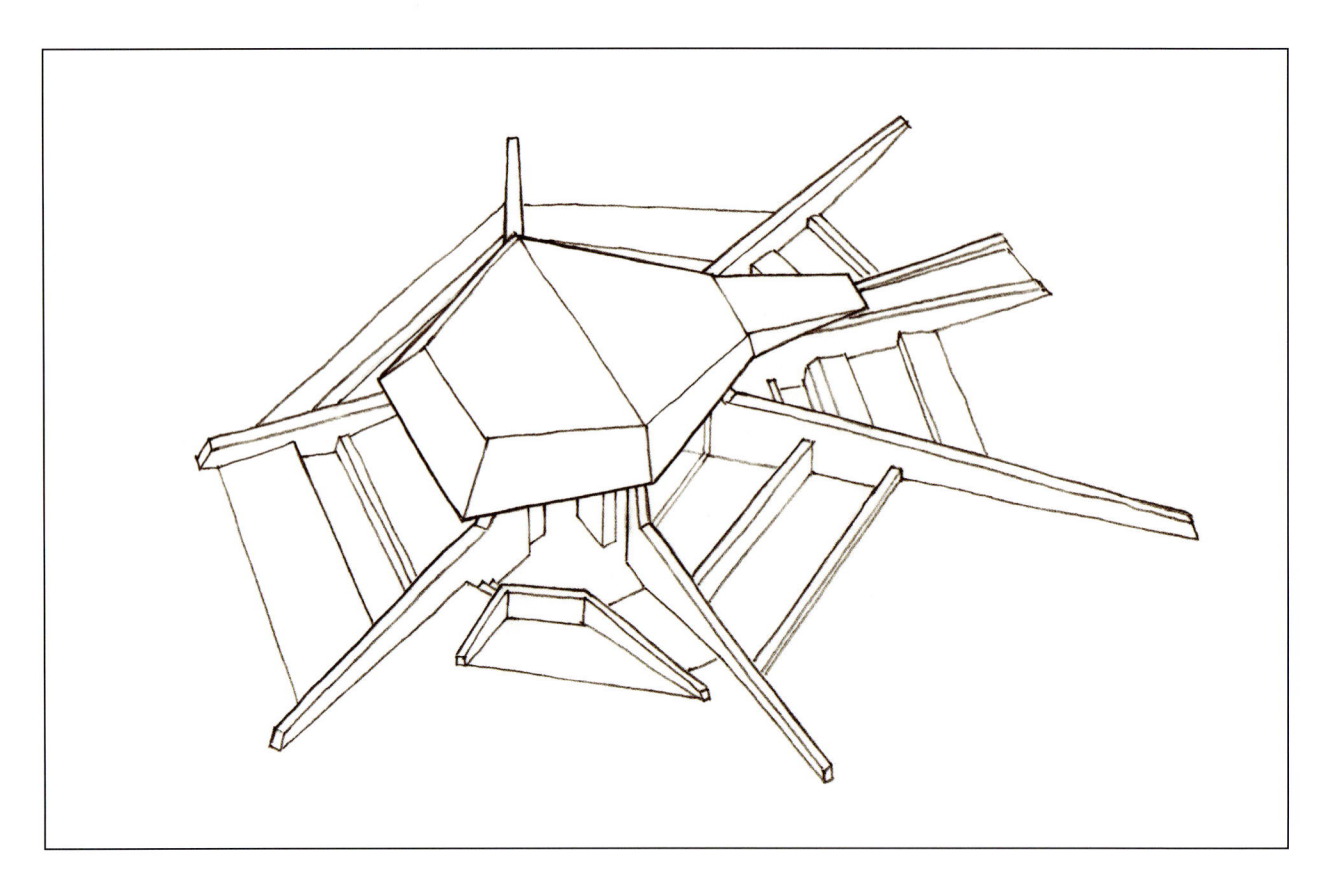

Spider house with organic gardens between radiating walls   1992

Roof variation for collecting and diverting rain water to cistern below house   1992

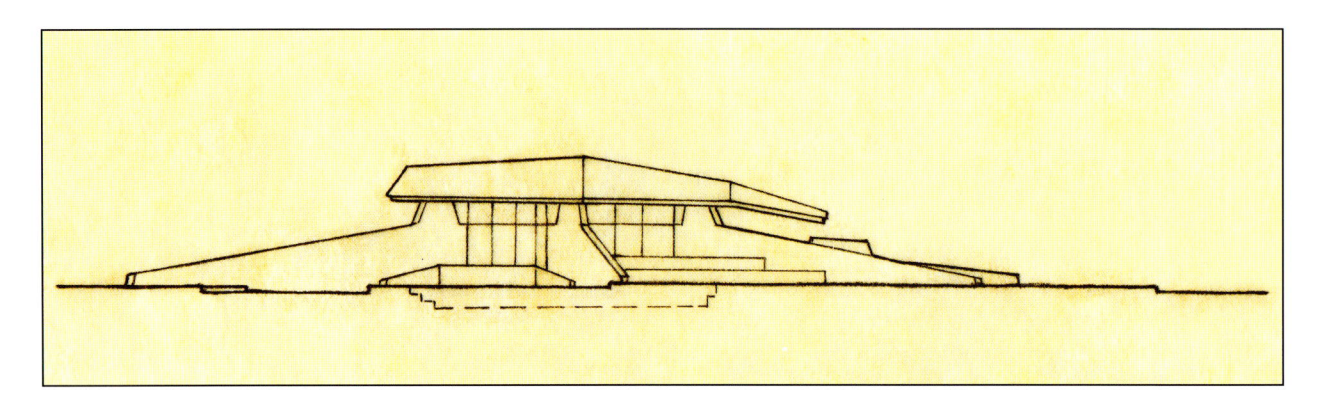

164 EVOLUTION

Study in planar forms   1994

Mendocino Coastal Residence

1992

Strong cold winds from the north, northwest – orient house to south for warmth

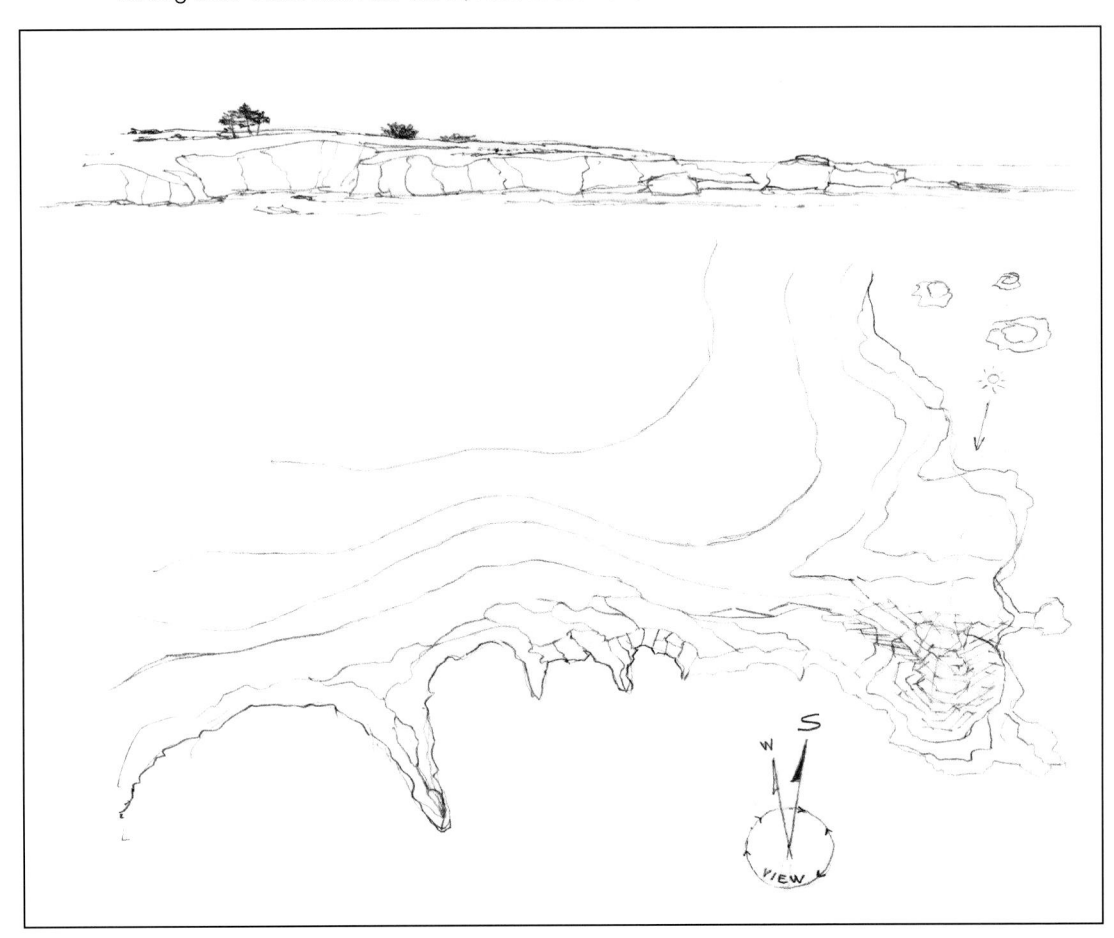

Incorporate top viewing element with protective arms to accommodate 360° view

166 EVOLUTION

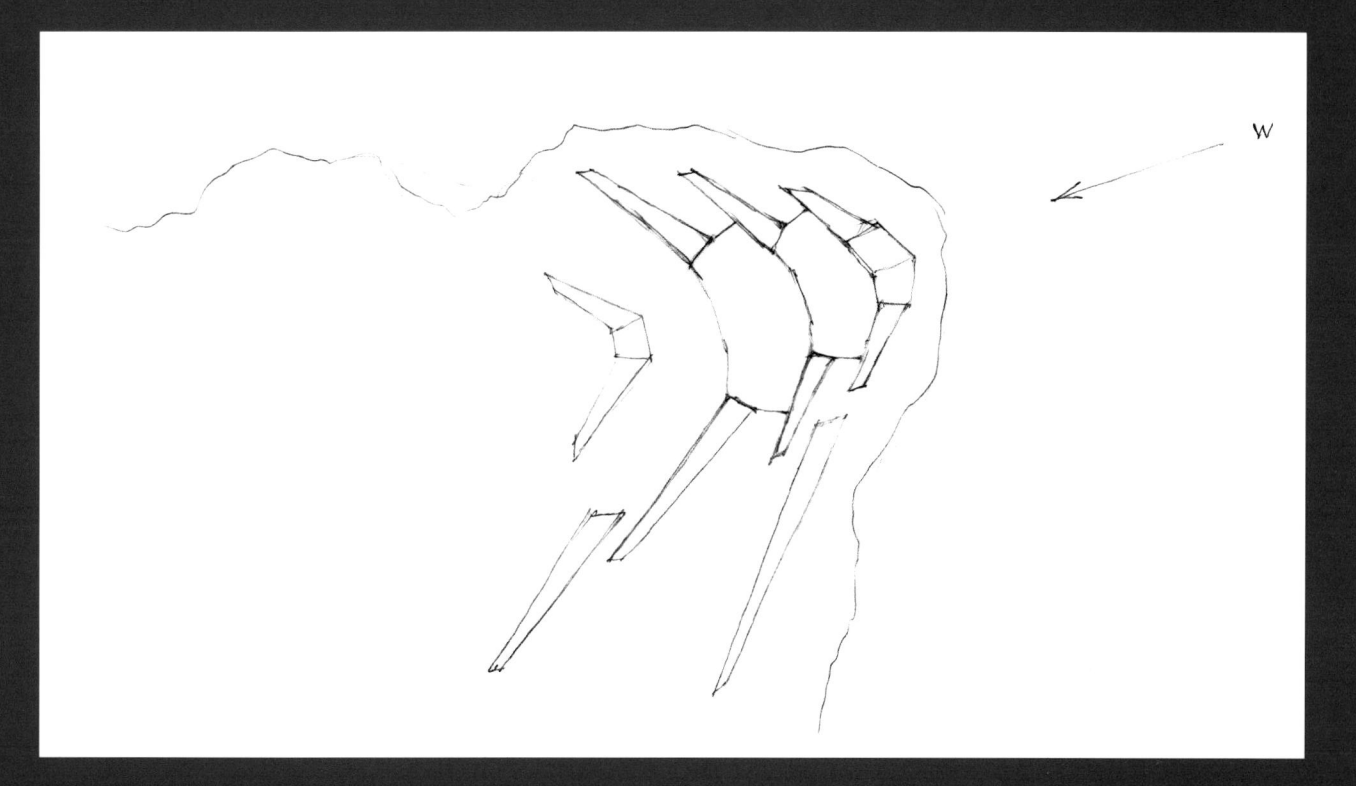

Structure is configured to allow the wind to flow over it with the least resistance

Building of layered planes as of a bird's wing

Fortified lock-down house providing protection from weather or intruders   1994

Massive earth connected base with moveable sky related top

Roof raises and lowers to afford protection / security

168   EVOLUTION

Building as top of hill   1992

Materials and colors integrate architecture with site
Add natural landscaping to fully integrate

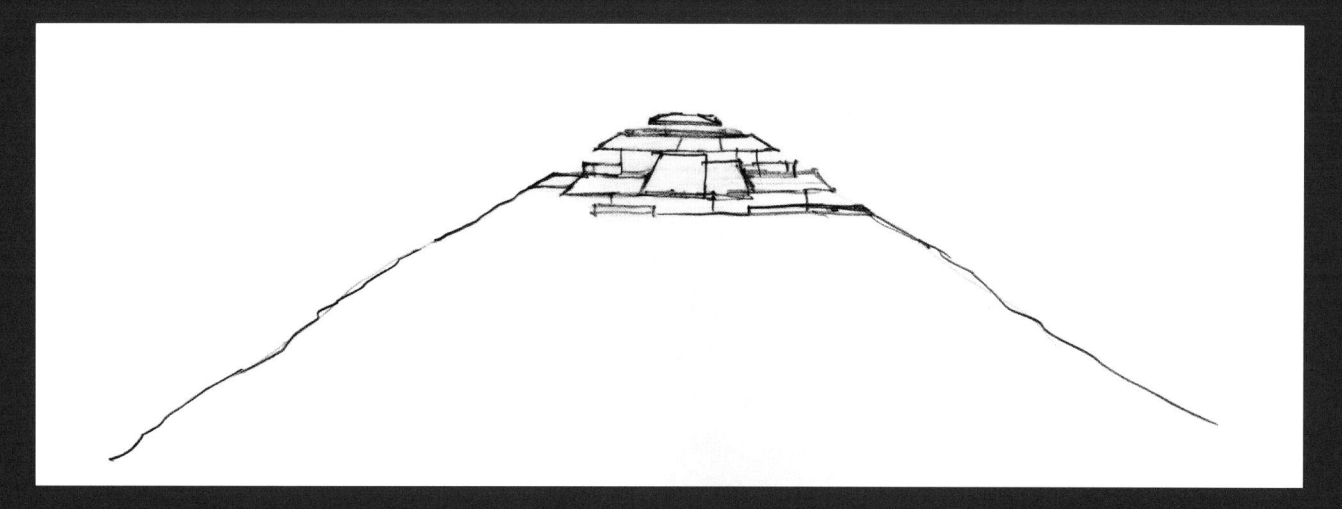

Sculptural sails unfurl to add the sky element

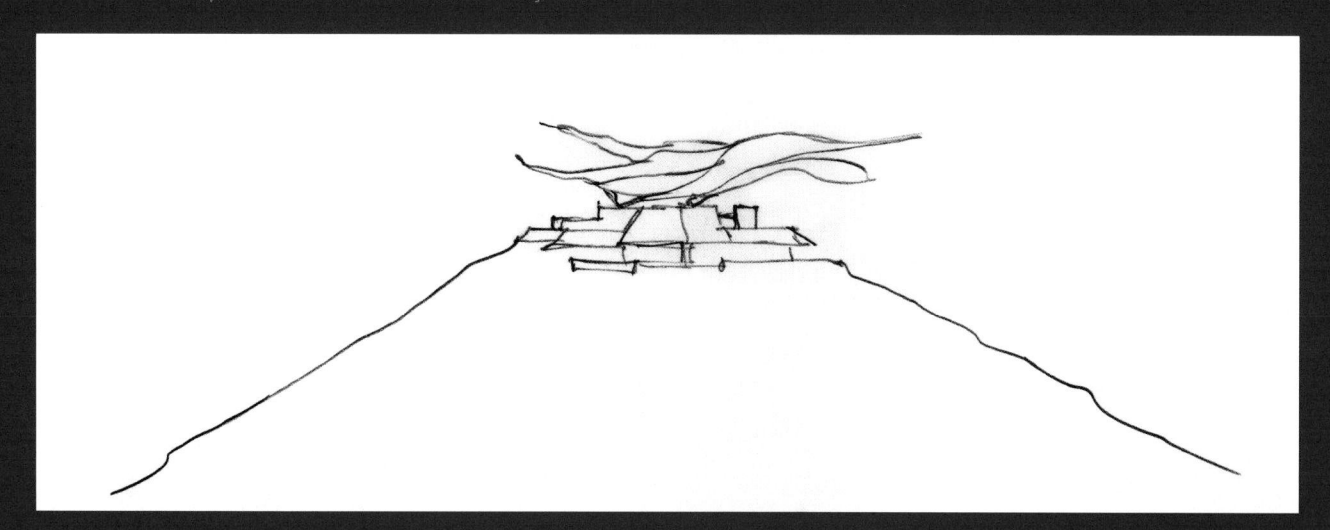

PRECEDENTS

REINFORCING PHILOSOPHIES . . .
Architectural theorists supporting this vision

Most of the following references focus on the architectural vision of earth and sky – others confirm my thoughts concerning symbolic imagery, integration with nature, and balanced ecological systems.

JORN UTZON

Jorn Utzon is a key figure in exemplifying, through his architecture, the relationship between earth and sky. He is the first architect to consciously have a vision that focused on earth and sky. Utzon started pursuing this interest in the late forties following several architectural tours to various parts of the world. Because of both his innate and early experiential influences he became aware of the relationship between earth and sky in nature (clouds forms over the sea), ancient man-made monuments (Mayan pyramids, Chinese caves), traditional oriental buildings (Chinese and Japanese houses), contemporary architecture (Wright's prairie houses), and modern sculpture (Henri Lauren's Aviator's Tomb). Again the adage – *to see what everyone else sees, but to think what no one else thinks* – applies.

"Platforms and Plateaus,"
Zodiac 10 **(1962)**

Platform:
Earth Element

"The Platform as an architectural element is a fascinating feature. I first fell in love with it in Mexico on a study trip in 1949, where I found many variations both in size and idea of the platform. . . . A great strength radiates from them." p. 114.

Utzon considered the "platform", the earth connected base, to be "the backbone of architectural compositions . . . in Greece, the Middle East, India and the Orient." p. 115.

Earth and Sky	"Chinese houses and temples owe much of their feeling of firmness and security to the fact that they stand on a platform with the same outline as that of the roof or sometimes even of larger size, depending on the importance of the building. There is magic in the play between roof and platform." p. 116.
Roof: Sky Element	"The roof can be hanging above, it can be spanning across or jumping over you in one big leap or in many small ones." p. 132.

Bayview House

Jorn Utzon sketches

Platform	"The floor in a traditional Japanese house is a delicate, bridge-like platform. This Japanese platform is like a table, and you do not walk on a table top. It is a piece of furniture." p. 116.
Earth and Sky	"The little mountain, Monte Alban, almost a pyramid, dominates three valleys outside the town, Oaxaca, in Southern Mexico. The top of the pyramid is lacking and leaves a great flat part. . . . By the introduction of staircase arrangements and step-like buildings on the edge of the platform and keeping the central part at a lower level, the mountain top has been converted into a completely independent thing floating in the air, separated from the earth [below], and from up there you see actually nothing but the sky and the passing clouds – a new planet." p. 116.

Monte Alban

Platform	"Some of my projects from recent years are based on this architectural element, the platform. Besides its architectural force, the platform gives a good answer to today's traffic problems." "In the Sydney Opera House scheme, the idea has been to let the platform cut through like a knife, and separate primary and

171

secondary functions completely. On top of the platform the spectators receive the completed work of art and beneath the platform every preparation for it takes place. . . . The buildings stand on top of the platform supporting each other in an undisturbed composition." p. 117

"Silkeborg Museum," *Zodiac 14* **(1965).**

Cave: Sky Connected

"The inspiration for the design of the museum emerges from a number of different experiences – among these, my visit to the caves in Tatting, west of Peking, where hundreds of Buddha sculptures and other figures have been carved in a number of rock caves at the river bed. These sculptures have all kinds of shapes – in contrast to, or in harmony with, the surrounding space. All the caves are of different sizes and shapes and have different sources of light. The old Chinese sculptors have been experimenting with all these possibilities, and the most fantastic result is one cave which is almost completely filled up by a Buddha figure with a face more than 20 feet high. Three narrow platforms connected with ladders give the visitor an opportunity to walk around and get quite close to this gigantic figure." p. 89.

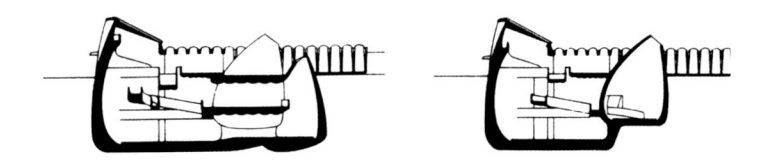

Silkeborg Museum

SIGFRIED GIEDION

Giedion was the first to recognize the significance of Utzon in the architectural modern movement. He was a professor at the Massachusetts Institute of Technology and later at Harvard University where he became Chairman of the Graduate School of Design. He was one of the most important architectural historians from the forties through the sixties.

Space, Time and Architecture **(1965).**

"It is not the independent unrelated form that is the goal of architecture today but the organization of forms in space: space conception. This has been true for all creative periods, including the present. The present space-time conception – the way volumes are placed in spacend relate to one another, the way interior space is separated from exterior space or is perforated by it to bring about an interpenetration – is a universal attribute which is at the basis of all contemporary architecture. . . . To this can be added another factor which is of no little importance and which lies at the basis of the best contemporary architecture. Its emanating force is generated by the respect it has given to the eternal cosmic and terrestrial conditions of a particular region. . . . This penetrating into the cosmic and terrestrial elements of a region I have elsewhere called the 'new regionalism.' The contemporary space conception and contemporary means of expression can reopen a dialogue with these unchanging elements." p. xxxvii.

"A new chapter in this edition, 'Jorn Utzon and the Third Generation,' deals with this changing approach to past history and the relations of his architectural generation to the founders of the modern movement." p. xliv

"The approach to the past always revolves around the same question: How did man in another time under other circumstances solve certain problems, and what were they? The buildings of primitive peoples are often closer to the architect of today than those of later cultures. So it is understandable that a ruin may sometimes express the essentials more immediately than a completely organized palace." p. 670.

"In 1948 . . . in Paris . . . he came in contact with the sculptor Henri Laurens. From him Utzon learned how one builds forms in the air, and how to express suspension and ascension. . . . [that same year] he went to Morocco. What most interested him there was the unity of village and landscape brought about by their identical material – earth. This created an unbroken sculptural unity between the environment and the up to ten-story housing." p. 672.

"Jorn Utzon was inspired by the great scale of the terraced buildings of the Aztecs and Mayas. In the late culture of Mexico, around 1000 A.D., he found a confirmation of something that had always slumbered within him. Several years later, in the article 'Platforms and Plateaus,' he refers to horizontal planes as a means of architectonic expression. . . ." p. 675.

"Jorn Utzon . . . possesses a double gift: he is able to have direct contact with the cosmic elements of nature and the past, and also complete control of contemporary methods of industrialized production – especially prefabrication. As a result he is able to detach prefabrication from its purely mechanistic attributes and bring it nearer to the organic." p. 678.

CHRISTIAN NORBERG-SCHULZ

Norberg-Schulz was one of the foremost architectural theorists and philosophers, particularly in the realm concerning earth and sky. He brought together in his writings Utzon, Heidegger, Bachelard, Wright and other key figures related to this line of inquiry. He was dean of the Oslo School of Architecture and earlier a visiting professor at the Massachusetts Institute of Technology.

***The Concept of Dwelling* (1984).**

"In the short story, Last Man Home, the Norwegian writer Tarjei Vesaas . . . suggests what is basic in the experience of a place. Thus he uses the words 'ground,' 'sky,' and 'horizon' to indicate its content. All places are determined by the ground on which we stand, by the sky above our heads, and by the limit of the horizon." p. 9.

"he [Vesaas] says that the house 'stands solidly on the ground,' 'as if asleep under the winds of the sky.' The house accordingly has something to do with earth and sky. . . ." p. 12.

"Centers may be 'landmarks' as well as 'nodes,' to use the terms of Kevin Lynch. . . . the center in general is experienced as a vertical axis mundi which unites earth and sky, since it is the point where all horizontal movement comes to an end. . . . the vertical is considered the sacred dimension of space. It represents a 'path' towards a reality which may be 'higher' or 'lower' than daily life, a reality which conquers the gravity of earth, or succumbs to it. The axis mundi is therefore more than a center on earth; being a connection between the cosmic realms, it is the place where a breakthrough from one realm to the other can occur. Human life takes place on earth under the sky, and the vertical is therefore experienced as the line of tension." pp. 22-23.

"Our discussion of human orientation shows that having a world does not only mean identification with the qualities embodied by things, but also orientation within the space they constitute. Space admits actions, and hence allows life to take place. As a 'between' of earth and sky, however, existential space is basically different from mathematical space. . . . Buildings, therefore, do not only gather the 'multifarious between' because of their built form, but also because they visualize the spatial properties of a situation. Any case of admittance thus represents a certain way of being between earth and sky . . . built forms are always understood in terms of their being between earth and sky, that is, their standing, rising and opening. The word 'stand' denotes the relationship to the earth, 'rise' the relationship to the sky, and 'open' refers to the interaction with the environment, that is, the relationship between outside and inside." pp. 25-26.

"The outside-inside relationship is first of all expressed through the treatment of the openings in the wall. In the wall, thus, earth and sky meet, and the way man 'is' on earth is embodied in this meeting. But the meeting of earth and sky is not only made manifest by vertical tensions. 'Earth' and 'sky' also imply concrete properties such as material texture, color and light. In general, morphology studies the concrete structure of floor, wall and roof (ceiling), or, in short, the spatial boundaries. The character of a form is determined by its boundaries." p. 27.

"A basic property of existential space is the distinction between horizontal and vertical, and accordingly the two directions play a constituent role within the language of architecture. The horizontal relates to the earth and the vertical to the sky, and thus they determine the kind of dwelling which a certain work of architecture makes manifest. . . . In the single work the type becomes manifest as an image or figure. The language of architecture thus comprises archetypes on all environmental levels." p. 29.

Introduction for *Poetics of Light*, Henry Plummer (A & U, 1987).

"The study of light . . . is something more than a mere investigation of illumination. Light and things belong together, and every place has its light. Light, things and places can only be understood in their mutual relationship. The phenomenology of things and places is also the phenomenology of light. In general, they all belong to the phenomenology of earth and sky. The sky is the origin of light, and the earth its manifestation. Therefore light is the unifying ground of the world." p. 5.

KENNETH FRAMPTON

Frampton is a prominent architectural scholar who has delved considerably into Utzon's work and its significance. He has for many years been a professor at the graduate school of architecture and planning, Columbia University, New York.

"Intimations of Tactility," *Architecture and Body* (1988).

"16. Earth. The tactile gravitates towards the earth, towards the horizontal, towards a technology of building that is timeless and archaic, towards pisé, adobe, ashlar and even rock itself. The work of Jorn Utzon exemplifies an architecture of the earth, set invariably against the 'canopy of the aerial.' It is an architecture of section predicated upon a decisive configuration in the ground, regardless of whether this profile is man-made or natural. The preferred natural forms are the mountain, the declivity, the escarpment and the cave; their artificial equivalents are the platform, the atrium, the terrace and the cistern. These forms are occasions in which the tactile emerges into its own, for the articulation of form resides in the texture of the ground. This is an esthetic which has to be decoded by the body. In Utzon's work one invariably rises onto an acropolis, enters into an atrium, descends an escarpment or penetrates a cave. Utzon's exemplary types may be readily listed: the Sydney Opera House, the Fredensborg Housing, the Elviria Complex, and the Silkeborg Museum. Archaic parallels can be drawn, and in some instances are cited by the architect: the Athenian Acropolis, the ziggurats at Uxmal and Chichen-Itza and the court of the Friday Mosque in Isfahan. For the paradigm of the cave evident in the unbuilt Silkeborg Museum, Utzon was to return to his experience of the Buddhist shrine at Tatung, China. . . ."

Silkeborg Museum

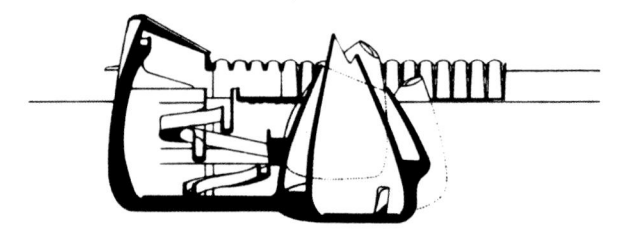

"18. Air. The archaic tradition of inscribing memory in the earth (cf. Heizer, Smithson) is to be complemented by the paradoxical monumentality of the aerial, as in the canopies of Utzon or even more astringently in the trellises, banners, kites and fireworks (cf. Christo, Piene) that are to be commonly found in Oriental culture . . . . A profound untapped expressiveness resides in this opposition between the earth and the aerial; a potential that cuts across history and culture to oppose the archaic gravity of the fixed to the volatile tectonic of light. This much already lies latent as a dormant poetic in Le Corbusier's Pavillion des Temps Nouveaux (1937)."

Studies in Tectonic Culture (1995).

"In many cultures, including that of China, one will find a typical opposition between a heavy weight masonry podium and a lightweight timber roof floating over it, as in Utzon's generic sketch of the podium/pagoda paradigm. We will encounter this formula in one Utzon scheme after another, where it invariably assumes the form of a shell roof or a folded slab structure suspended over a terraced earthwork." p. 248

Sketch of Chinese temple: roof and platform

"a profound feeling for an inflected landscape shaped by topography, climate, time, material, and craft, and hence for an architecture engendered in large measure by natural forces, is a fundamental principle of Utzon's architecture. . . . As to the inspiration that Utzon derived from nature, we may cite Kjeld Helm-Petersen's appreciation of Utzon's Kingo housing to the effect that '[for] this artist there is no essential difference between a city organism and a plant organism.'" p. 250.

"Utzon's short stay in Morocco in 1948 was already indicative of his affinity for the Orient. There he became involved with designs for a gravity-fed paper mill and a stepped housing scheme [in Morocco], both being inspired by indigenous prototypes. What impressed Utzon about the Moroccan vernacular was 'the unity of village and landscape, brought about by their identical material - earth.'" p. 253.

"As I have already remarked, Utzon's architecture may be read in terms of the Semperian[*] formula of the earthwork versus the roofwork. This countervailing but complementary opposition generally appears in his work through the spectrum of three different type forms of increasing hierarchical complexity, each type being largely determined by a variation in the roof. . . . the Silkeborg Museum is something of an exception since it comprises an earthwork that is sunken into the ground and roofed by a mixture of folded-slab and shell form construction." pp. 260-261.

* Harry Mallgrave and Wolfgang Herrmann, *The Four Elements of Architecture and Other Writings by Gottfried Semper*, 1989.

MARTIN HEIDEGGER

"Building, Dwelling, Thinking," *Poetry, Language, Thought* (1971).

Heidegger was one of the foremost existential philosophers of the twentieth century.

"Standing there, the building rests on the rocky ground. This resting of the work draws up out of the rock the mystery of that rock's clumsy yet spontaneous support. Standing there, the building holds its ground against the storm raging above it and so first makes the storm itself manifest in its violence. The luster and gleam of the stone, though itself apparently glowing only by the grace of the sun, yet first brings to light the light of the day, the breadth of the sky, the darkness of the night. . . . It clears and illuminates, also, that on which and in which man bases his dwelling. We call this ground the earth. What this word says is not to be associated with the idea of a mass of matter deposited somewhere, or with the merely astronomical idea of a planet. Earth is that whence the arising brings back and shelters everything that arises without violation. In the things that arise, earth is present as the sheltering agent." p. 41.

"To dwell, to be set at peace, means to remain at peace within the free, the preserve, the free sphere that safeguards each thing in its nature. The fundamental character of dwelling is this sparing and preserving. It pervades dwelling in its whole range. That range reveals itself to us as soon as we reflect that human being consists in dwelling and, indeed, dwelling in the sense of the stay of mortals on the earth. . . . . But 'on the earth' already means 'under the sky.' Both of these also mean 'remaining before the divinities' and include a 'belonging to men's being with one another.' By a primal oneness the four – earth and sky, divinities and mortals – belong together in one. . . . Earth is the serving bearer, blossoming and fruiting, spreading out in rock and water, rising up into plant and animal. When we say earth, we are already thinking of the other three along with it, but we give no thought to the simple oneness of the four. . . . The sky is the vaulting path of the sun, the course of the changing moon, the wandering glitter of the stars, the year's seasons and their changes, the light and dusk of day, the gloom and glow of night, the clemency and inclemency of the weather, the drifting clouds and blue depth of the ether. . . . The divinities are the beckoning messengers of the godhead. . . . The mortals are the human beings. They are called mortals because they can die." pp. 147-148.

"man dwells by spanning the 'on the earth' and the 'beneath the sky.' This 'on' and 'beneath' belong together. Their interplay is the span that man traverses at every moment insofar as he is as an earthly being." p. 221.

GASTON BACHELARD

The Poetics of Space (1958).

Bachelard held, for many years, a chair of philosophy at the Sorbonne in Paris.

"The reader who is alive to the accompaniment of cosmic poetry that is always active beneath the psychological story in Bosco's novels, will find evidence, in many pages of this book [L'Antiquaire], of the dramatic tension between the aerial and the terrestrial.
By following Henri Bosco, we shall experience a house with cosmic roots. This house with cosmic roots will appear to us as a stone plant growing out of the rock up to the blue sky of a tower." p. 22.

"the house Bosco describes stretches from earth to sky. It possesses the verticality of the tower rising from the most earthly, watery depths, to the abode of the soul that believes in heaven." p. 25.

VICTOR CHRIST-JANER

"Constituent Imagery," Perspecta 17 (1980).

Christ-Janer was an acclaimed architect who was also a professor at the graduate school of architecture and planning, Columbia University, New York.

"'Where the Earth Meets the Sky'
In an attempt to attach a special meaning to recurrent images and to suggest that the image operates uniquely and meaningfully in support of the psychological equilibrium, the image of earth and sky presents itself as all important. The image of earth and sky has its roots so deeply grounded in the psyche as to give to this image the first priority. It is one in a series of seminal recurrent image considerations in this paper and is discussed first because it forms the setting upon which all history is acted out. This image suggests a case where the physical setting demands man's response in order to live in the world. The response takes form as either intuitive action or as an act of intentionality. If the intuitive response has its origins in the unconscious or preconscious, it operates simultaneously with conscious intentionality to produce the possibility of change in the earth-sky configuration. This change, as an act of intentionality, I refer to as the act of building or 'making' an act of poietics [creating]." p. 11.

PRECEDENTS

▪ ▪ ▪ ▪ ▪ RELATED STRUCTURES
Historic buildings exemplifying these principles

Architecture throughout history has symbolically depicted the idea of earth and sky. Forms were expressed, especially in the beginning, as earth connected elements with the sky implied, while others, later on, expressed both earth and sky.

Of the many architects through history whose structures incorporated the imagery of earth and sky, none that I can find, save Utzon, have left a record of their thoughts related to this vision in the form of writings and/or drawings. For the rest this idea seems to have been operating on a subliminal level, but still expressed in their work.

JORN UTZON

**Sydney Opera House,
Sydney, Australia
1957 – 1973**

Floating roof forms over earth connected platform

source unknown

**Silkeborg Museum,
Silkeborg, Denmark
1964 (design)**

An in-the-earth building with vertical sky connections

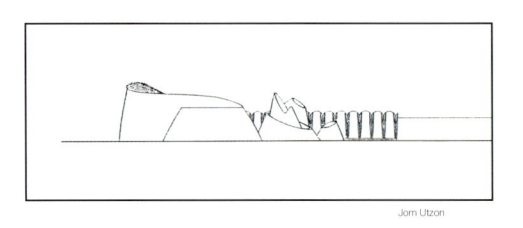

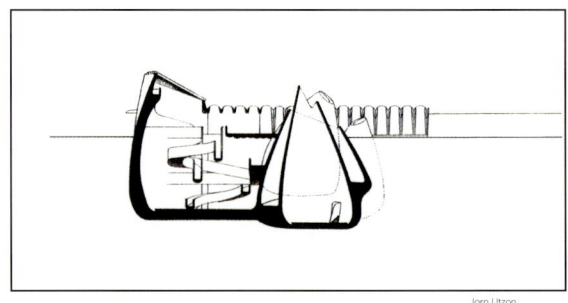

Jorn Utzon

Jorn Utzon

180 EVOLUTION

FRANK LLOYD WRIGHT

**Robi House,
Chicago, Illinois
1909**

Roof forms floating over multilevel base elements

Hedrich Blessing

**Falling Water,
Connellsville,
Pennsylvania
1936**

A restatement of earth forms as floating sky related elements above

Hedrich Blessing

LE CORBUSIER

**Notre-Dame-du-Haut,
Ronchamp, France
1955**

Freeform roof floating above massive earth related masonry walls

Prithwish Neogy

MIES VAN DER ROHE

**Bacardi Office Building
Santiago, Cuba
1958**

Space frame roof structure over a raised platform base

EERO SAARINEN

**Dulles Airport,
Chantilly, Virginia
1962**

Sky related floating roof suspended over a platform base structure

ALVAR AALTO

**Shiraz Art museum,
Shiraz, Iran
1970**

Earth related building expressed as an extension of the land contours

GIO PONTI

**Pirelli Building,
Milan, Italy
1955**

Two embracing earth related vertical building slabs with a floating roof top

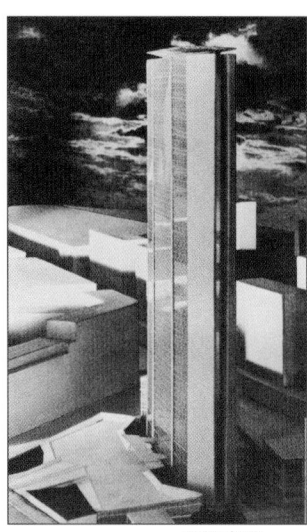

BHUTAN HOUSE

Thimphu, Bhutan
1920

Floating roof over wood and rammed earth house base

CAPPADOCIA

Göreme, Turkey
1000 B.C.

Natural earth connected tufa stone bases with sky related basalt tops

STONEHENGE

Wiltshire, England
2500 B.C.

Earth connected vertical stones with sky related cross members

PYRAMIDS

Giza, Egypt
2500 B.C.

Pyramidal forms as a restatement of mountains and the earth

SYNTHESIS

ESENCE ▪ ▪ ▪ ▪ ▪ ▪ ▪ ▪ ▪
A balance of forces

Synthesis is the bringing together of parts so as to form a whole – whereas *analysis* is the opposite, the separation of a whole into parts to understand its nature and workings. To achieve synthesis in its purest form is to approach the *essence* of a thing, to find that harmonious balance of all the forces acting upon it.

This balance of forces can sometimes happen in a natural way when circumstances are such that individuals are forced to take the course of least resistance, especially if physical and material resources are limited. A prime example is *indigenous architecture*, which comes close to an essence of expression. There is an efficiency of design and construction influenced by multiple factors.

The most determinant of these is *place* – the physical site on the face of the earth. One cannot discuss earth and sky, the terrestrial and the cosmic elements, without discussing "spirit of place," the essence embodied in a location. The earth in a particular place can be looked upon as a coded message – full of clues, earthbound information and skybound information. The following factors are determined by place:

light	sounds
colors	smells
sun orientation	climate
topography	materials
plants	structures
wildlife	context
water	culture
geological formations	history

When, out of necessity, these factors are taken into consideration, as is the case with indigenous architecture, the resultant structures integrate naturally with the local landscape. The architecture has a unity, it feels right, it belongs.

Bernard Rudofsky points out in *Architecture Without Architects* – the architecture of primitive people is often fundamentally better than that of the present.

As can be seen in the following images, indigenous architecture has, in terms of colors, materials and forms, a natural unity and integration with the surrounding environment. It has many lessons to teach us.

Trulli House Complex, Alberobello, Italy

Himalayan House, Bhutan

Rural Farm House, Hungary

Ruins fall into the realm of indigenous architecture. They are intriguing, inspiring and significant in so many ways. Ruins are earth connected imagery – solid to the ground, fragmented and airy to the sky. The earth is reclaiming the man-made structure, pulling it back into her bosom. Ruins can be seen as pieces of art, sculpture in balance with the forces from above and from below.

Christopher Woodward, the author of *In Ruins*, states that the viewing of a ruin is "a meditation on time, transience, and humanity." What Woodward puts forth as the observer's required participation is very close to my view of *abstract art*. "A ruin is a dialogue between an incomplete reality and the imagination of the spectator." And he goes on, "Each spectator is forced to supply the missing pieces from his or her own imagination and a ruin therefore appears differently to everyone."

Ruins are very important inspirational sources for my own architectural work.

Corfe Castle, Wareham, Dorset, England

Tantallon Castle, North Berwick, Scotland

Chaco Canyon, New Mexico

Architecture, the man-made, has an effect on *place*. The changes made indelibly reconfigure the landscape. It is our responsibility, as humans first and as architects second, to enhance and not destroy a *place* by what we create.

We leave testimony of our existence as a society – we contribute to the continuum. The threads of the unconscious human psyche continually reemerge in built form.

It is more advantageous to have a creative approach that operates on a philosophical level rather than on merely a form level. An approach which is flexible and fluid to all the variables can accommodate any *place* on the planet.

Building materials and colors from the locale
Abha, Saudi Arabia

Architecture reflective of surrounding tree forms
Stinson Beach, California – Val Agnoli, Architect

Monastery of Docheiariou, Greece

Poetry distills language to its essence. The term poetry is often used to describe any creative pursuit, whether it be literature, art, architecture, music, dance or others, that strives toward the inherent nature of a thing – its spirit. When this is achieved it is readily evident in its beauty, balance and simplicity.

Architecture, on its highest level, is the pursuit of poetic form. As with literary poetry, it employs images and symbols to achieve its essence. These are the common language of the psyche that transcends the purely physical.

Joseph A. Burton, an architectural historian who focused on Louis I. Kahn, concluded from Kahn's writings that, "the architect must practice his discipline as a poet and search for the appropriate visual symbols. In Kahn's mind, the art of architecture is a poetic language. It is nonverbal, consisting of physical ciphers meant to be read. Architecture 'speaks' through silent but evocative, corporeal images directed to the eye."

The closer one can bring something to its essence, the more meaningful it will be over an extended period of time. It approaches the timeless.

SYNTHESIS

▪ ▪ ▪ ▪ ▪ ▪ ▪ ▪ ▪ FLEXIBLE / FLUID
Allowing the design to achieve wholeness

The only permanent thing in life is change. With this in mind, whatever one is creating should be thought of as an evolving organism, even though it may be inert or mechanical in nature. The thing, object, idea under consideration is changing and growing in the course of its development, and will eventually come to its own resting place. One is continually defining his vision throughout the process, while at the same time allowing for it to move in any direction.

Staying flexible is particularly important in architecture where there are thousands of forces acting on a building: aesthetics, place, culture, function, construction, cost and so on. One has to let the structure flow, with controlled guidance, into its own being.

In my work I try not to categorize myself. To do so would put a psychological limitation on what I pursue or attempt. I want all possibilities open to me. I think of myself as one who creates, not exclusively an architect. I design and invent what interests me – books, photographs, learning tools, educational systems, metal forges, cars, motorcycles, computer operating structures, engines, furniture, buildings and cities. To me they are all interconnected. Many of the same principles that control one apply to another.

To remain flexible it is important to take respites, change focus, do a pleasurable activity – which allows the conscious mind to turn off and the unconscious to engage. The unconscious mind is the place where creative thoughts make breakthroughs, and even extraordinary leaps.

Charles Darwin had a nature walk constructed on his property where he would go when confronted with a difficult or seemingly unsolvable problem. He would focus on the walk and the wonders of nature around him. Darwin claimed that invariably ideas and solutions would present themselves.

Flexibility is another way of dealing with ambiguity – the unknown. It allows the time for more clues / solutions to present themselves while maintaining confidence that answers will emerge. I find this unhurried natural course to be the most effective way to balance forces and achieve essence.

Town of Al-Hajra, Yemen – In balance with the natural environment

III

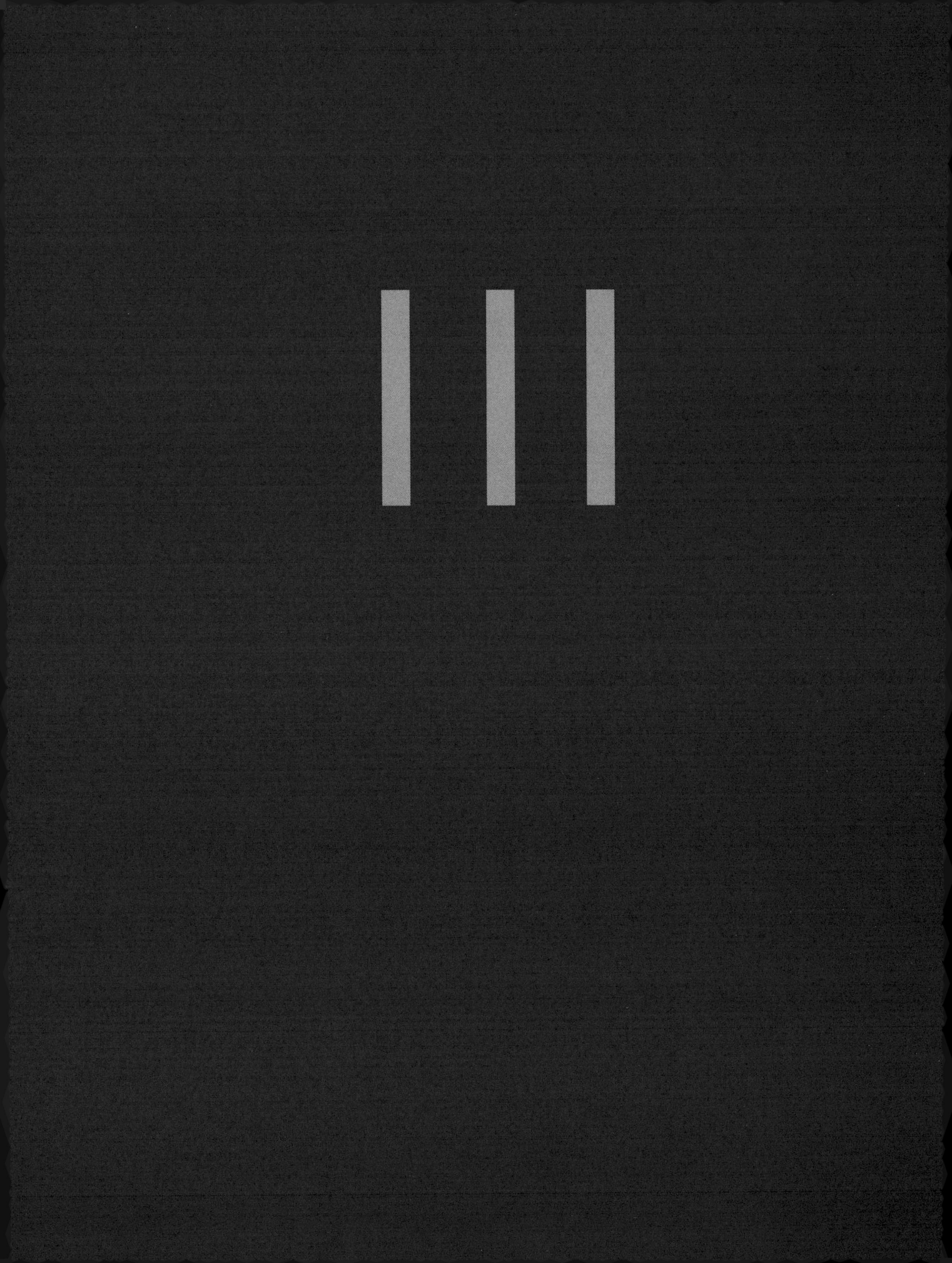

THE REALITY

Forms and expressions made whole

Sources, influences and manifestations culminating in an idea defined

From architecture and urban planning to sculpture and functional objects

PRINCIPLES

HUMAN . ARCHITECTURAL . DESIGN
Personal guiding criteria influencing expression

All creative acts start with the individual and his general life principles. These principles define who we are and extend outward in the directions we want to pursue; they are what we hold to be true, right, and of value at any specific moment in time. We commit to them but allow for evolution and readjustment as we gain insight and understanding into a particular situation or subject area. Since life is constant change, it behooves us to be flexible and fluid to maintain a position of equilibrium in all we do.

It is difficult to clearly separate *human*, *architectural*, and *design* principles. They are interconnected and flow one into the other.

HUMAN

Basic personal beliefs affect everything in life. We each have a unique set of values and parameters that we live by, whether we are aware of them or not. Just look at your siblings who came from the same parents and grew up in the same environment; how differently some of them pursue life. In this same regard, closely observe your extended family, your friends, co-workers, and/or fellow students. Note their political views, religious beliefs, aesthetic sensitivities, living spaces, who they admire, physical activities, and entertainment choices and you will quickly realize how their individual beliefs affect all that they do.

I give only a sampling of my personal beliefs and values as examples, not as they would apply to someone else. Variations and combinations will be different for everyone.

In examining my own approach, I have a tendency to break things down to their simplest terms – in life, in creative endeavors, in architecture and in the design process. The two most important human principles I have come to live by are:

Treat others as you would want to be treated.

Covers most moral issues

Utilize your natural talents and abilities.

Be in touch with your true spirit

What follows are a few other factors that are important to me – not in the category of principles, but they still govern my behavior.

Nature

Beauty

Creativity

Love

Friends

What each of these means to me affects my entire life.

ARCHITECTURAL

The more profound the thought process, the more meaningful the architecture. The thought process sets up the conditions for both conscious and unconscious pathways, allowing for the flow of ideas. Design is not just an intellectual exercise, however; the intellectual brings us to the point where the unconscious can engage.

With meaning we arrive at the essence of a particular thing, in this case a work of art. The irrelevant is stripped away.

The meaning behind something is almost always multileveled. The considerations in architecture are endless, but narrow considerably when passed through the filter of one's individuality and uniqueness. By tuning into our preferences and intuitions we develop a set of priorities that guide us through the creative process.

Creative works involve **multiple considerations**. When designing a letter opener the variables are few, maybe twenty, as opposed to architecture where there are thousands, even tens of thousands. This may sound overwhelming, but is quite manageable when the following principles are kept in mind.

Order of priorities

Arrange the considerations in the order of personal preferences.
This is the uniqueness one brings to the work of art.

Flexible and fluid
Allow for the many factors that will have an influence on the final outcome. Guide the process but let the work – building, painting, photograph – flow into its own being.

Faith
Have faith in your ability to succeed. I find that part of faith is to just keep moving forward with the assumption you have the power to succeed. If you are where you should be, reaching beyond what you know, real creative breakthroughs can occur. There will always be doubt; when this happens I usually recall what Herman Hesse wrote: "I . . . learned by experience that faith and doubt belong together, that they govern each other like inhaling and exhaling. . . ."

Umbrella concepts play a large part in my thinking. They are part of the idea of overviews in combination with wholeness. Umbrella concepts are broad groups of integrated principles that apply to various creative situations helping to make the work whole. Again they are related to what one deems important – the uniqueness factor. Umbrella concepts can vary in scope from all-encompassing to a limited realm, as in the range exemplified below.

I first envision architecture with the broadest of umbrellas – **the earth and the sky.** The earth is the base element; the sky is the aerial element, with human activity occurring between the two. The broader the umbrella the more one can do under it in terms of form and expression. The earth and sky umbrella is the major commonality of my work.

Man between earth and sky, as it implies, takes into consideration man as an integral part of the **total ecosystem**, from the leaf to the universe, with the idea of creating architecture that, among other things:

Is in harmony with nature
Produces balanced microsystems
     – buildings
     – cities
Conserves resources
Fulfills human psychic needs
Has physical permanence
Maintains simplicity

On a smaller scale, I use **concepts of territories** in organizing a building. I do not see buildings in terms of floor plans, but rather as areas with defined boundaries. In the case of a residence, these areas range from the *public* (living, dining, kitchen and family room), to the *semi-private* (children's bedrooms and play areas), to the most *private* (master bedroom and sanctuary).

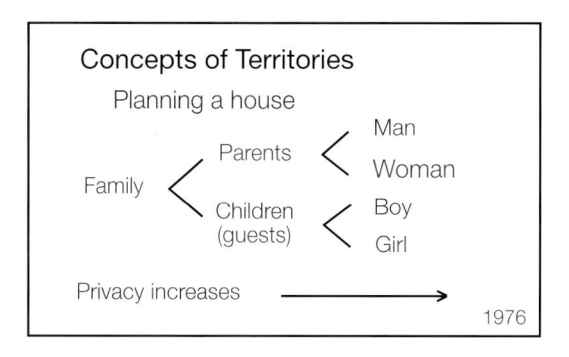

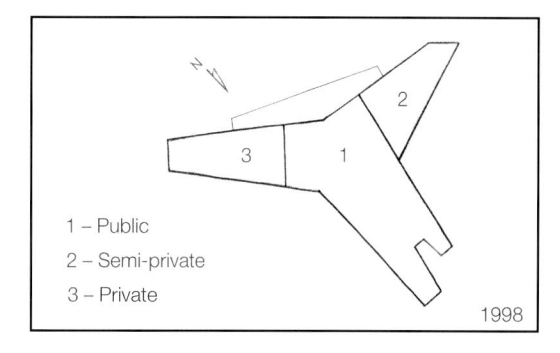

Territories index card

Hawk Hill House territories (full plan p. 239.)

These different territories can sometimes be separated by level changes, floor textures, and / or distance. For instance, a guest is less likely to wander into someone's personal space when he or she has to lift a leg to step from a hard surface to a soft surface. Building territories are not necessarily specific to particular occupants, but can be more universal in their application and use. Buildings usually outlive the people they were designed for and often their original designated functions change.

DESIGN

As with any skill, we develop our design abilities over time, starting with small unsure steps until we accumulate the tools, the experience and the facility to put them together with confidence. This does not happen instantly, except in rare cases where an individual can draw from proficiency in other similar fields or has an innate capability. It is not important where one starts, but how far he goes in his quest. This requires determination, discipline, and faith.

A few words about tools – **tools** are essential to any creative process whether it be architecture, sculpture, music or cooking. The foremost of these is the ability to record one's thoughts, ideas and mental images. *Drawing, photography, notebooks and sketch cards* are the recording tools I find to be the most useful and applicable to my circumstances.

Drawing

Drawing is an indispensable tool no matter what you do in life and it is also a language understood by most people around the world. A drawing is a very effective way to record and / or communicate ideas and images from the conscious and unconscious mind. The act of drawing itself stimulates and pulls ideas from the unconscious.

Photography

Photography is a valuable tool – important in many ways: It records information and captures what you find significant – natural forms, buildings, people – for immediate or future reference. It is one of the best tools for learning aesthetic principles, by repeatedly composing within a framed format. And, it puts you in touch with yourself. When taking photographs thoughtfully you are looking in a mirror – to your inner self. Creative photographer, Richard Benson, explained it as "the instantaneous net that is cast out onto the world, grabbing up . . . information. And . . . the synthesis that the photographer makes with the camera, the eye and the finger. The decision as to where the net is thrown. And the moment it's thrown. And the meaning of all the things as they sit together in the frame." This leads to photography as an art form.

Notebooks

Notebooks can be organized with a structured format that affords the maximum freedom for any combination of materials to be assembled: text, drawings, photos, cutouts, tracings. My preferred arrangement is a flexible three ring notebook cover, in a solid color, with blank white paper. At the top of each entry, I put a title (underlined), then the material / information / drawings to be included, followed by the date, and if applicable, references and / or influences. This allows me to organize the material, know when I thought of it and what caused me to think of it. I have different notebooks for different categories. In planning a trip, I put together a travel notebook for that trip. Other separate notebooks include photography, architecture, sculpture, teaching and mechanical devices.

Index Cards

Blank 3x5 index cards are a flexible and portable version of the notebook. I use a small flat leather holder for my cards allowing the whole assemblage to fit into a pocket without being bent or crushed. This packet of several cards is always with me for one never knows when inspiration will strike. The same structured format used for the notebook applies to the index cards: title, drawing and/or text and the date.
The cards themselves can be organized into a file system arranged by title or by date, or the contained information can be transferred to the large notebooks for development and expansion depending on need and preference.

One's ability to **concentrate** is of prime importance in the pursuit of any creative activity. Concentration occurs when we are lost in our thoughts, when we are totally committed and focused to the exclusion of all else. It is a mental place, just past the conscious veil, inside the mind. 'Allow' yourself to flow with the course of least resistance in a relaxed and unpressured way; it is as simple and as difficult as holding the same thought. The subject matter is the thing to focus on – not the thought process.

Concentration can occur under various circumstances, sometimes spontaneously, but in most cases under structured conditions. Accidental or spontaneous concentration is nice when it happens, but not something one can count on. It can occur while sitting on a rock, under low tree cover, looking into the rhythmic movement of a stream or while standing on a cliff overlooking the setting sun as it sinks into the misty horizon. These are gifts that on occasion can be repeated.

With structured conditions, there are numerous scenarios and approaches involving commitment and the setting up of circumstances that consistently give results.

One might like the quiet of her studio in the evening, at the drawing board, under a pool of light, with the sound of soft conducive music coming out of the darkness.

Whereas, another wants to be at the local gathering place in the morning, where he is fixed to his seat, at a small round table, drinking tea. Only through concentration can he get beyond the ambient noise level and deep into his work.

And yet another might go into controlled contemplation by sitting upright in a comfortable chair, closing the eyes, quietly relaxing the body and clearing the mind, then calmly thinking about the subject to be focused on.

Many avenues to concentration could be employed by a single individual.

Intense concentration is a capacity characteristic of great thinkers, writers, artists, inventors. Prime examples are Newton, Darwin, Michelangelo and Einstein. True concentration opens pathways to the unconscious – the source of the most profound creativity. Concentration leads to inspiration.

Developing an understanding of **aesthetic principles** is not only mandatory for artists, but is of great benefit to anyone. This sensitivity leads to an appreciation of the beauty in our world. Aesthetic awareness enhances life.

To put aesthetic principles in proper perspective as they apply to art and architecture one can go back to Marcus Vitruvius – to his criteria for judging art: *firmness, commodity, and delight* (see p. 42). Aesthetic principles relate to *commodity* which deals with function – the function to communicate, among other things, beauty, which in turn contributes to the *delight* factor.

The principles of aesthetics are generally referred to in schools as **basic design**, which is comprised of numerous elements – elements that we investigate and explore separately, but in the end put together selectively in relationship to one another – creating a wholeness of expression.

Some of these elements / principles are listed below. For further investigation, there are many excellent books available on the subject of aesthetics / basic design, which is a whole study area in itself.

Form	Simplicity
Space	Contrast
Light	Scale
Unity	Value
Balance	Line
Proportion	Texture
Composition	Color
Rhythm / Repetition	Motion
Emphasis / Focal Points	Structure
Edge Conditions / Boundaries	Wholeness

Initially one learns the principles. As time passes they will order themselves to reflect one's perception of the world. If one were to use or combine all of the aesthetic principles at once, a visual "smorgasbord" would be produced, not pleasing to the eye. Each individual must seek his own preferences. Some things will be naturally emphasized more than others.

How we approach anything is dependent on our **attitude**. I have two handmade signs pinned up in my studio, "Attitude is everything" is the most prominent. It puts me in the mental place of having a 'can do' mind-set with which there is no limit to what will be accomplished. 'Can do' leads to motivation which in turn leads to enthusiasm. By shifting your attitude, you will improve your life. The other equally important sign is of a William Blake quote, "Execution is the chariot of genius." One must commit to "doing it" – in this case the creative process.

The **creative process** (or as it is referred to in the architectural world, *the design process*) is, in its essence, the translation of ideas (abstract thought) into physical reality (form). It is a continual process of absorbing and reflecting. There are as many ways to accomplish this as there are individuals.

The ways of approaching the creative process are generally consistent but can also vary depending on the mysteries of the psyche. There are rare times, now that I have many years of experience, when an idea for something will enter my mind in its complete form, with the details – the whole process happening instantaneously.

In most cases the creative process follows a sequence one invents to suit his or her own uniqueness. It can be thought of as a kind of exploration that begins the moment one conceives of an idea to create something. This initial idea is not the concept. The concept is an approximate image of the end product. With the *idea* in mind, one proceeds to absorb as many factors as possible concerning the work to be created. Look for clues, particularly from the site. Keep in mind that the final outcome will be determined by the factors already inherent in the variables. Stay flexible and fluid throughout. Have faith in your intuition – knowing the results will flow from the unconscious realm.

The artist must attune himself to that which wants to reveal itself and permit the process to happen through him. Martin Heidegger, philosopher.

In gathering the facts and information – **the design considerations** – one begins to assimilate the material into his unconscious. It helps to keep an open mind to allow for the unencumbered flow of thoughts and ideas, which naturally leads to connections.

At some point during this process one intuitively develops a **concept**, a mental image of what he wants to create. It can be vague and general in nature or approach the definitive. The concept is particular to a project, it embodies one's vision, but varies depending on conditions: site, location, resources, building program and numerous other factors.

The concept is a specific theme toward which one is moving, continually absorbing and reflecting, making decisions and judgments. The closer one gets, the more defined the design becomes.

Concept Sketches

Desert School

Concept: *block sun – collect north light*

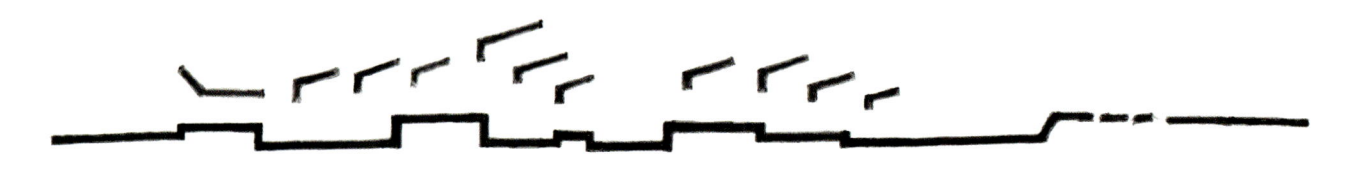

Section

Roadside Service Complex

Concept: *expression of flow – protection from noise and from sun*

Site Plan

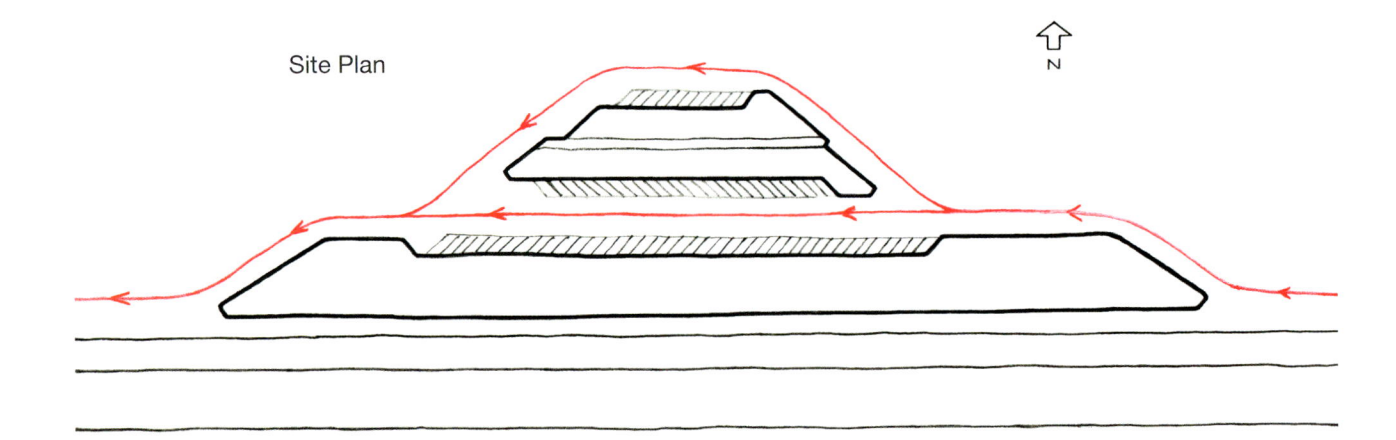

Section

I begin by asking clients to tell me not only their physical and functional needs, the building program, but images of what they want and just as significantly, their fantasies and dreams related to the project. Everything is taken into consideration and reflected in the design.

In addition to the building program, there are multiple design considerations from which the concept will be born. These are the same considerations one further explores when developing and fulfilling the concept.

My architectural design considerations fall into two major categories:

General – including, but not limited to:

    Aesthetics – perceptual beauty
    Territories – functional layout
    Sequences – spatial movement
    Order – visual and structural framework
    Integrity – material expression
    Methods – construction systems

Specific – including, but not limited to:

    Site – a place on earth
        Spirit of that place   Water
        Orientation – sun – light   Climate
        Colors – surrounding   Context – man-made
        Land formations   Natural environment

Earth connection
Sky connection
Fire
Water
Cave entry
Sanctuary
Natural interiors
Interior / Exterior connection

All these factors are synthesized by my unconscious to eventually be expressed through my hand, onto paper, into reality.

Design from the inside out and from the outside in simultaneously and let the variables meet where they may. If one is fluid and flexible throughout the whole process the work will evolve naturally into its own being.

Alvar Aalto's buildings, especially his earth connected plans, come closest to this way of thinking. He brings together the site and its physical characteristics with the building's functional requirements. He was one of the early modernist architects to harmoniously balance the internal and external forces acting upon a building.

It is interesting to note that his sensitivity to the site and particularly land contours may be related to the fact that his father was a map maker – again, the importance of early childhood influences.

Aalto's plans are the commonality of his work. It is the plan that generates the upward three dimensional quality of his expression, which varies dependant on contextual conditions.

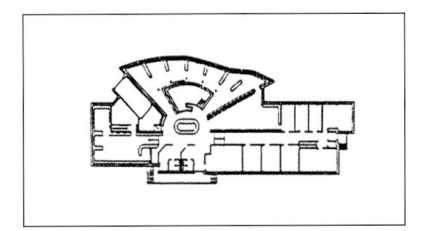

Seinajoki Library, Finland. Alvar Aalto

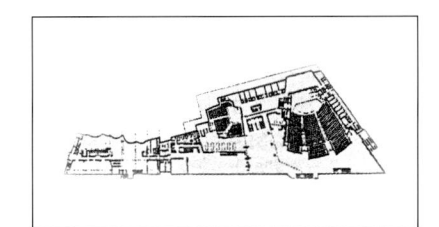

Finlandia Hall, Helsinki. Alvar Aalto

There are two considerations that will evolve and follow their own course:

Personal expression – it is an extension of who you are. You cannot seek it, it is a by-product of what you do and your attitude in doing it, provided you are true to your nature.

Capturing the period in which you live. You are a product of your time, it will take care of itself as long as you are not purposely trying to express a past age or time such as Greek, Classical or Gothic.

Although *there are no rules in the creative process*, there are guiding principles that have been established over the ages regarding what works and is visually successful. The process and the results are different for everyone. In the end, each person must do it his or her own way. *You are your greatest resource.*

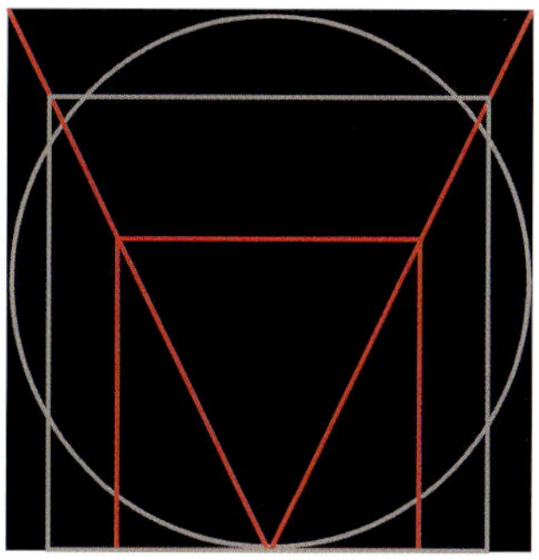

EXPRESSIONS

ARCHITECTURE . . . .
Inspired by natural forms

The following **EXPRESSIONS** are the design work of Louis O. Roberts

Earth connected natural rock formations at Pinnacles National Monument, California

Natural forms translated into earth-sky architecture with added roof structure   1991

Rock formations known as "Hoodoos" located in the Badlands of Alberta, Canada

Earth-sky human habitat derivative of the natural rock "Hoodoos"

1992

207

Stony landscape reminiscent of architectonic structures – *"to see what everyone else sees but think what no one else thinks"* see page 24

Aerial view of stone shaped house, garage, terraces and outcroppings on a sloping site

1992

208 REALITY

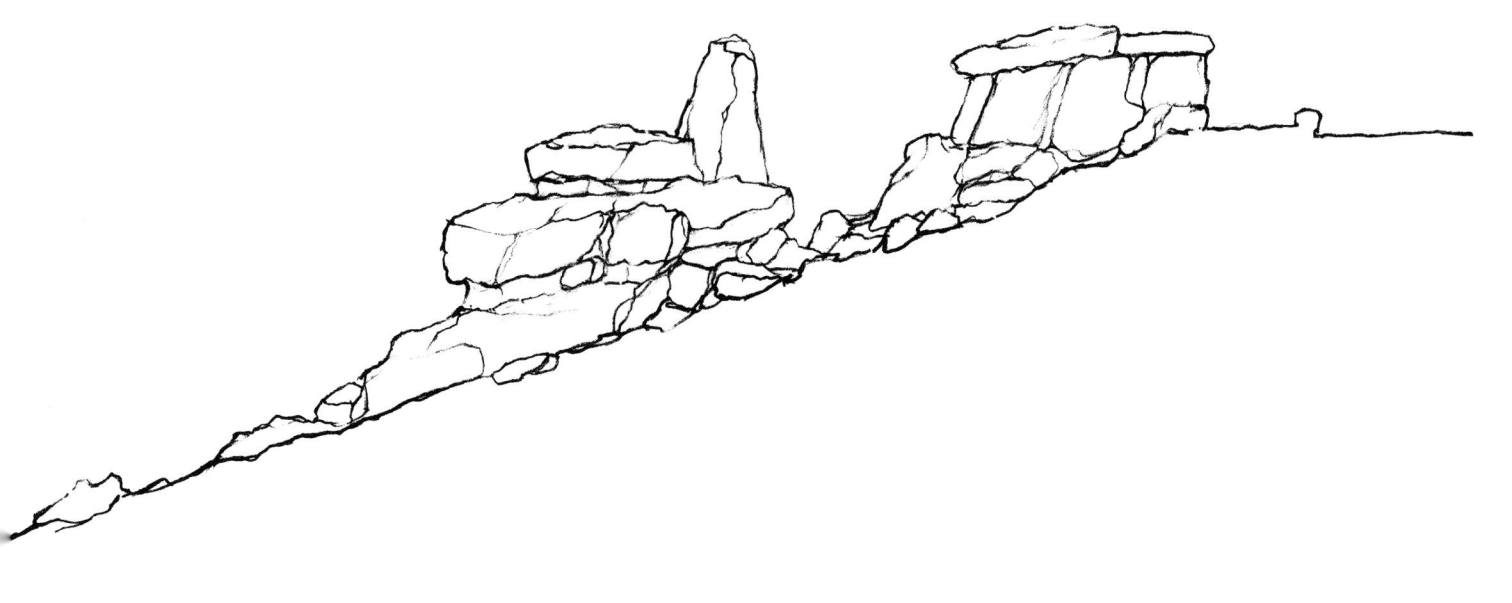

STONE / BOULDER HOUSE Conceptual 1992

Earth connected stone configured residence with garage adjacent to road

The various construction elements making up the building

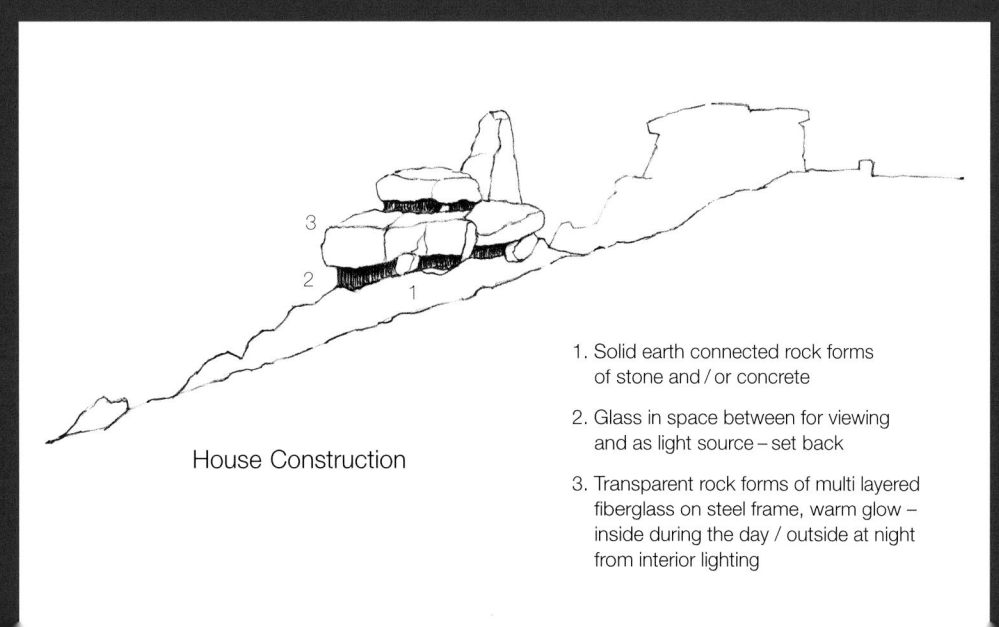

House Construction

1. Solid earth connected rock forms of stone and / or concrete

2. Glass in space between for viewing and as light source – set back

3. Transparent rock forms of multi layered fiberglass on steel frame, warm glow – inside during the day / outside at night from interior lighting

EXPRESSIONS

ARCHITECTURE . . . . . .
Inspired by ancient man-made forms

MEGALITH HOUSE   Conceptual   1991

Carmel Valley, California

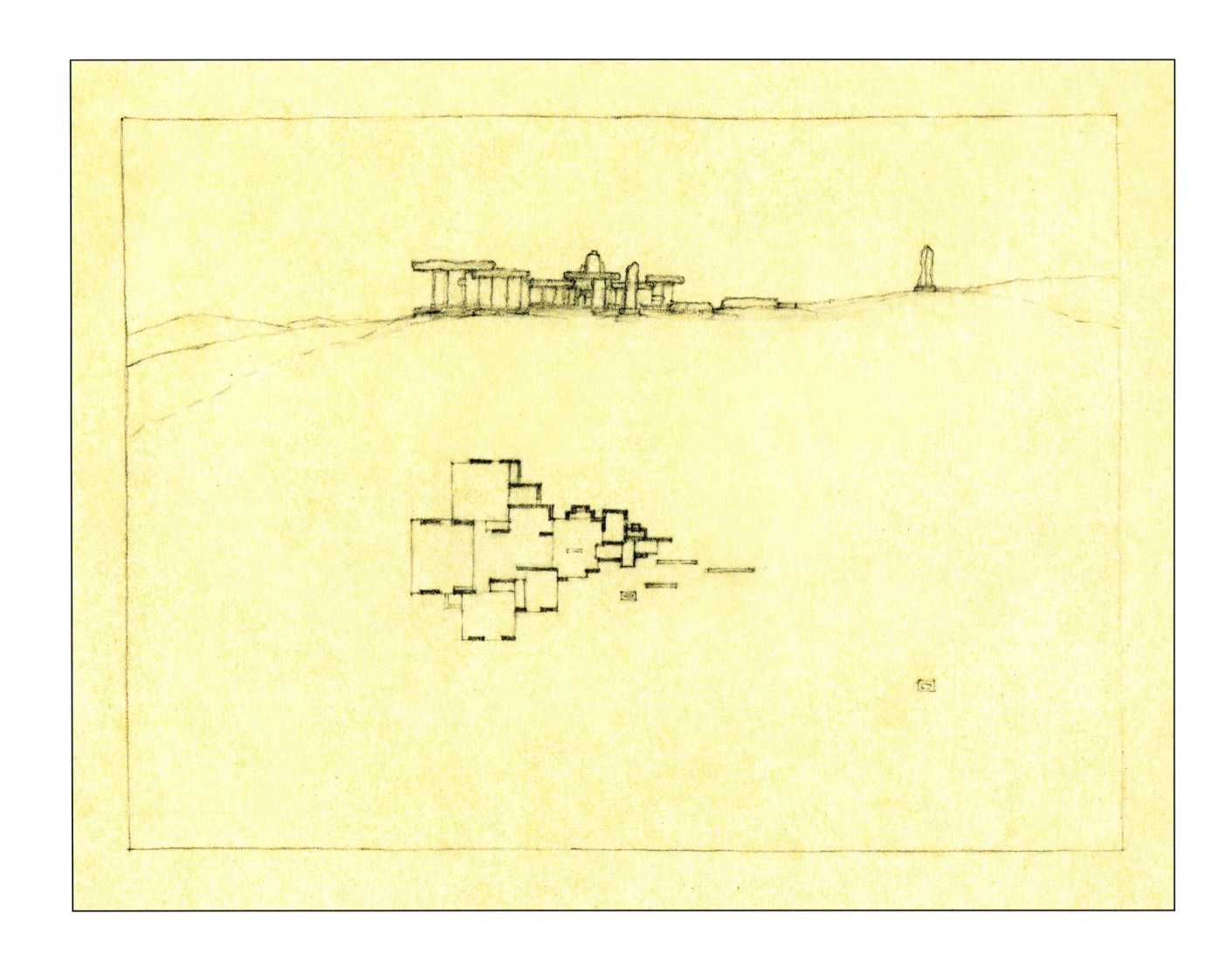

Conceptual sketches of Megalith House on hilltop

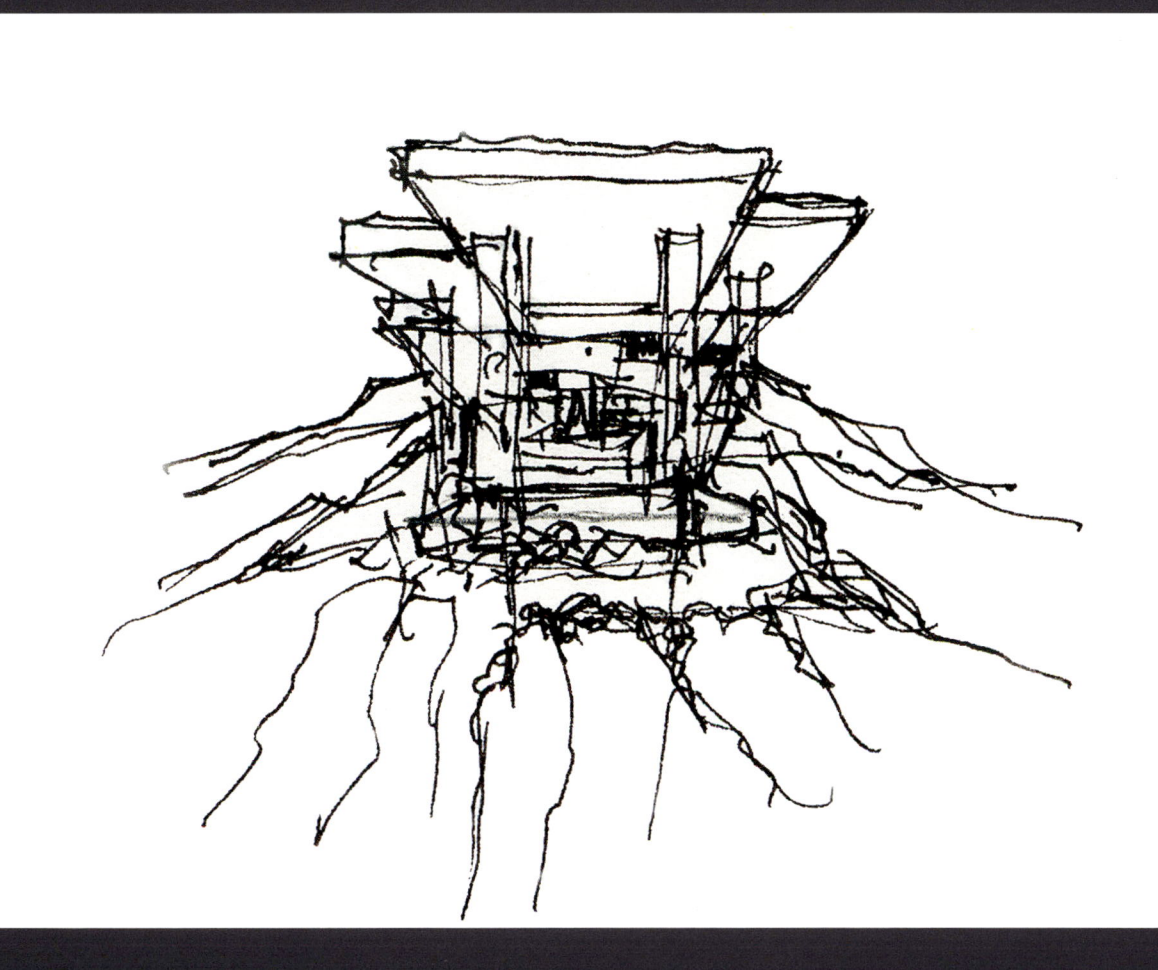

West elevation with the winter solstice sunrise aligning with megaliths

South elevation with megaliths as fireplace chimney mass and as entry marker

Water circulates from interior basin at entry through various slots in the floor to exterior corner pool; water and fire are integral parts of the house

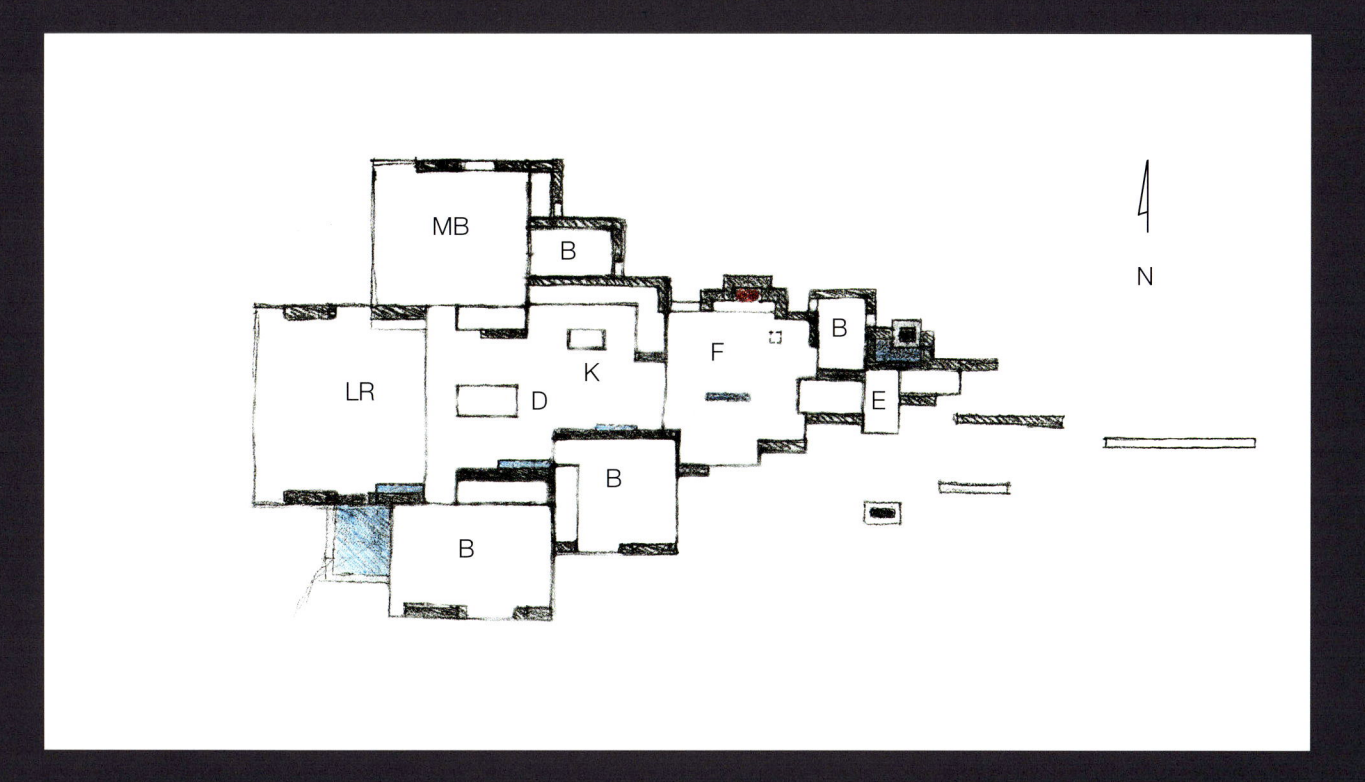

213

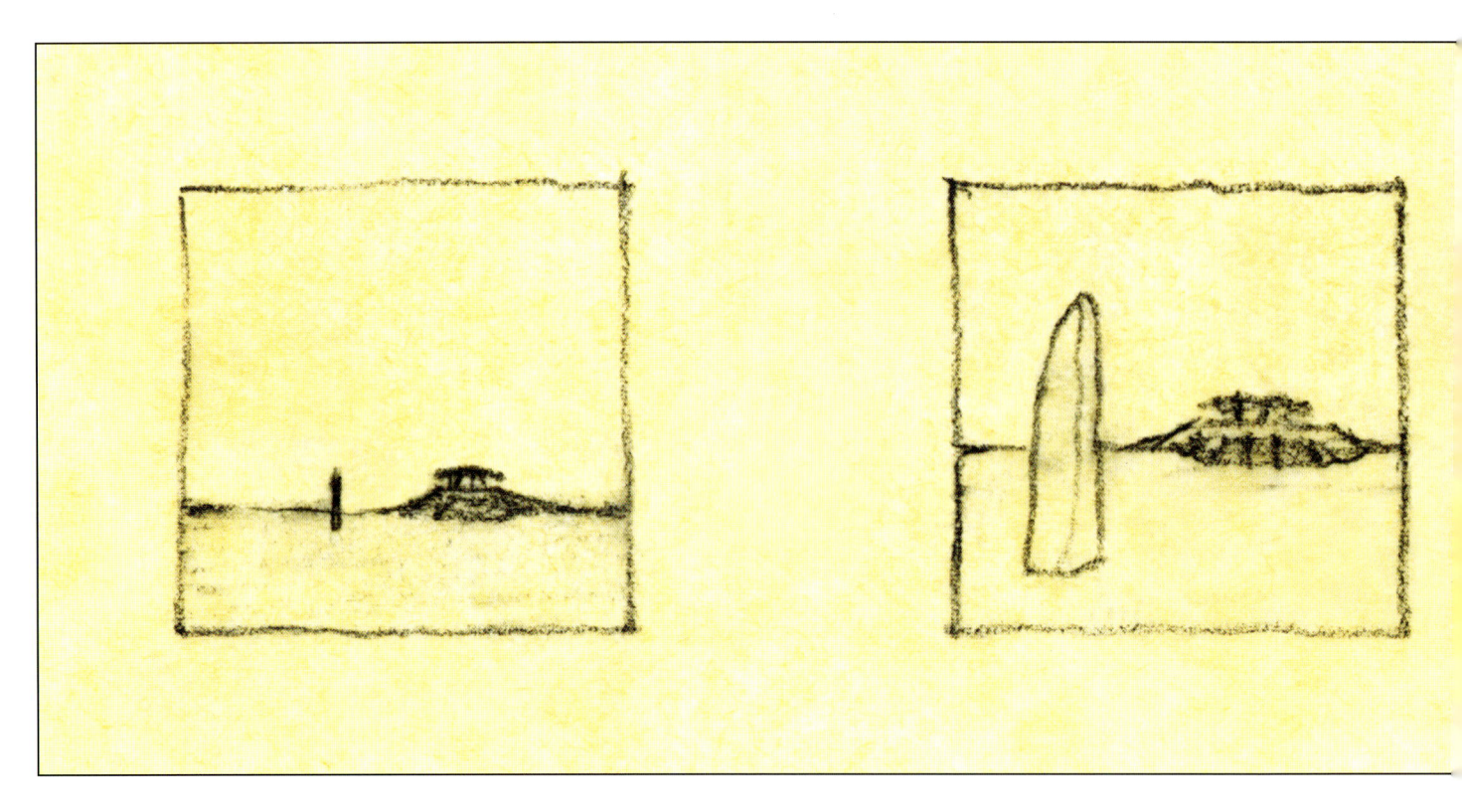

A series of experiential perspectives approaching the house

DOLMEN / MEGALITH HOUSE   Conceptual   1993

214 REALITY

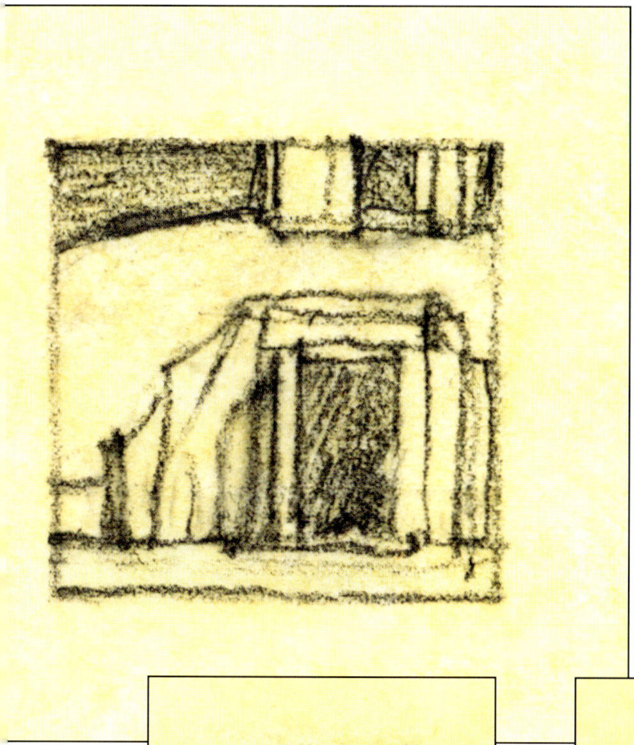

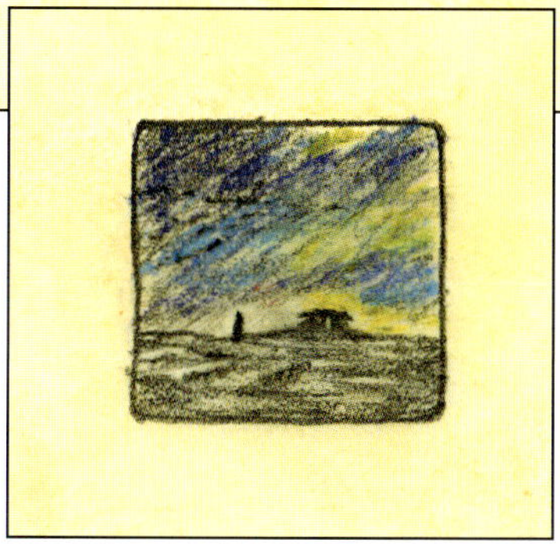

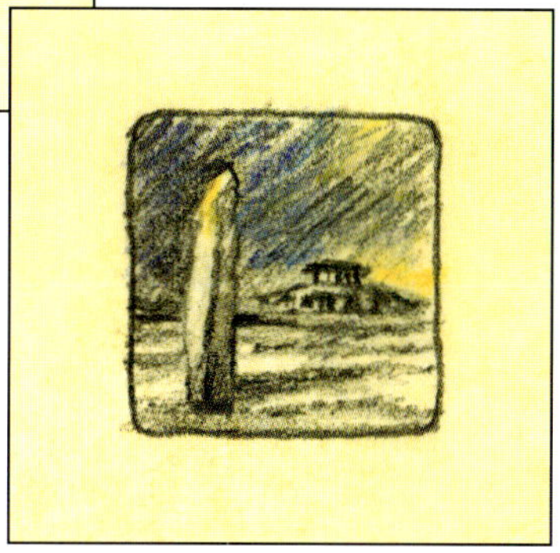

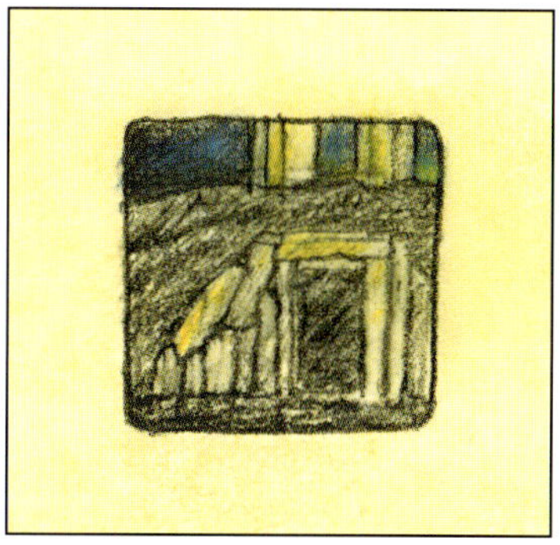

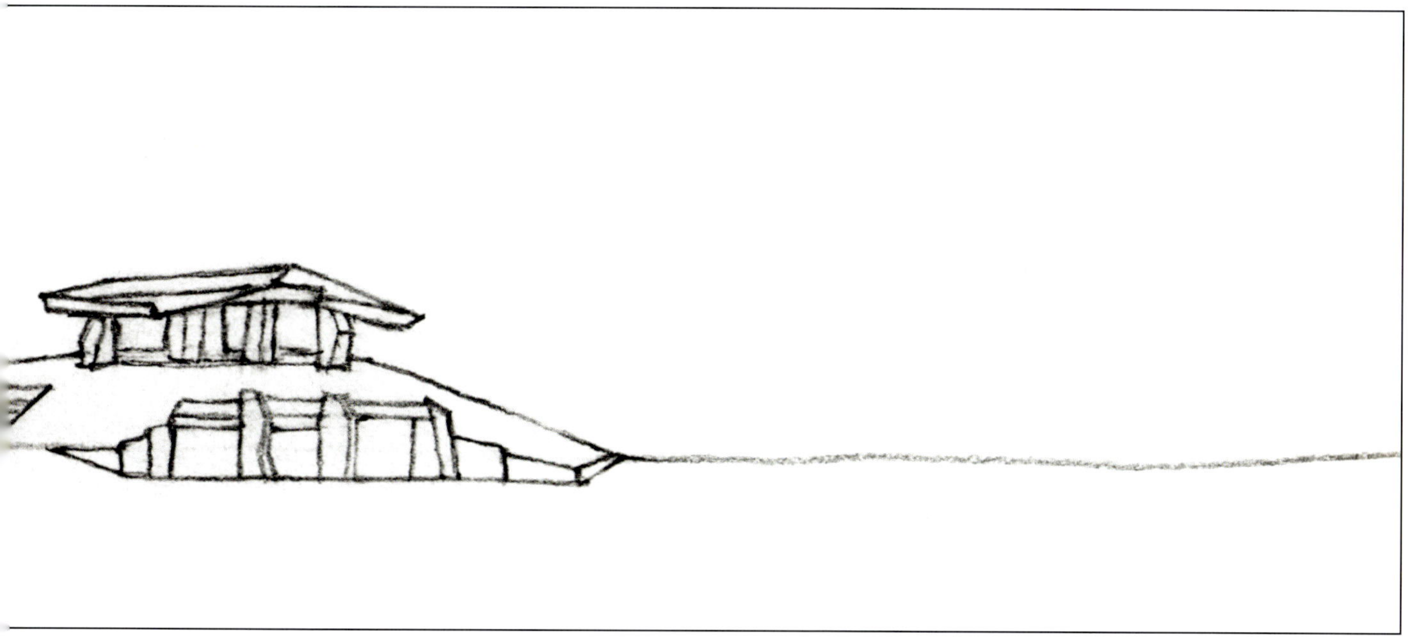

EXPRESSIONS

ARCHITECTURE
Earth expressed – sky implied

COASTAL CLIFF HOUSE Conceptual 1994
California Coast

Structure anchored to the vertical and horizontal earth with multiple concrete and metal planar elements

Moveable metal framed panels deflect wind and control sun shade

Study sketches of various form arrangements

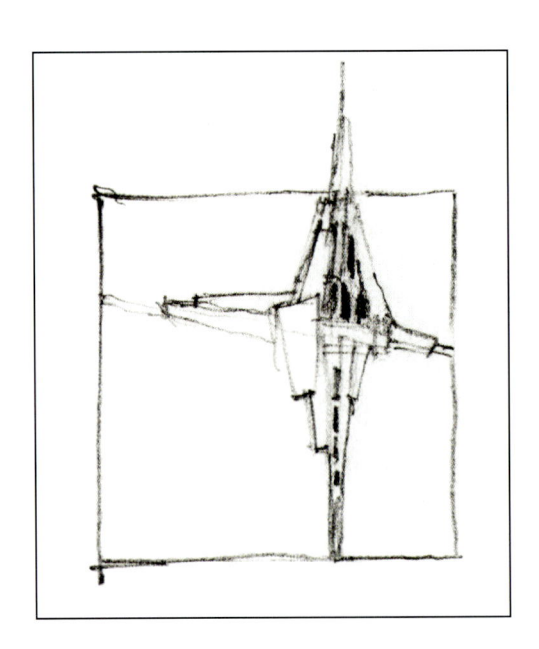

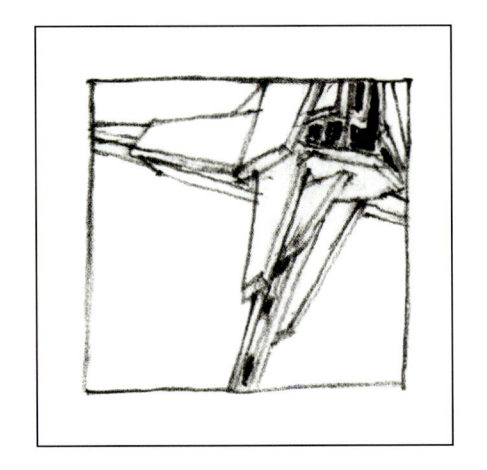

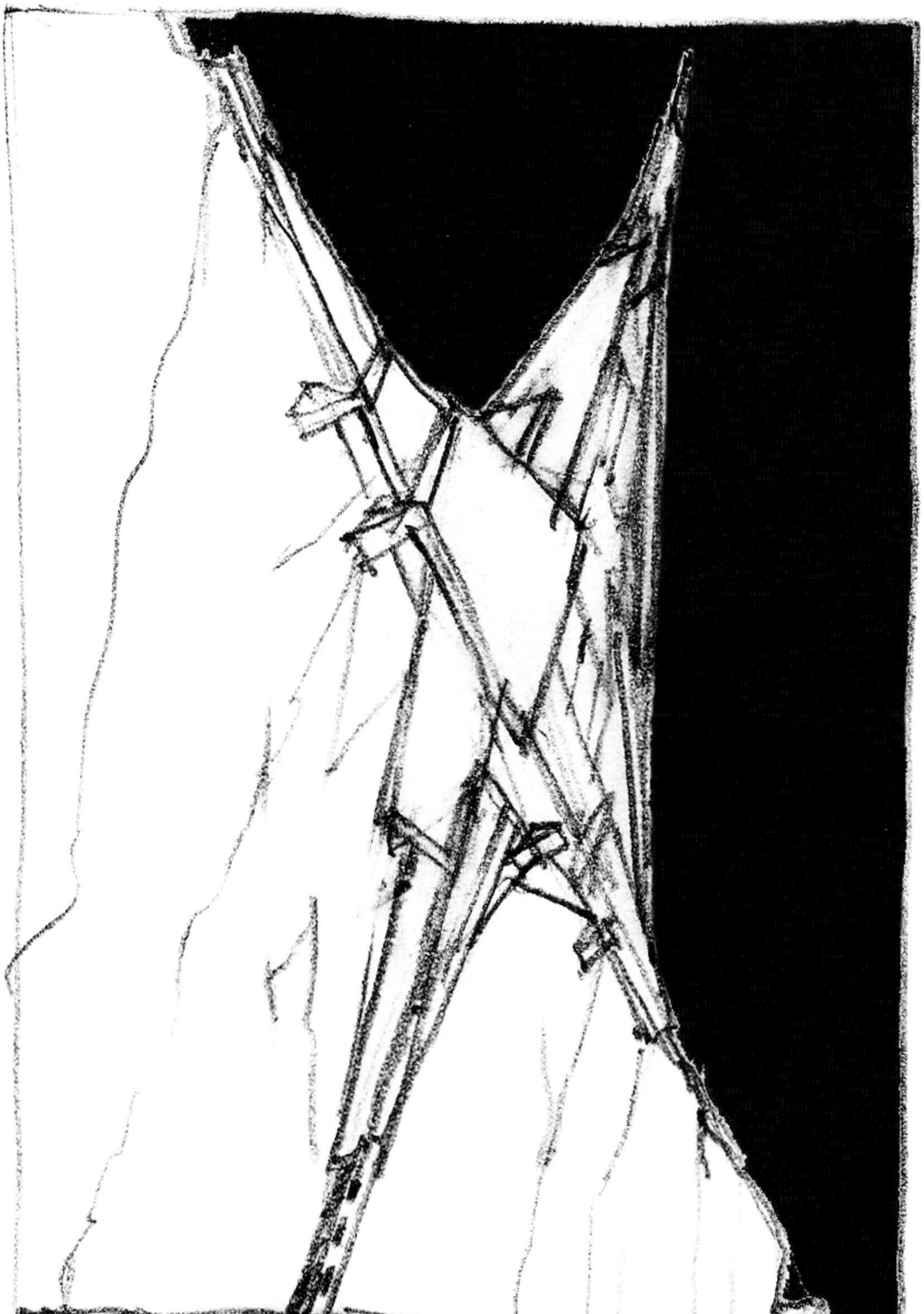

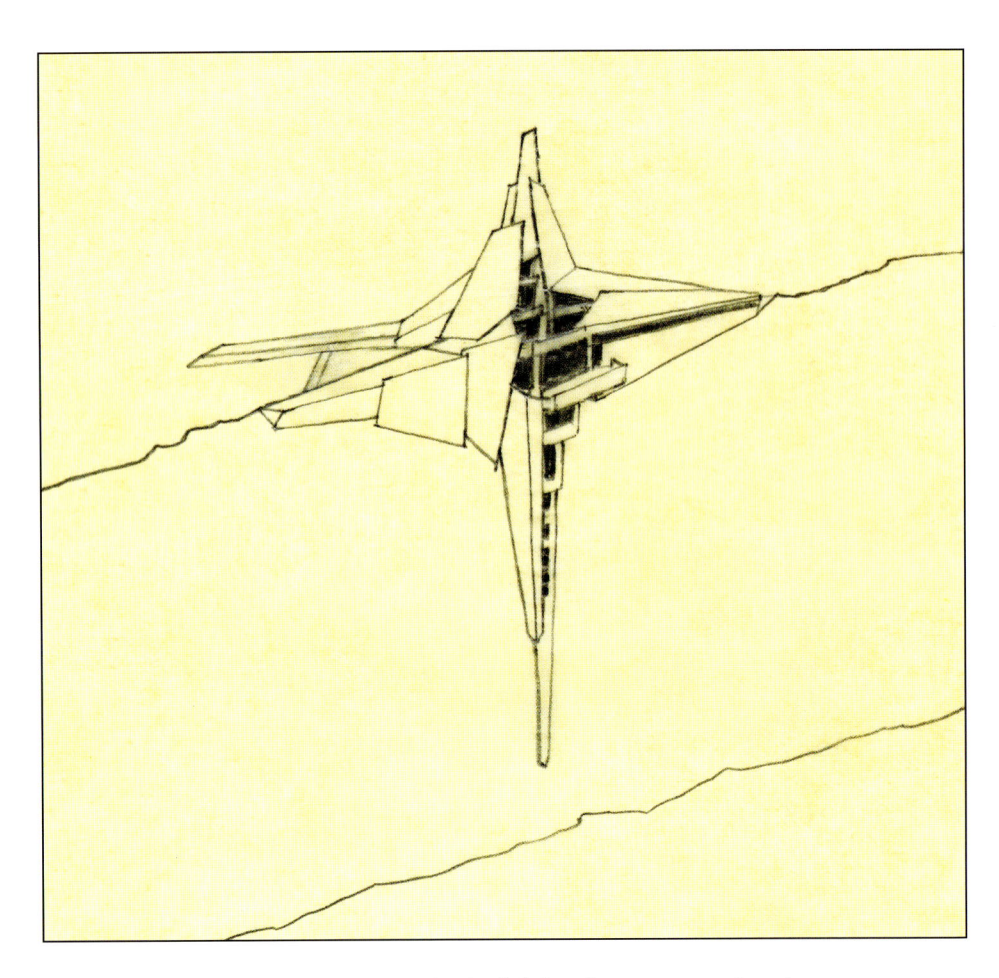

Developmental sketches – more clearly defining the component parts

Plan study – with anchor elements secured into the granite bedrock

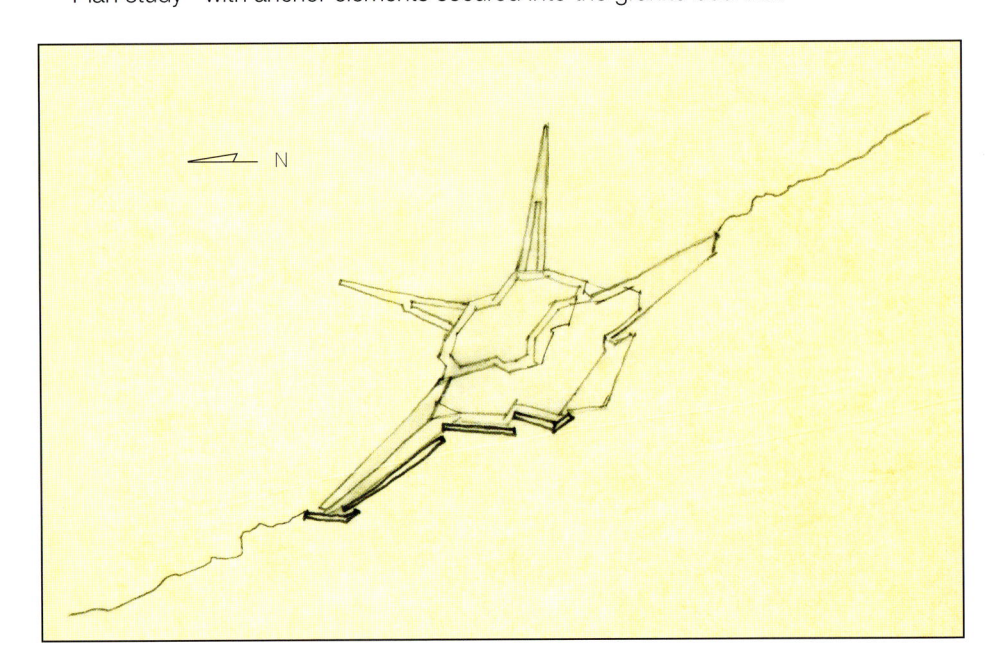

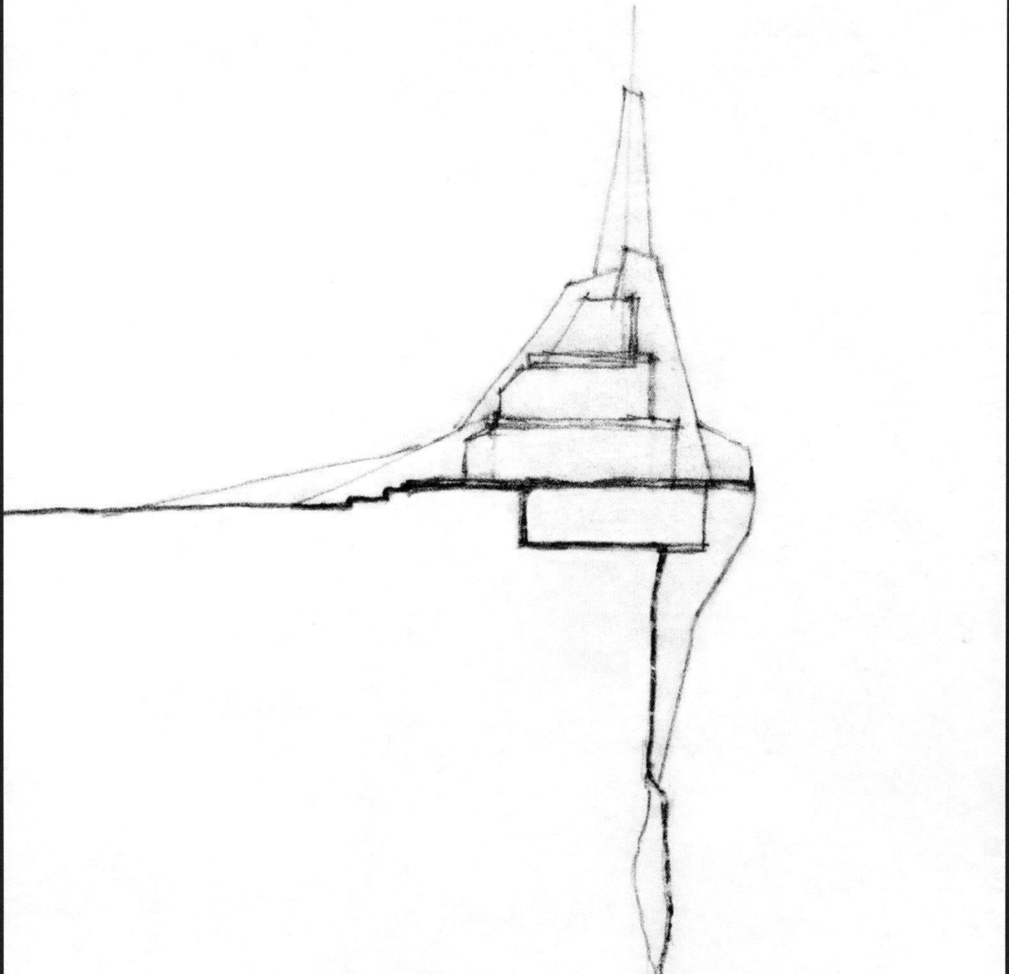

HIGHRISE TOWERS   Conceptual   1994

Earth connected skyscraper with an impenetrable exterior skin

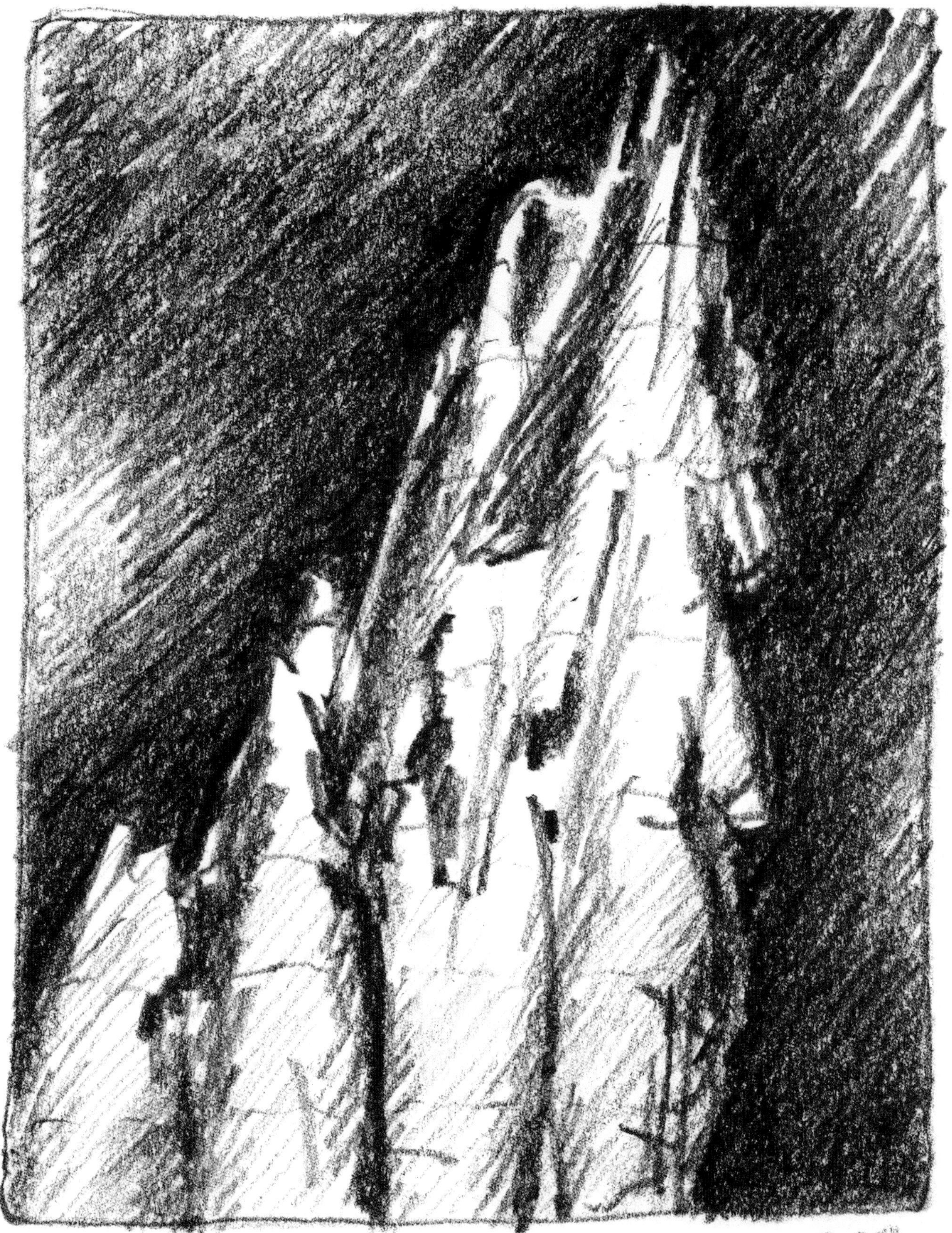

The underlying structure of the highrise is built of interlocking vertical fins covered with an impenetrable transparent woven carbon-fiber skin

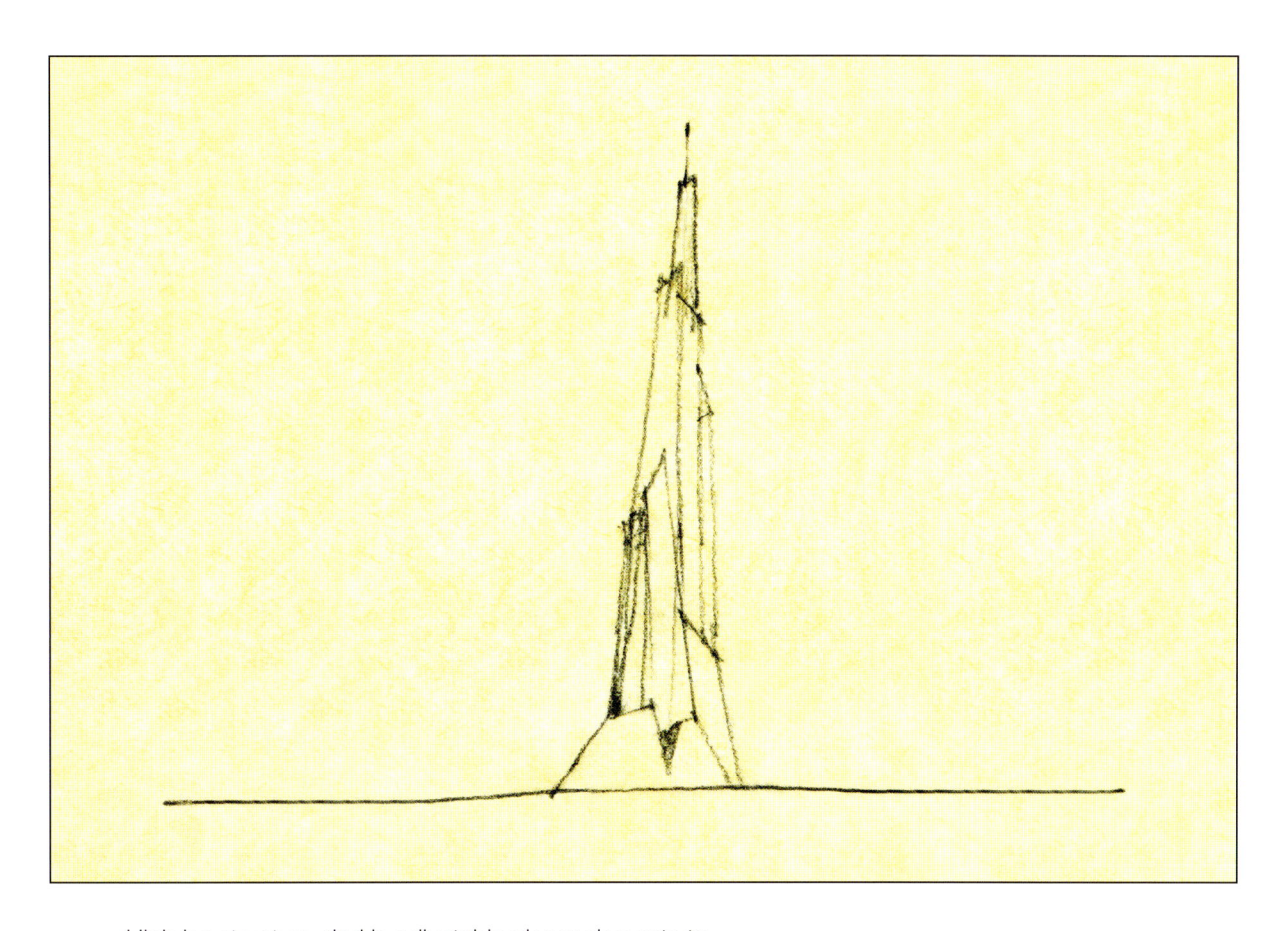

Highrise structure clad in adjustable planar elements to accommodate a balanced internal ecosystem

Building in the exposed window configuration

EXPRESSIONS

. . . . ARCHITECTURE . . . .
Earth and sky expressed – energy between

OAKLAND HILLS RESIDENCE　　　Conceptual　　　1991-92
Oakland, California

House overlooks San Francisco and the Golden Gate Bridge

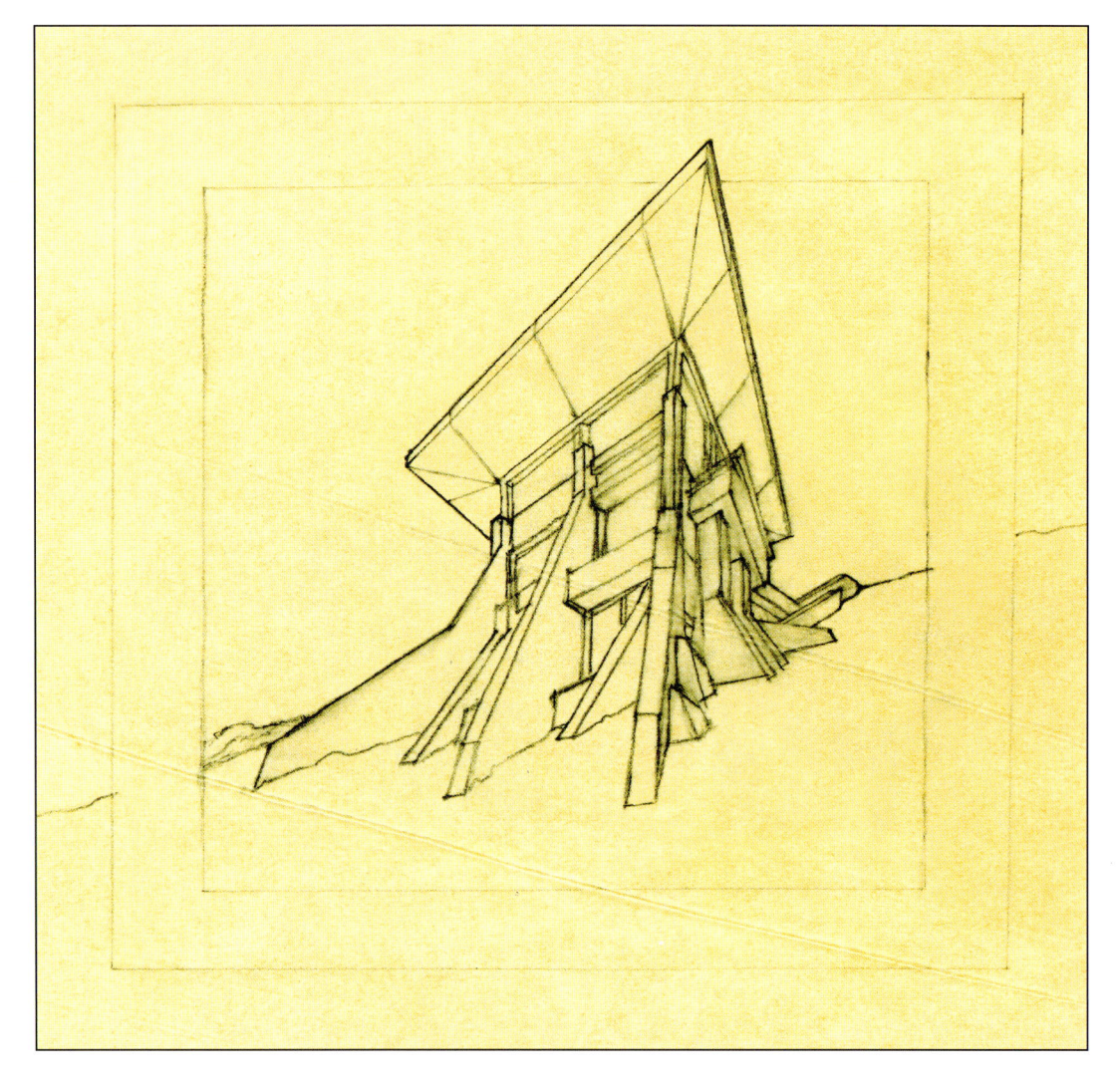

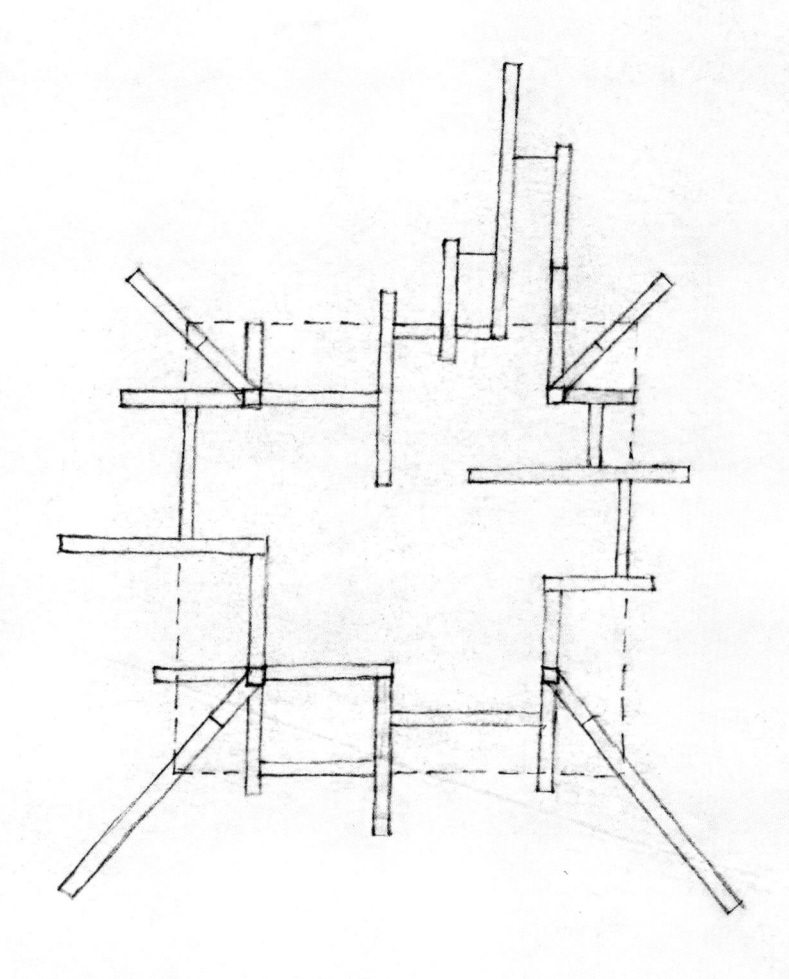

Early sketch of south elevation and earthquake resistant structure

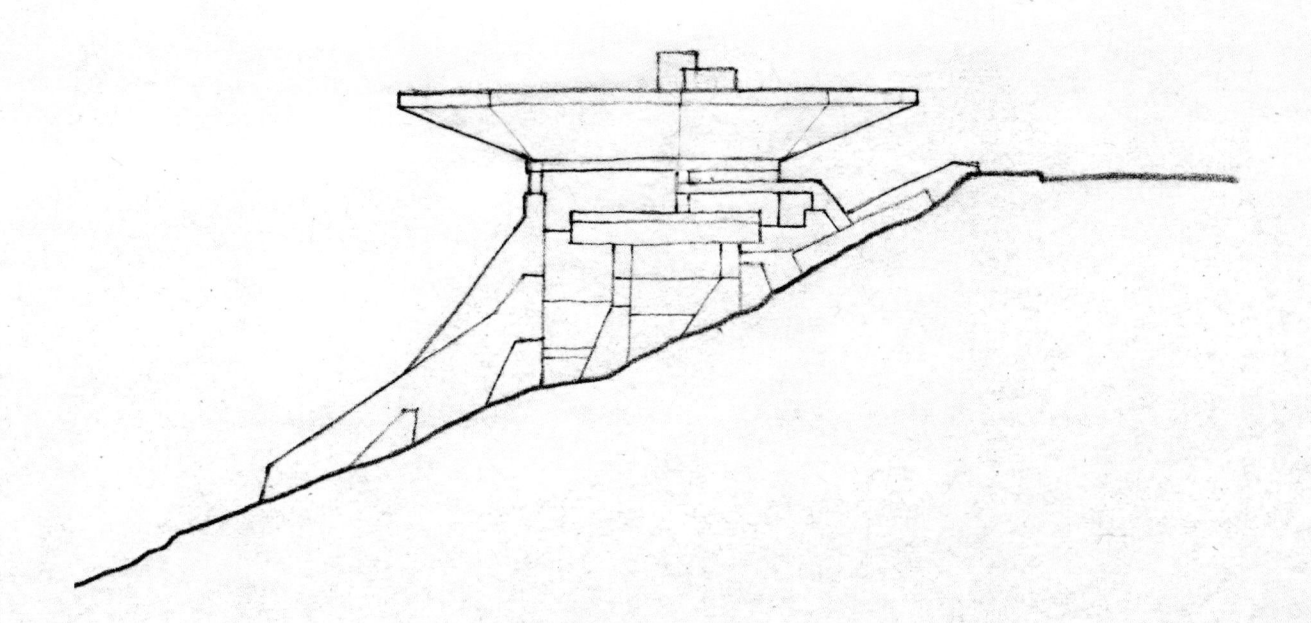

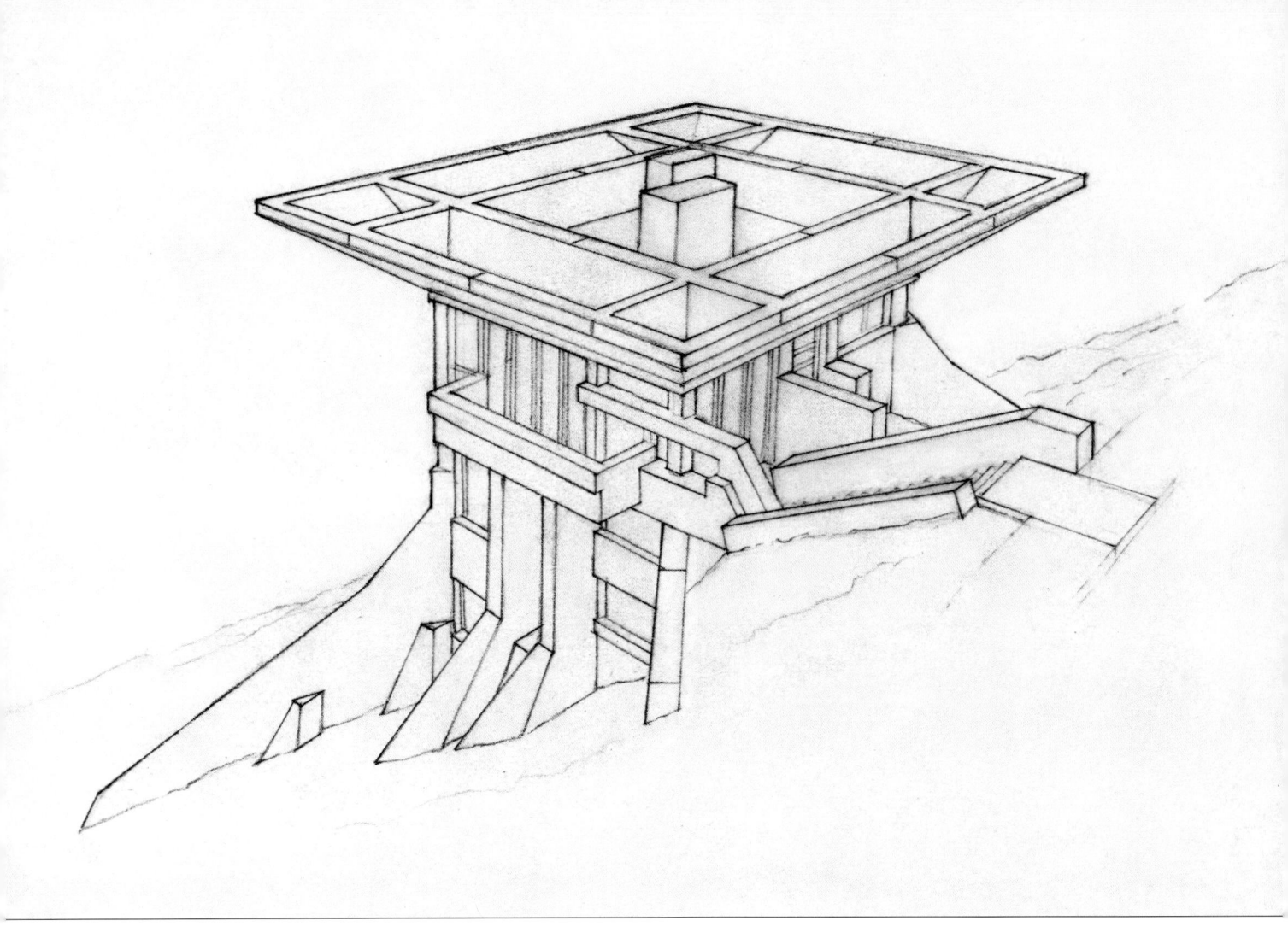

Aerial view to the northwest

West elevation

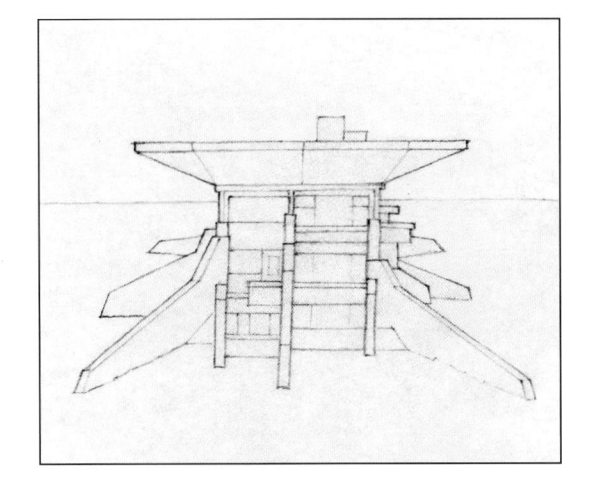

226 REALITY

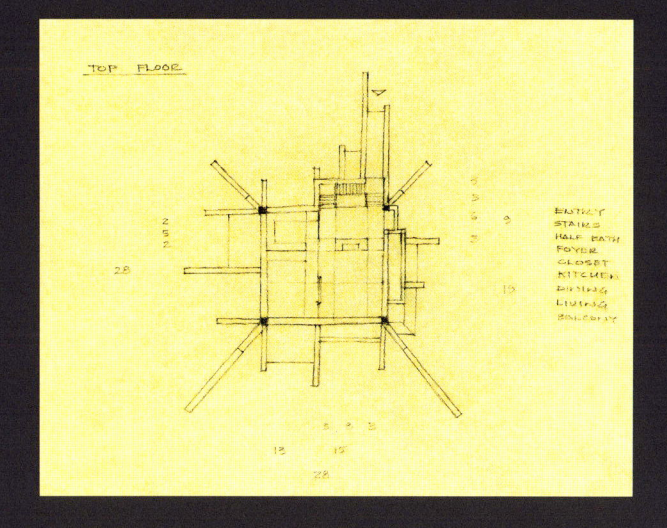

Sketches of house levels and territories with rough dimensions and possible room uses

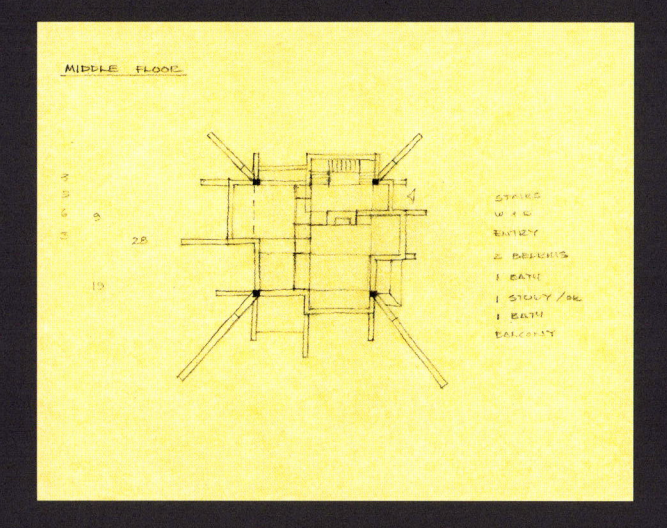

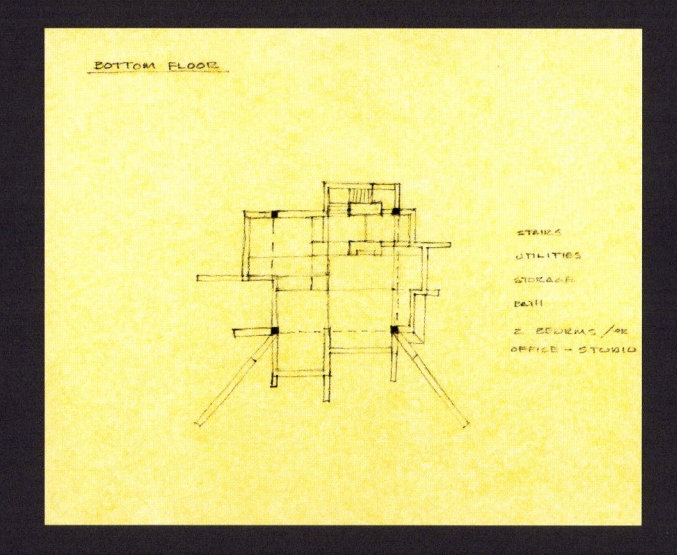

227

Other possible variations on the same earth-sky concept

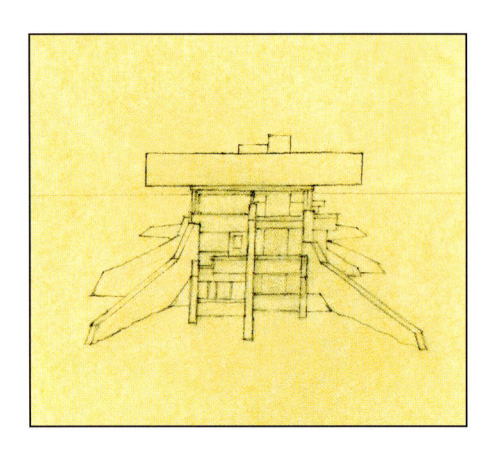

Above and below – building incorporates a rectilinear slab roof

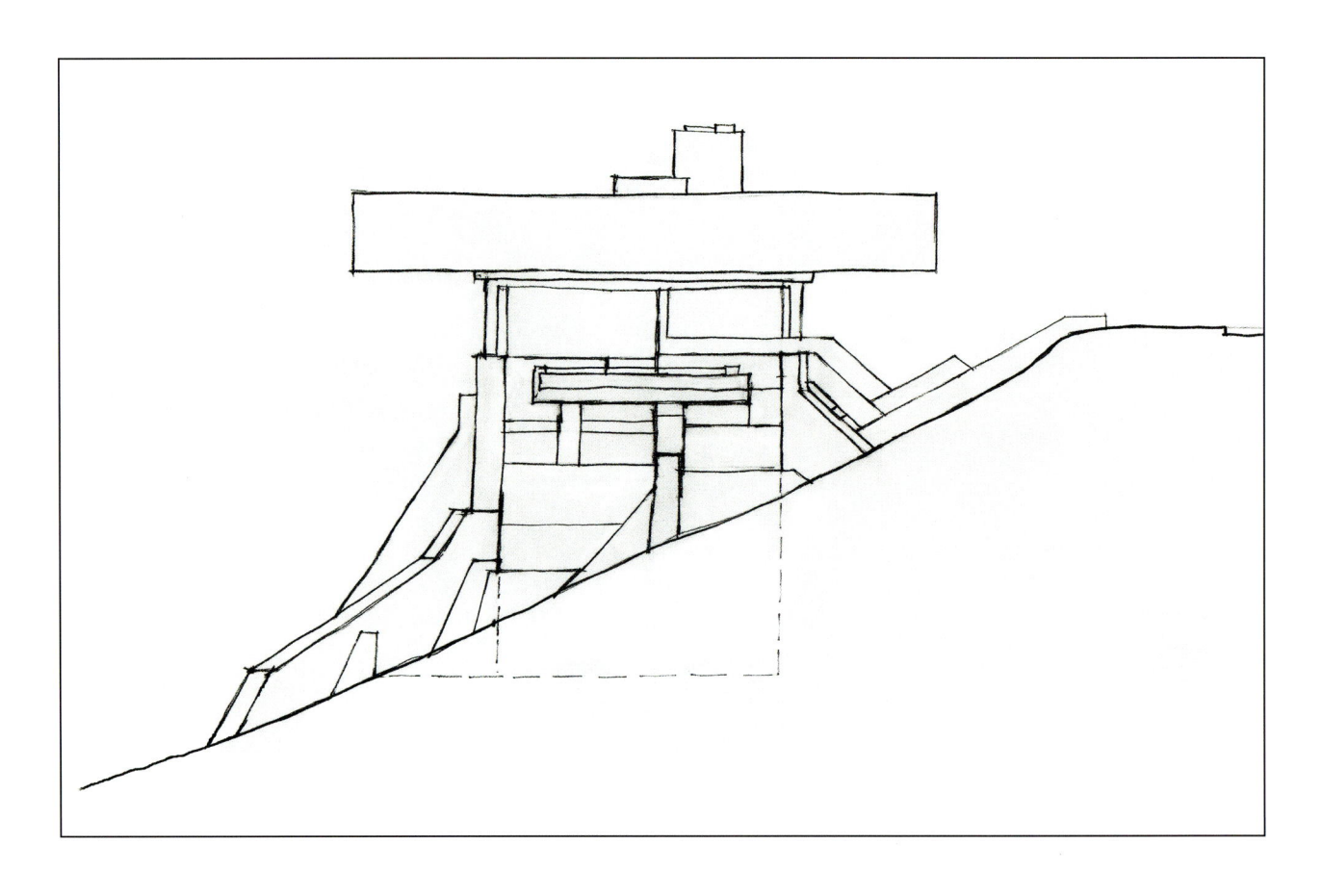

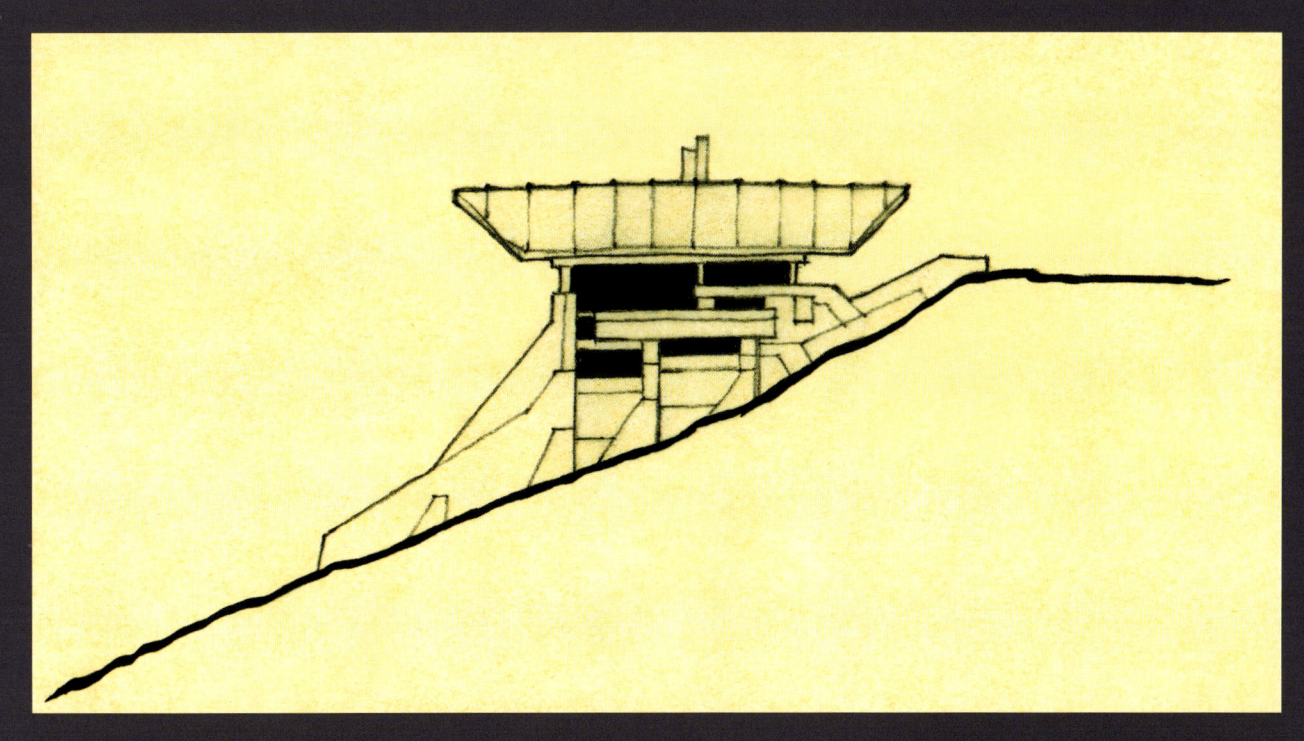

Building employs a sky related metal roof giving contrast to the concrete base

Building is reconfigured using planar elements with the addition of a sanctuary atop

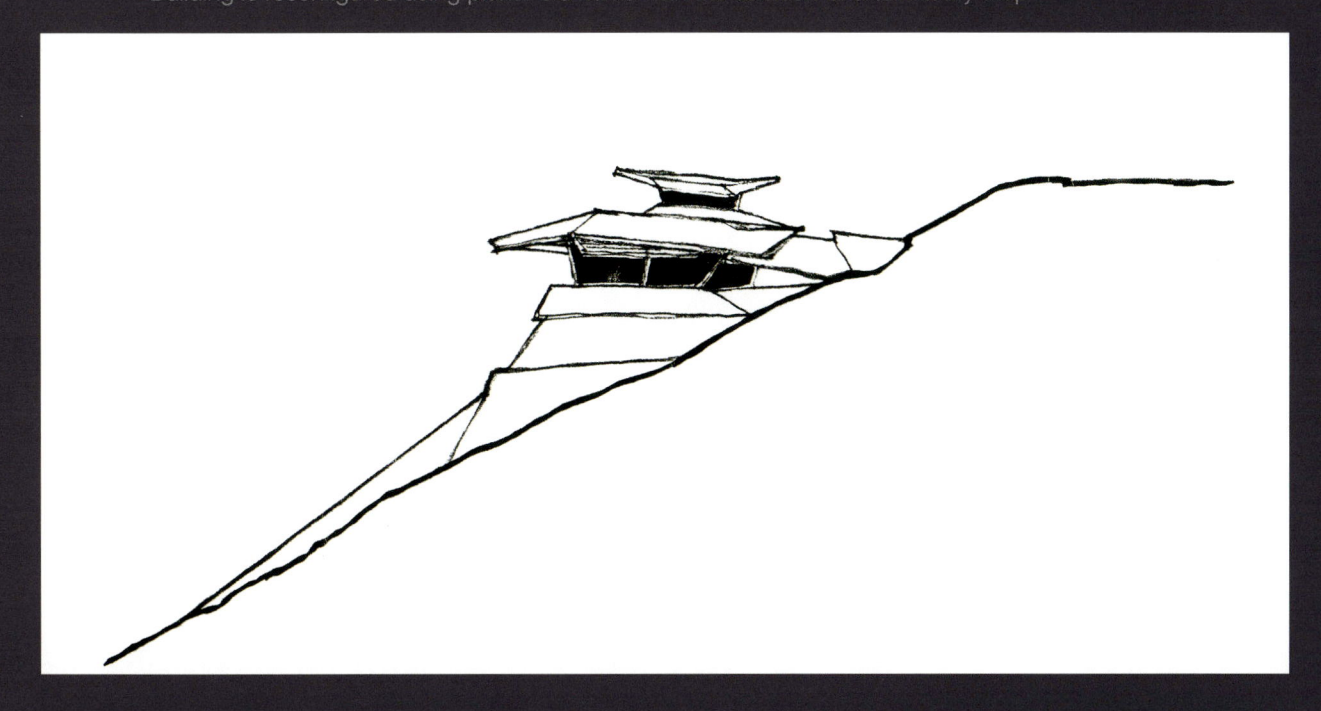

NAVARRO RIDGE HOUSES   Conceptual   1993-94
Mendocino County, California

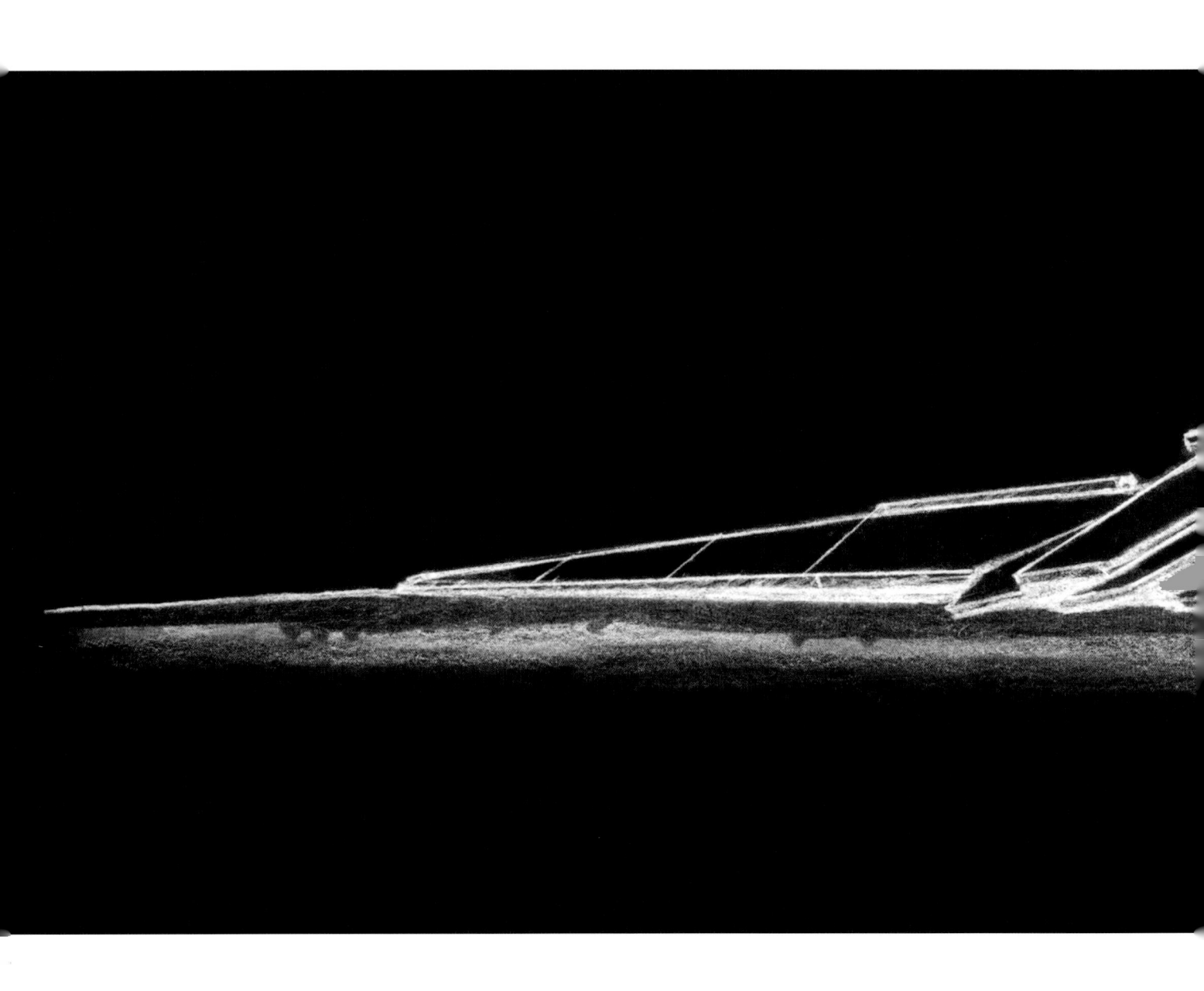

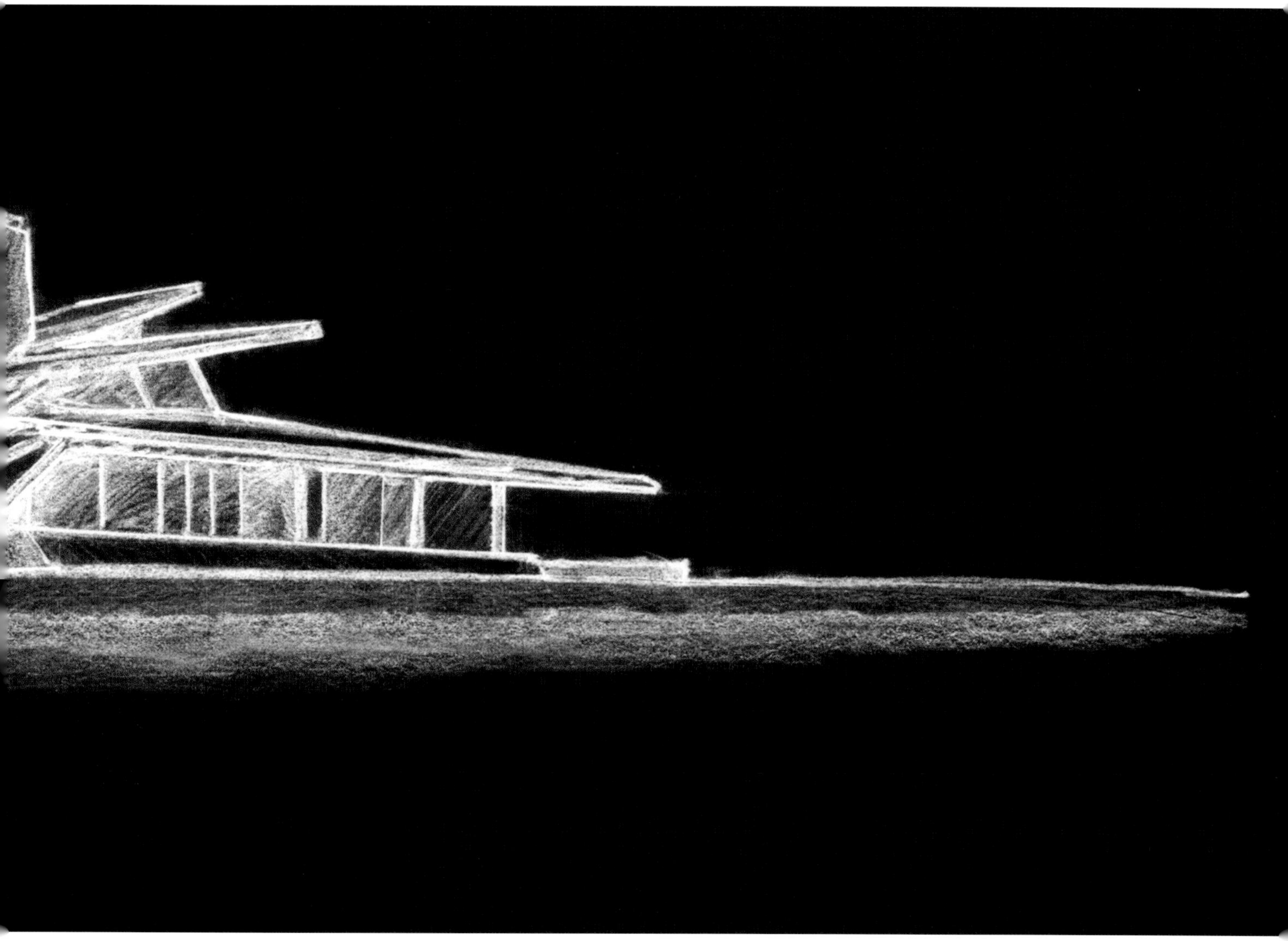

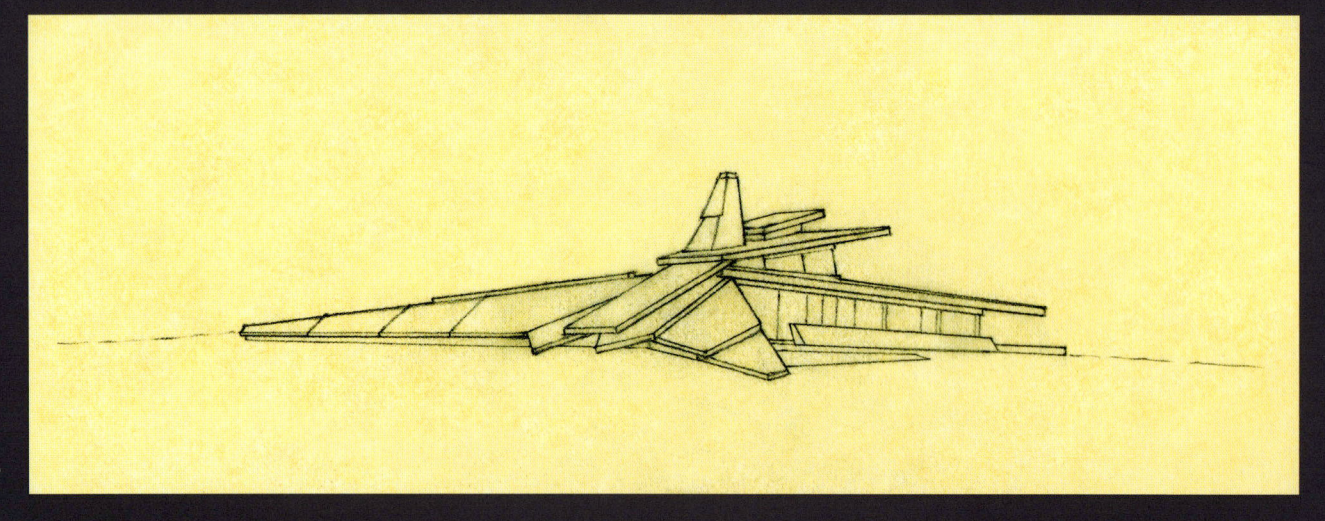

Westerly elevation showing winged panels affording protection from north winds

Three part building construction system

Corten Roof

Steel Frame

Concrete Base

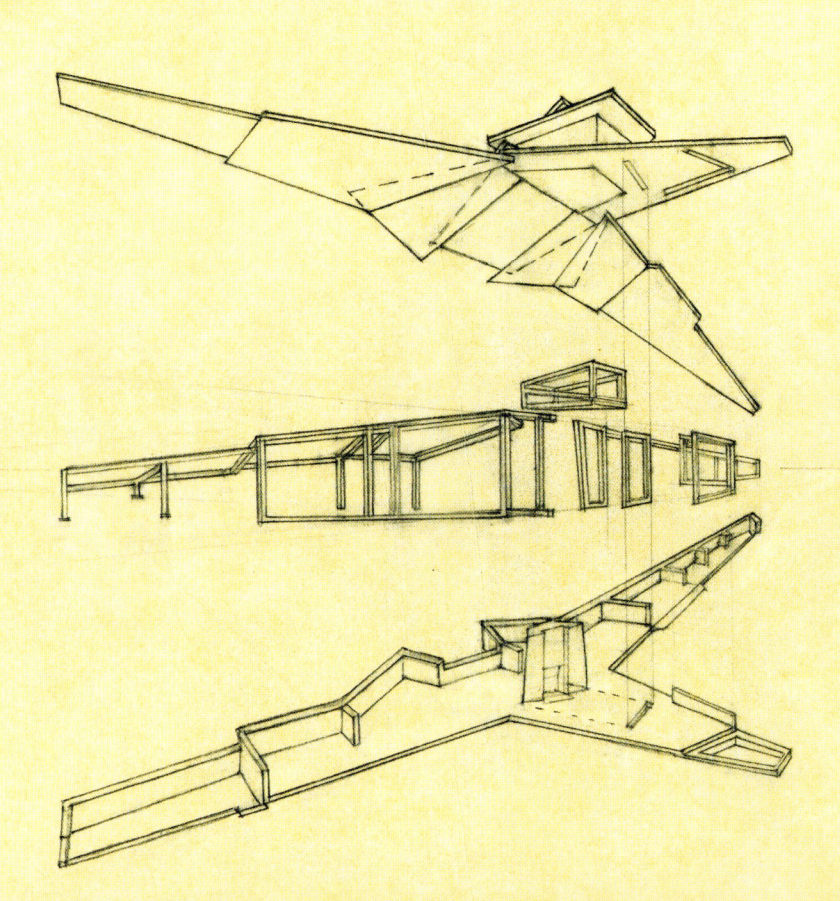

Studios

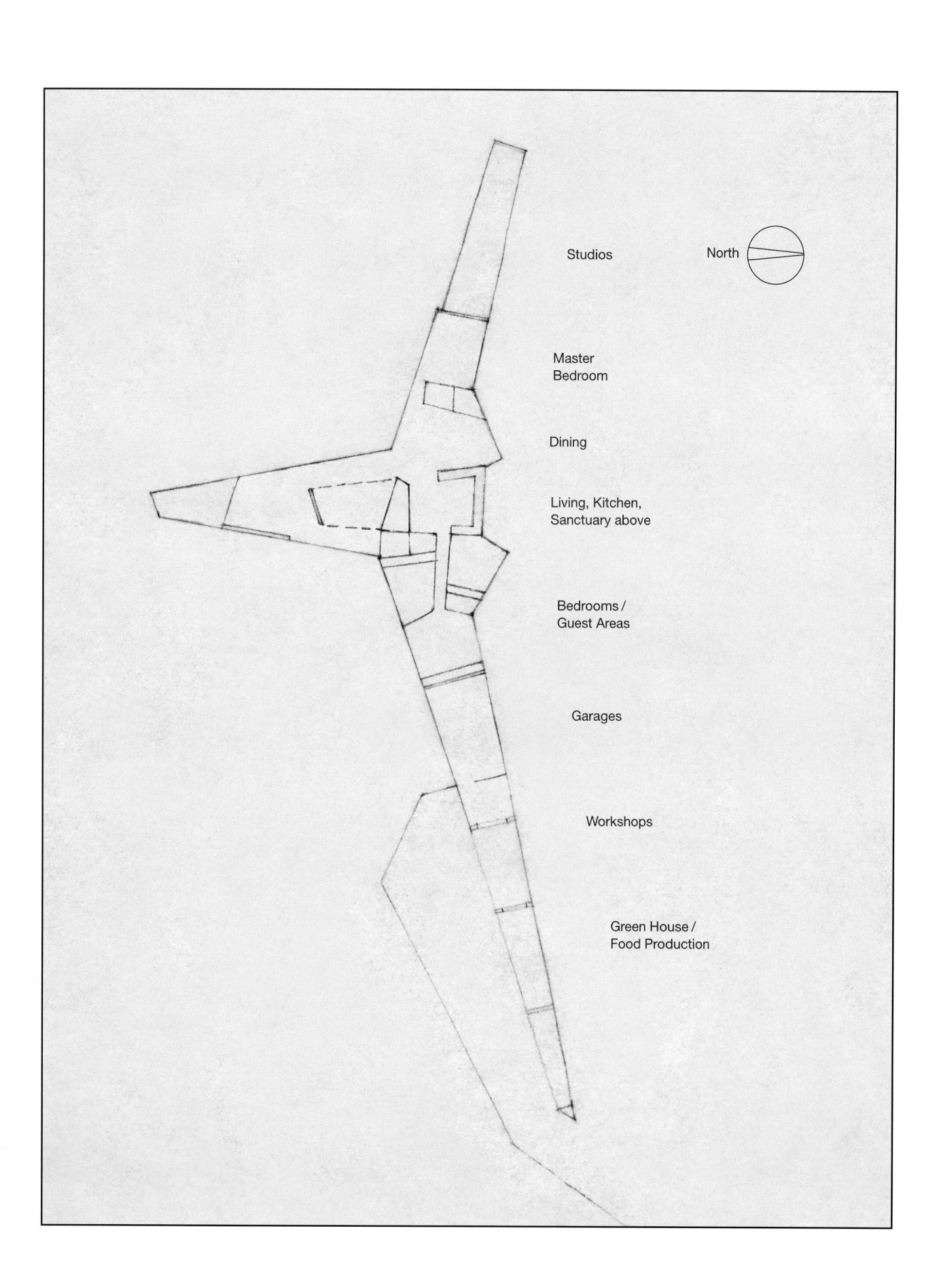

North

Master
Bedroom

Dining

Living, Kitchen,
Sanctuary above

Bedrooms /
Guest Areas

Garages

Workshops

Green House /
Food Production

Roof plan

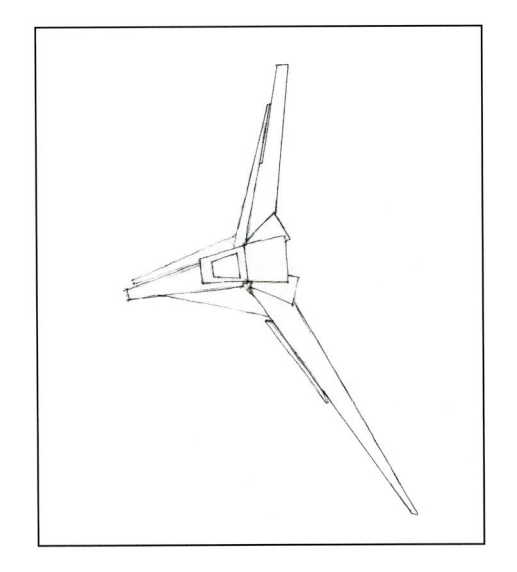

East elevation

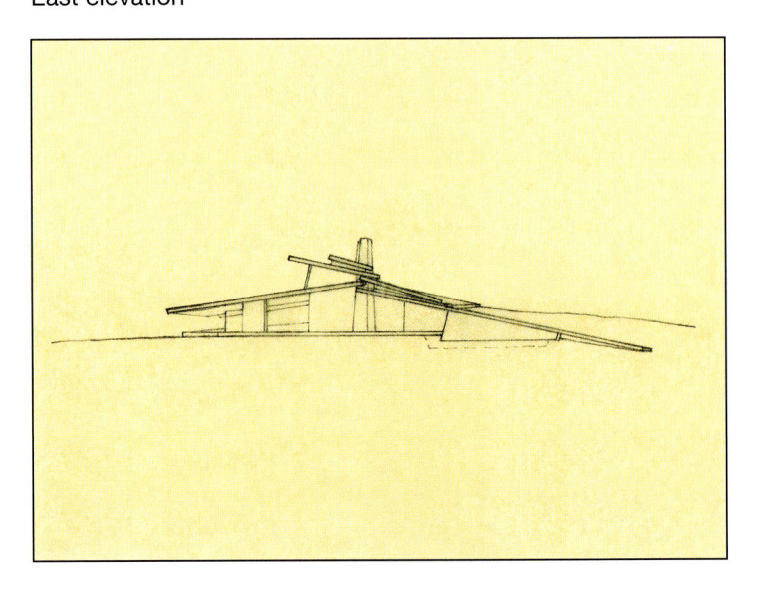

Living core layout grid

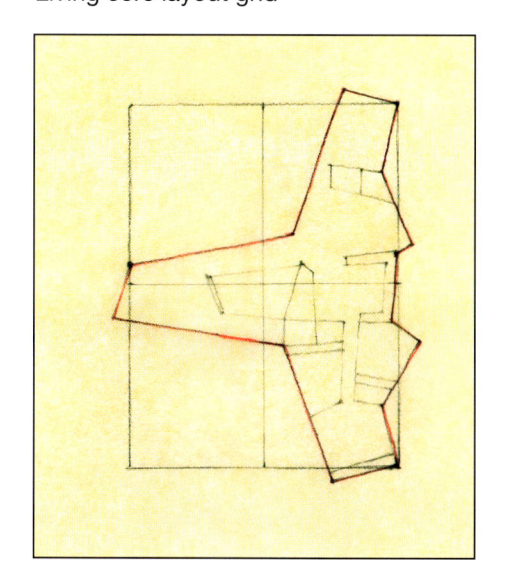

Section looking west

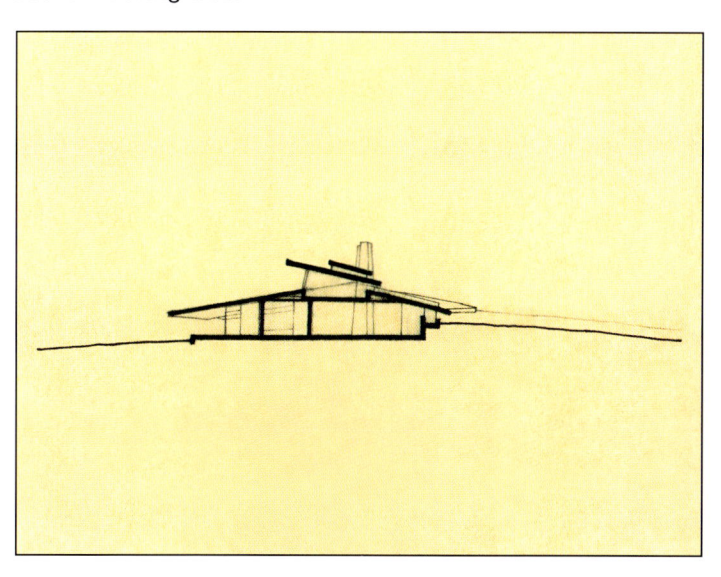

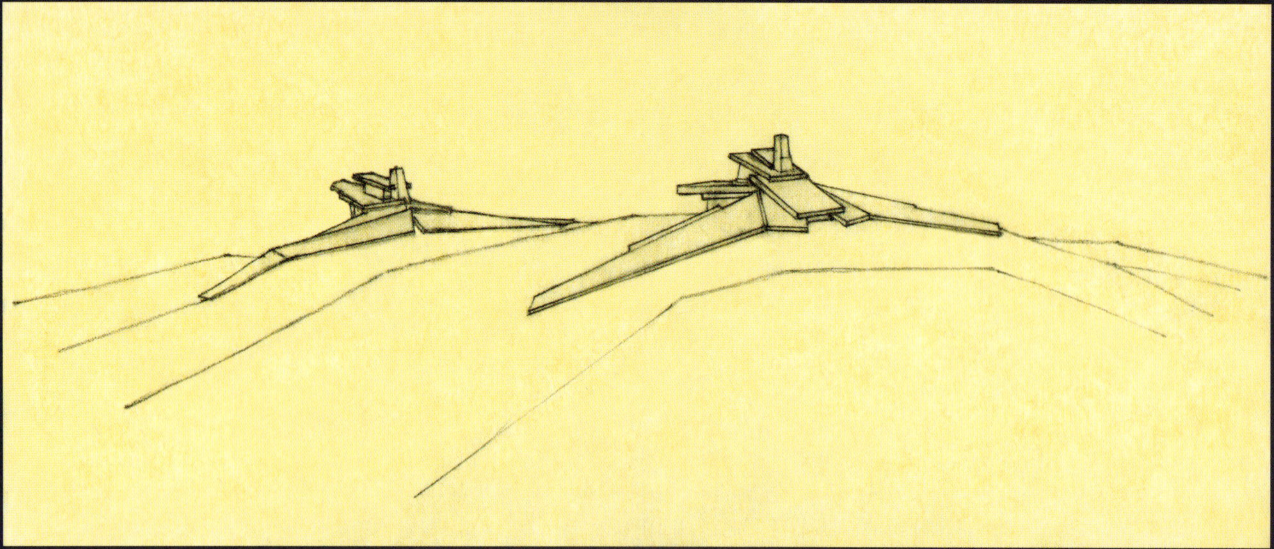
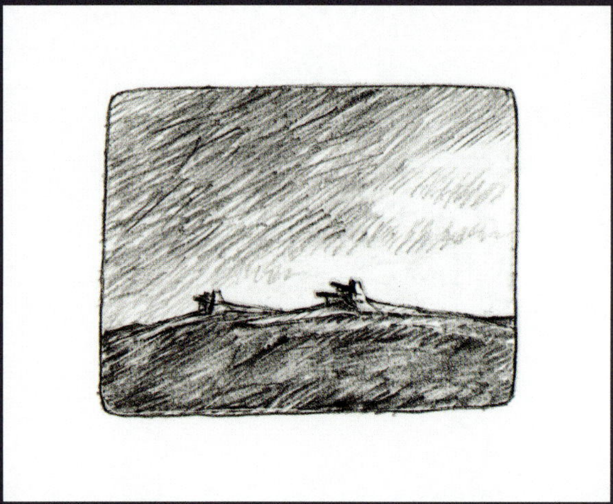
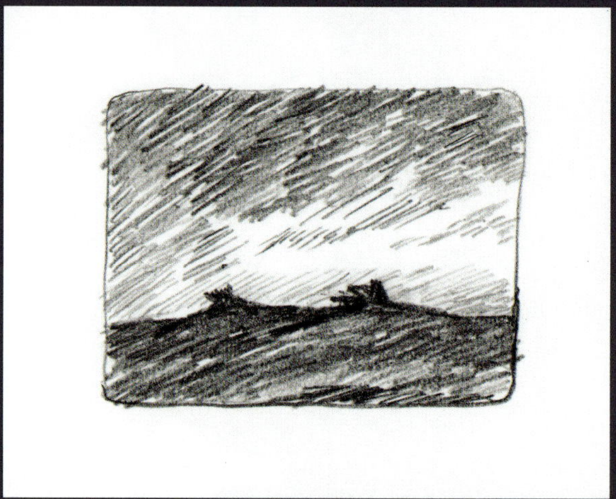
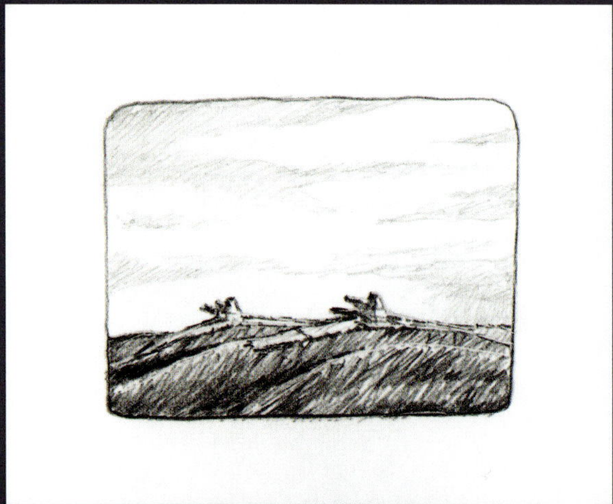
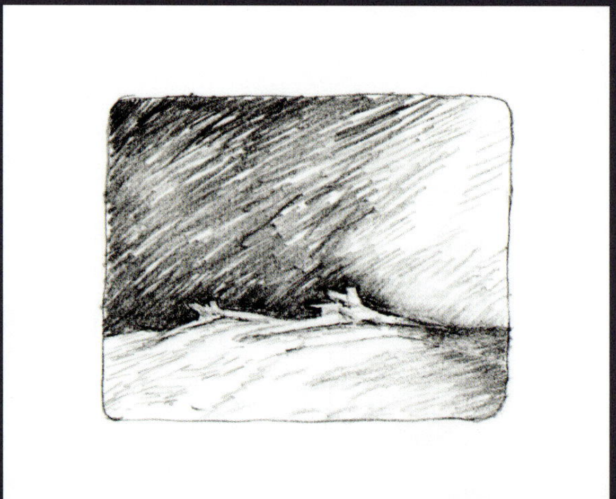

East elevation

Exploring another variation on this same general house concept

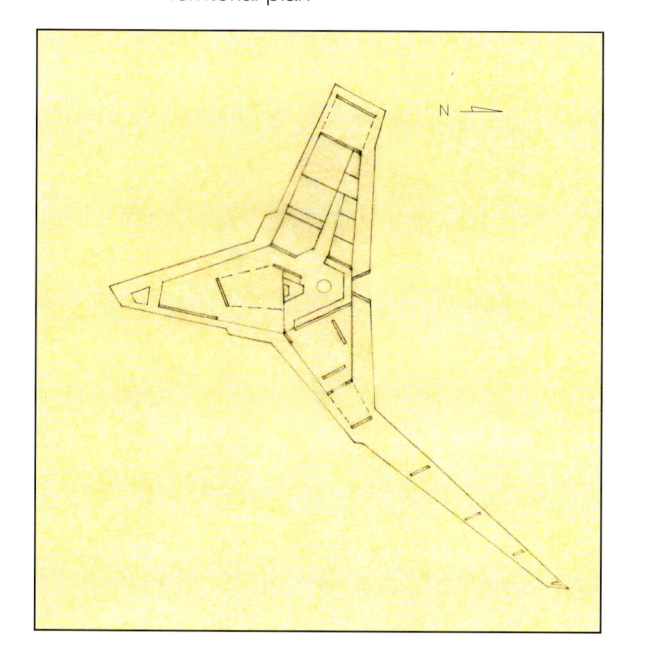

Territorial plan

Roof plan

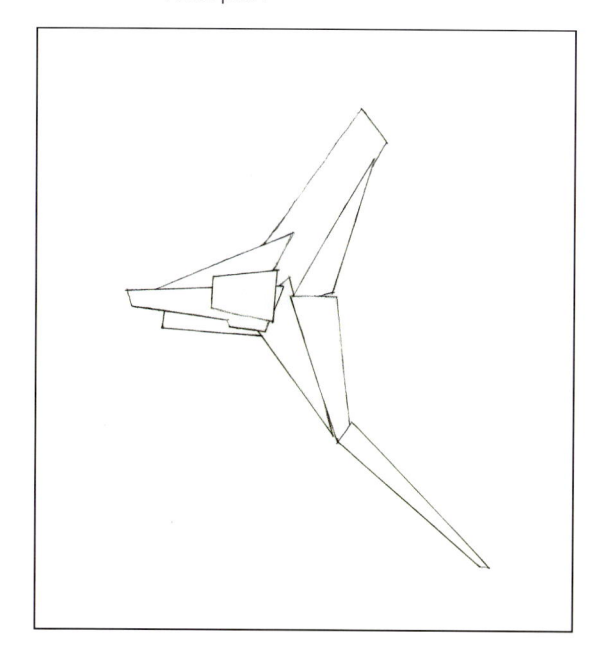

237

HAWK HILL RESIDENCE   3600 Square Feet Plus   1998-2000
Coastal California

Louis O. Roberts, architect

Aerial view of model indicating megalith alignment with the chimney to summer solstice
Driveway, turnaround, garage, storage areas and utility room on lower level

Roof from above in the model with driveway and turnaround

Floor plan (see p.197 for territorial divisions)

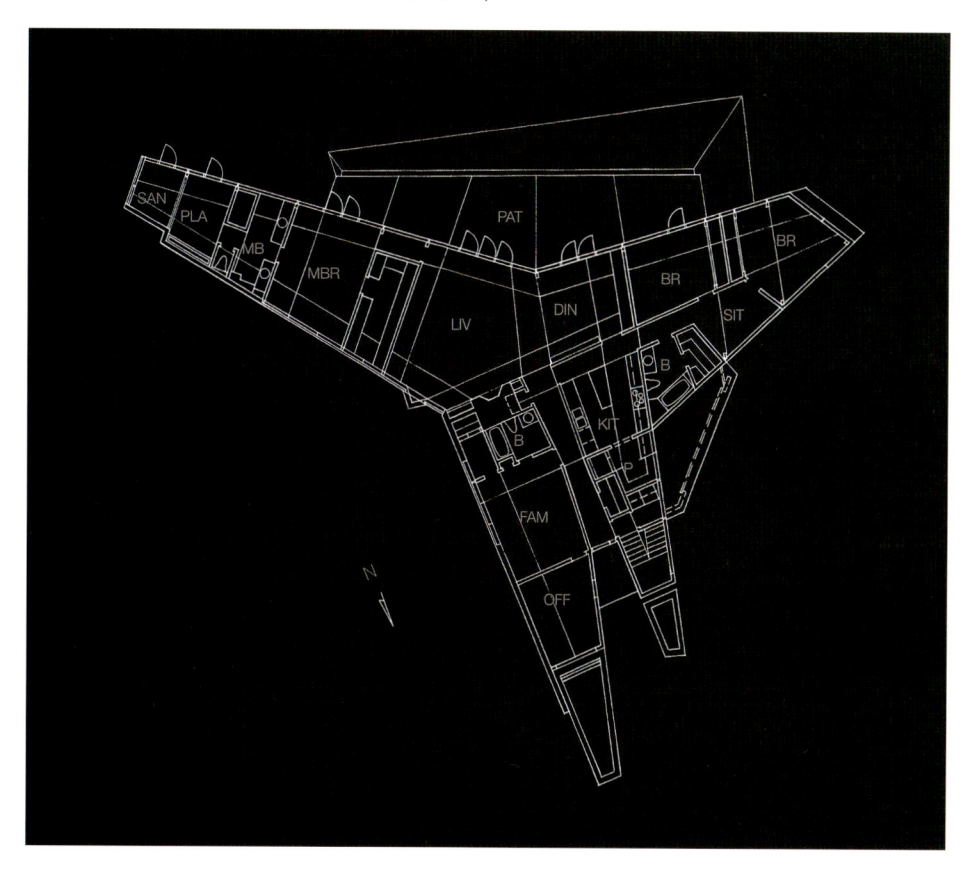

239

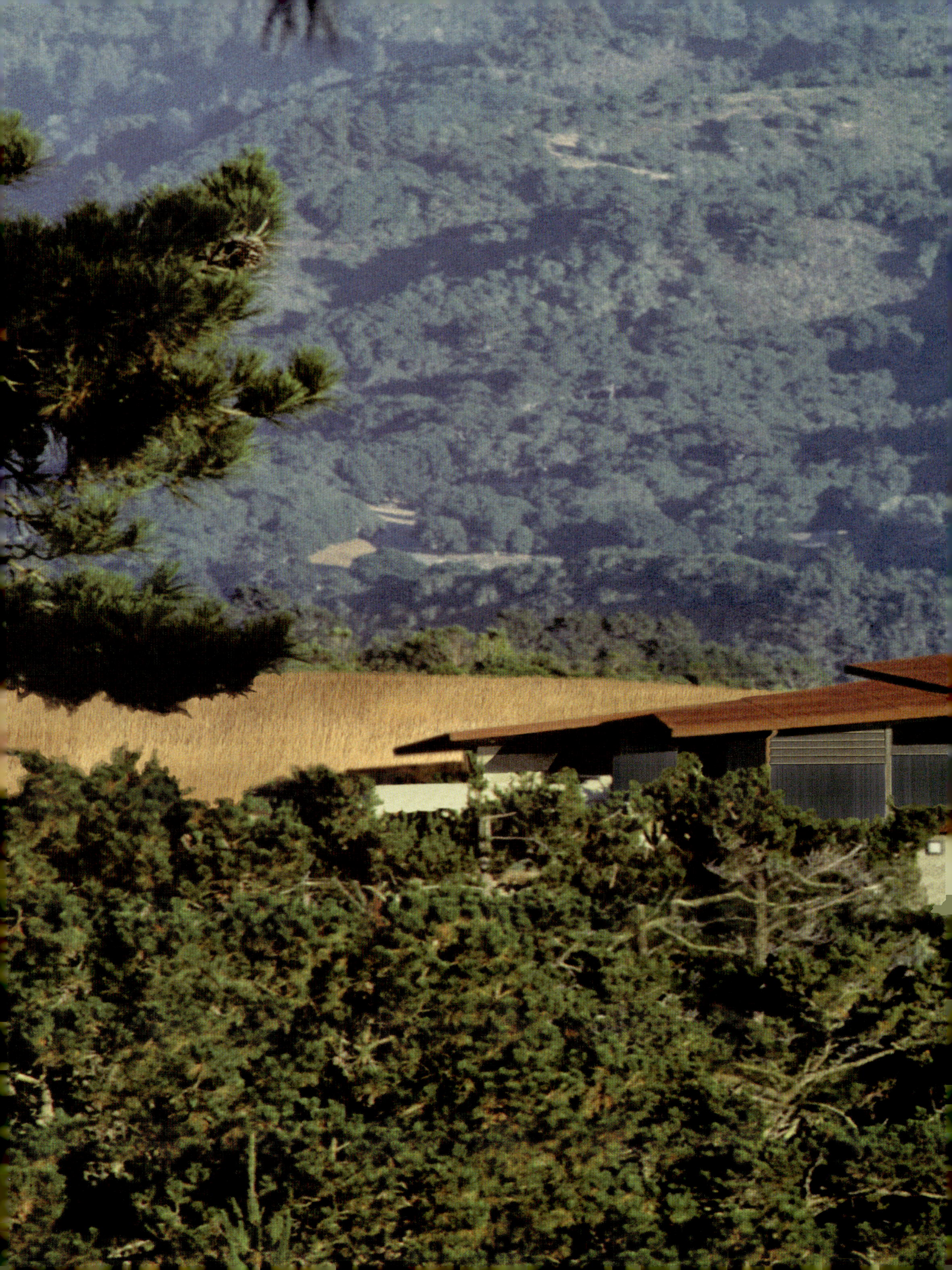

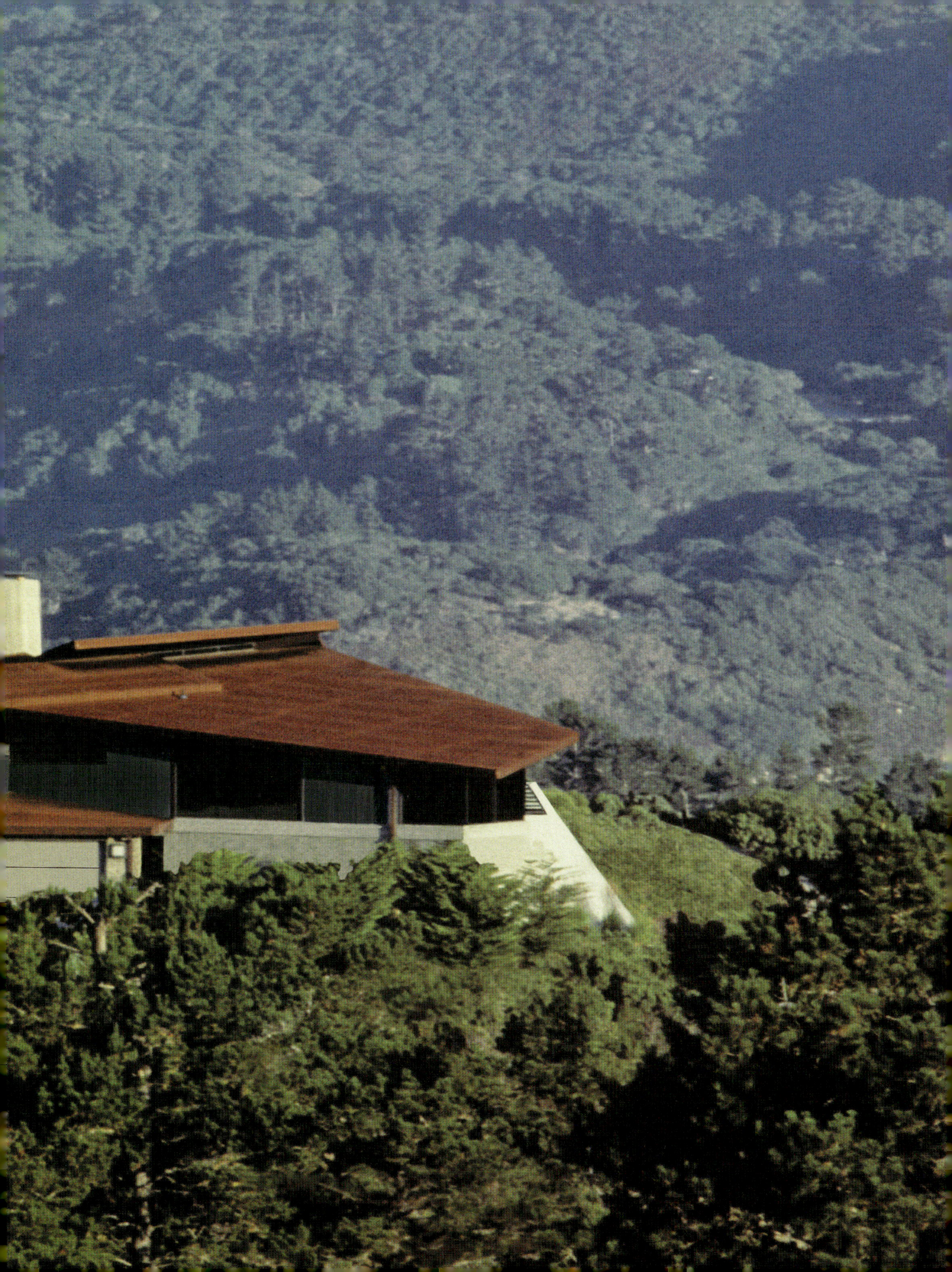

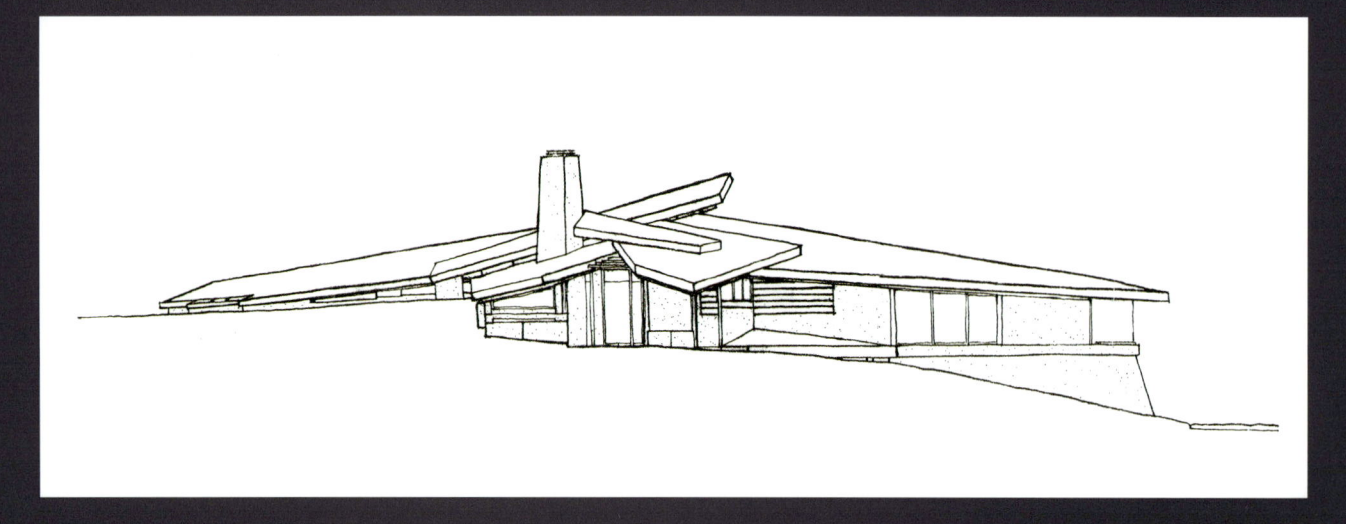

North Elevation showing entry and roof outline reflective of the approaching hill form

The *vision* behind this design is that of earth and sky – a roof form floating above a massive ground connected base. The roof *expression* is derived from the forces in nature: the curve of the hill, ice jams, and tectonic plates.

Since this is a multilayered *concept*, the considerations integrate and flow together to become a whole. They include: symbolic imagery, nature, sculpture / form, site conditions / views, plan territories and others as outlined on page 203.

Colors and *materials* were chosen to help integrate the building with its natural setting. Material integrity was maintained by making the base material the finish material, and every intersection of form and materials was detailed for visual and structural balance. Systems were invented for: roof panels and cladding, windows and doors, water elements and invisible tracking to accommodate lights, speakers and sprinklers.

West elevation with stepped windows design to diffuse / fractionalize sun's reflections

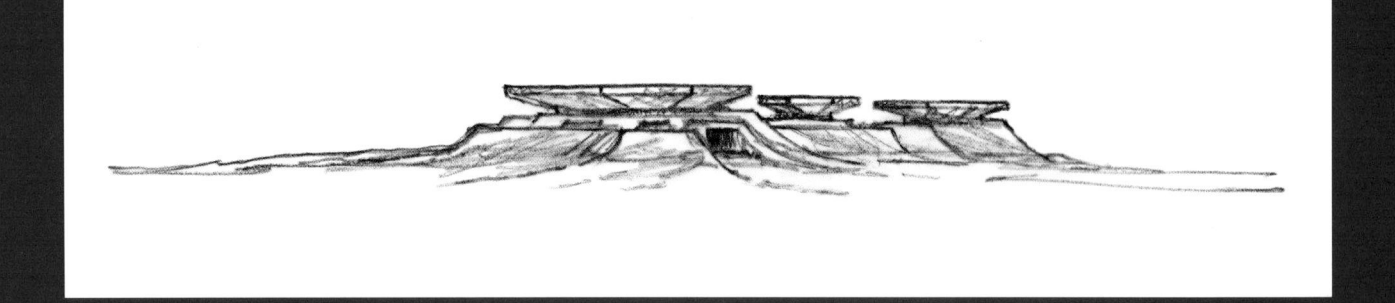

TEXAS RESIDENCE   Conceptual   1997
Midland, Texas

Plan in rough form showing wing walls dividing the various territories

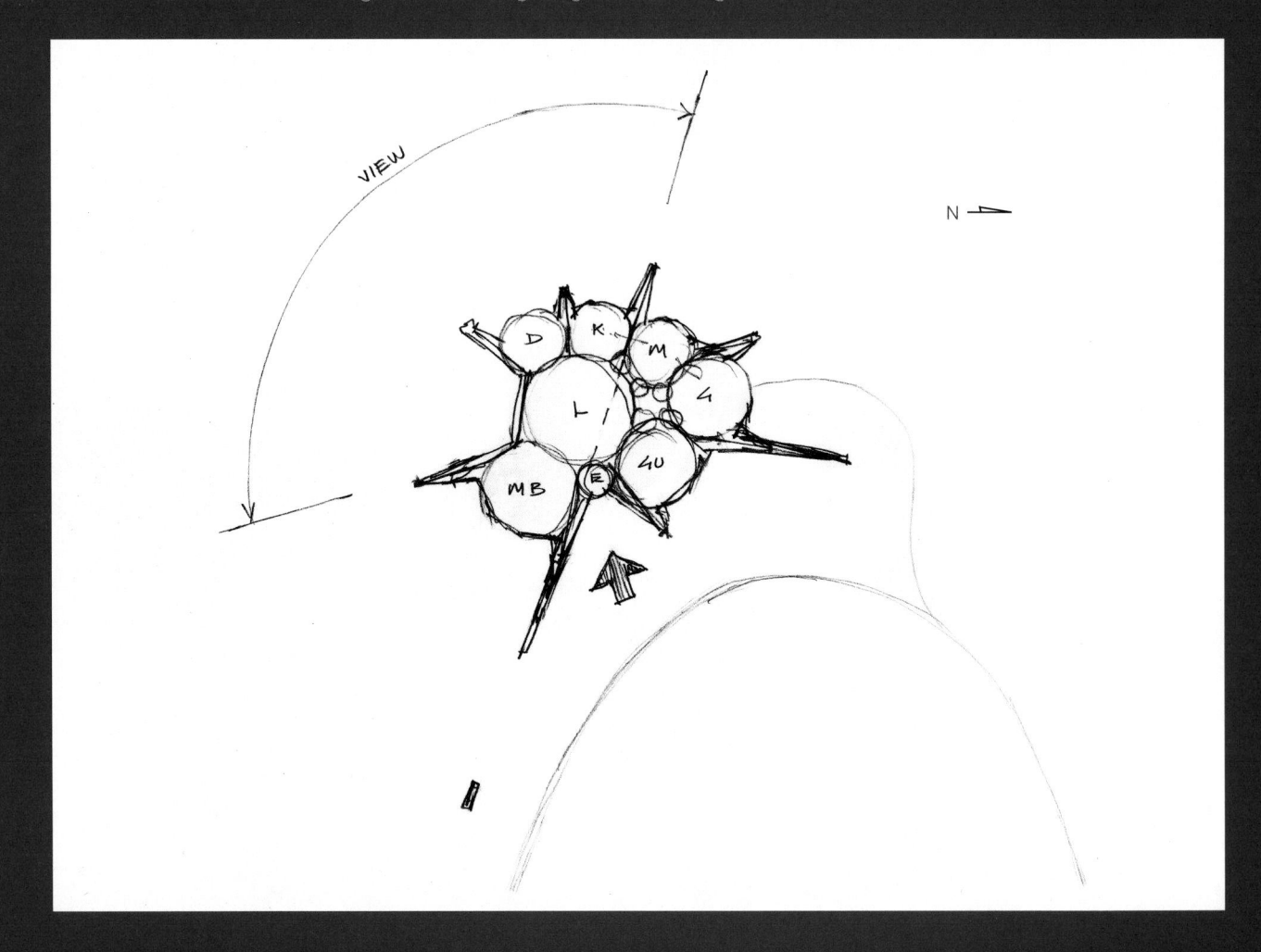

244 REALITY

Drawings are purposely allowed to follow their own course

Various studies for this earth-sky house on a central Texas plain

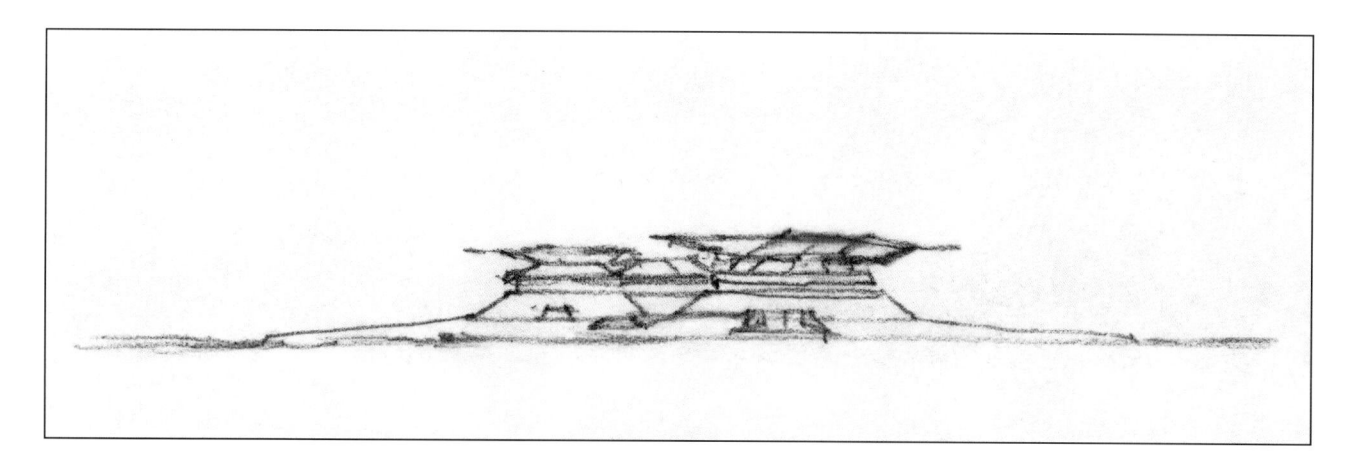

245

EXPRESSIONS

. . . . URBAN PLANNING . . .

Earth expressed as cityscape

Idea sketch for futuristic city

Point Sur, California has an almost identical natural rock base configuration as Mont Saint Michel, France – hence, one could envision in this unique *spirit of place* a modern day National Cultural Village / urban environment.

1993

Urban vehicle accommodation – parking
This concept can best be understood by thinking of Mont Saint Michel as being built on a multileveled parking structure rather than on solid rock – as illustrated above. Parking structures such as these can be thought of as varying horizontal man-made contours added to the natural landscape, either to enhance or neutralize what exists.

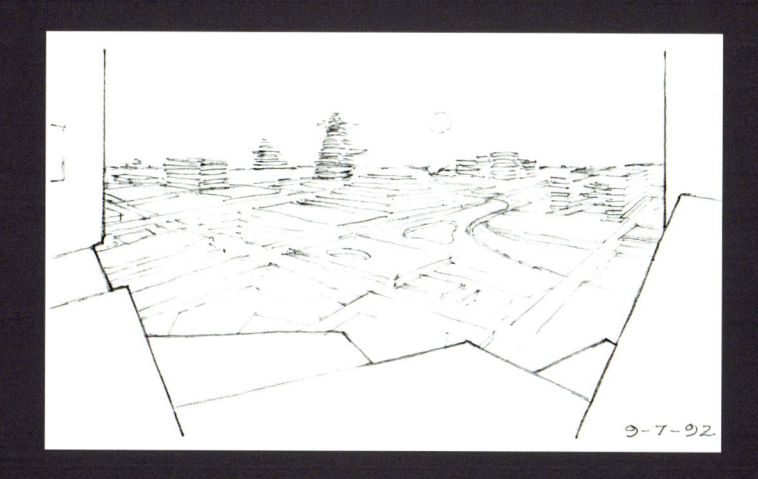

247

Eroded honeycomb stone forms could be the shape of cities to come

Nature's highrises – harmonious in color and form with the surrounding landscape

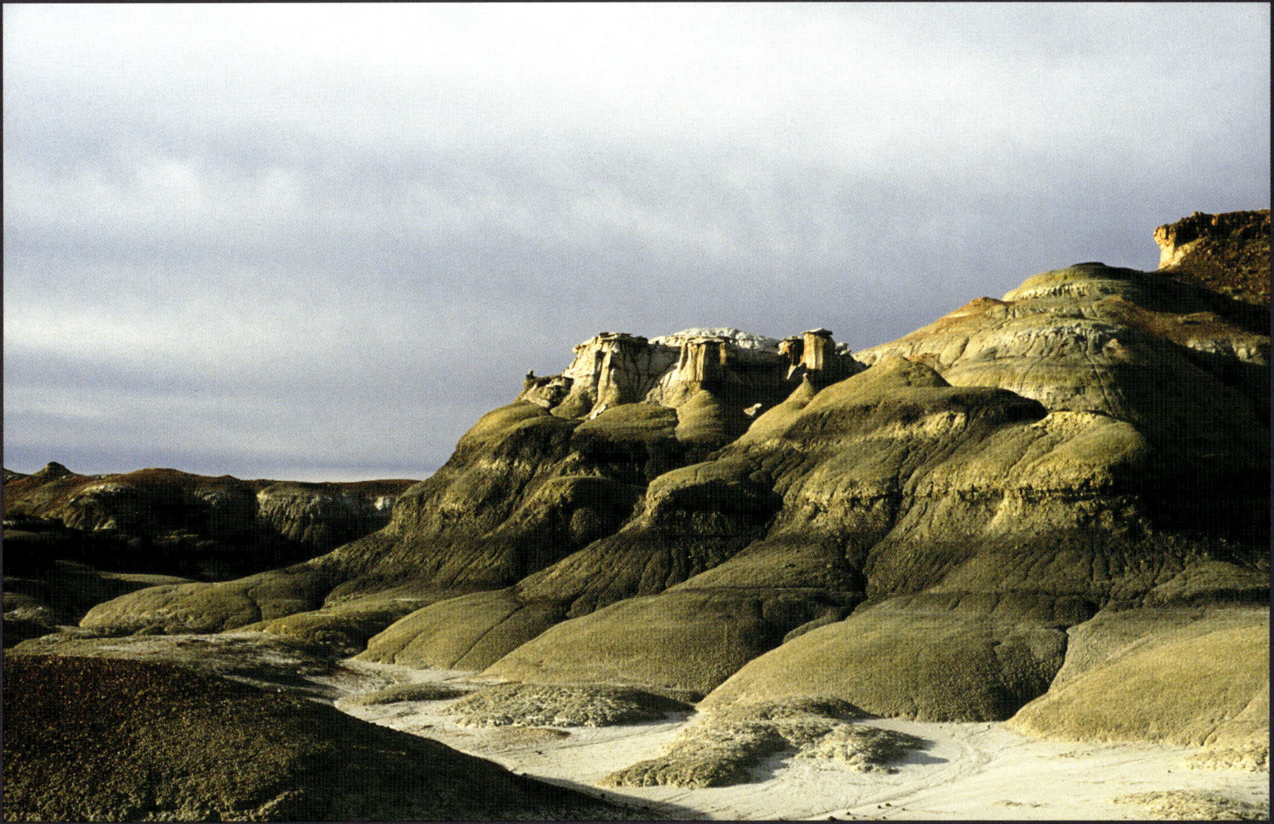

EXPRESSIONS

▪ ▪ ▪ ▪ ▪ ▪ ▪ **OBJECTS** ▪ ▪ ▪ ▪
Furniture – an extension of architecture

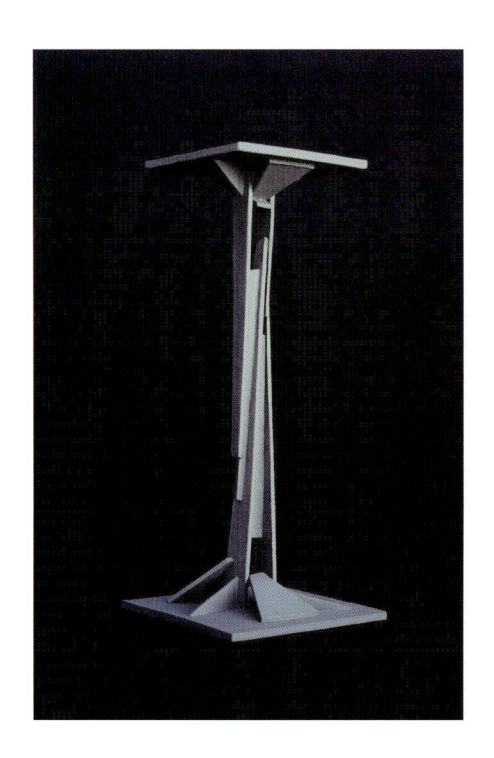

Planar metal pedestal with house model   1994

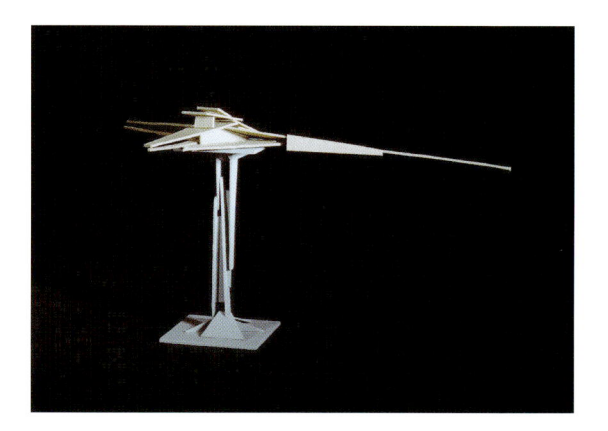

Kitchen work table with floating wood top and metal base

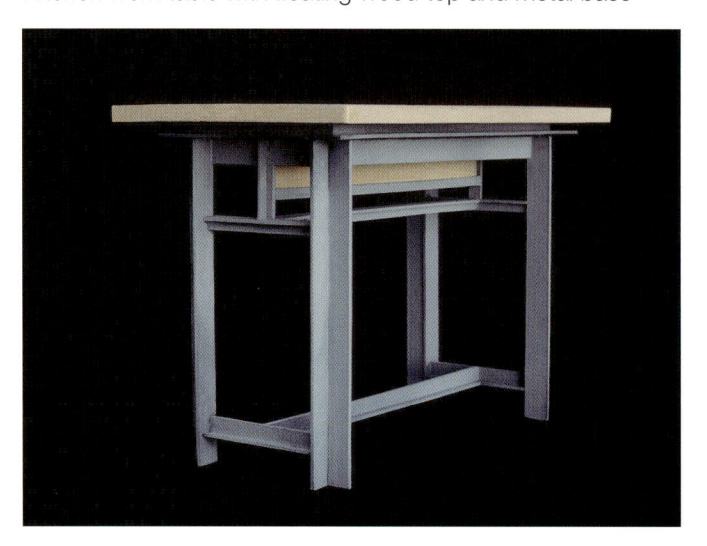

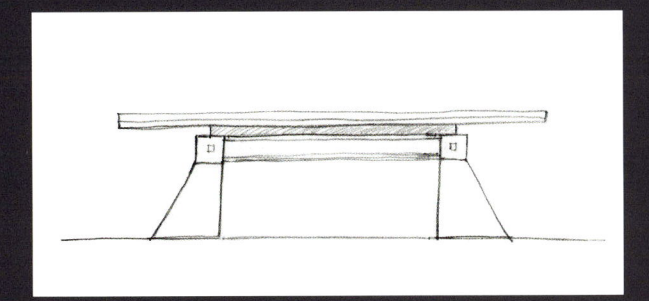

Dining table with floating top – legs below

Earth-sky tree lamp

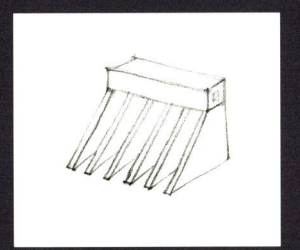

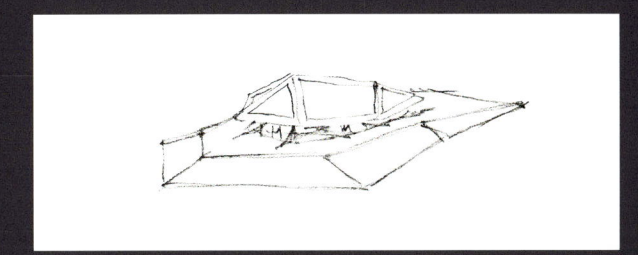

Low lamp with floating glass shade

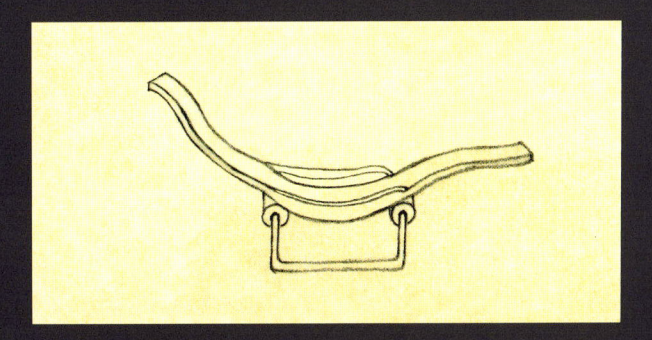

Adjustable lounge chair with headrest variations

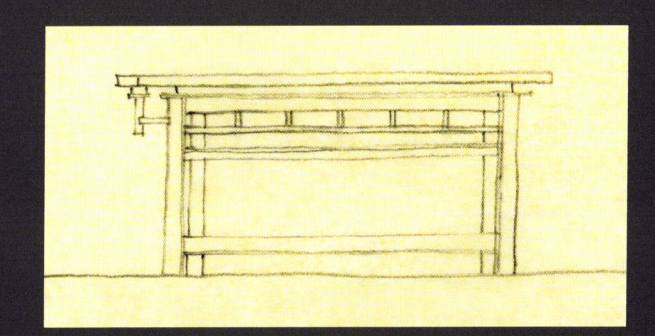

Kitchen work table, above and below

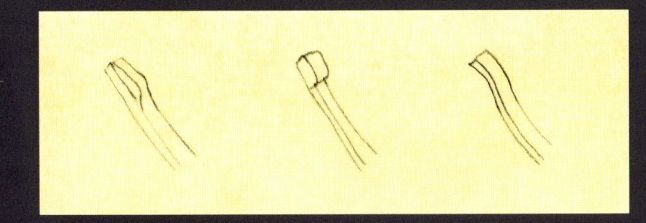

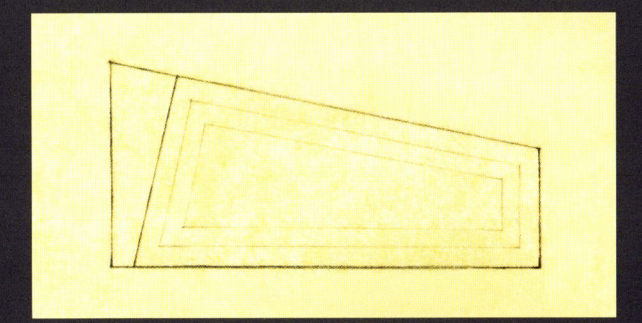

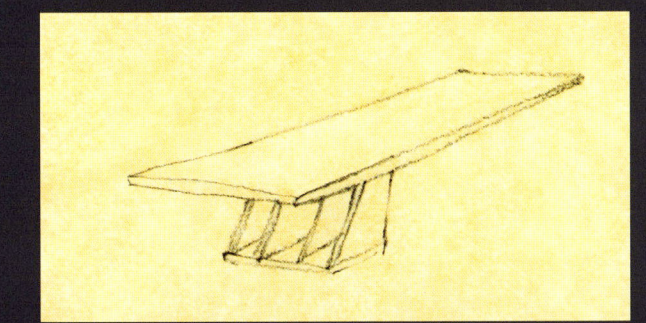

Cantilevered dining table, left and below

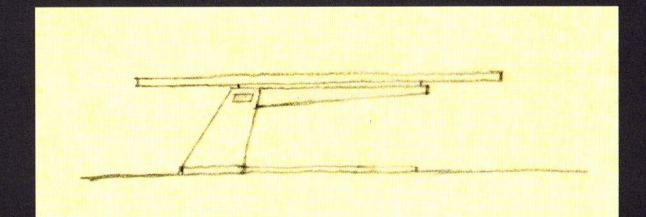

EXPRESSIONS

· · · · · · · · · **OBJECTS** · ·

Sculpture – non functional form

BRONZE BUST OF COLE WESTON – Photographer   1995

Early cardboard mock-up

Final patinated bronze bust with structural rib

As a study in abstract planar forms this bust can best be interpreted by my revised version of what Christopher Woodward stated concerning *ruins* (p. 186) – [*Abstract art*] *is a dialogue between an incomplete reality and the imagination of the spectator. Each spectator is forced to supply the missing pieces from his or her own imagination and [the art] therefore appears differently to everyone."*

Profile showing positive and negative spaces

Three quarter perspective

EXPRESSIONS

▪ ▪ ▪ ▪ ▪ ▪ ▪ ▪ ▪ ▪ OBJECTS
Mechanical – industrial form and function

MOBILE PROPANE METAL FORGE 2003

Maintains 2000 degrees internally

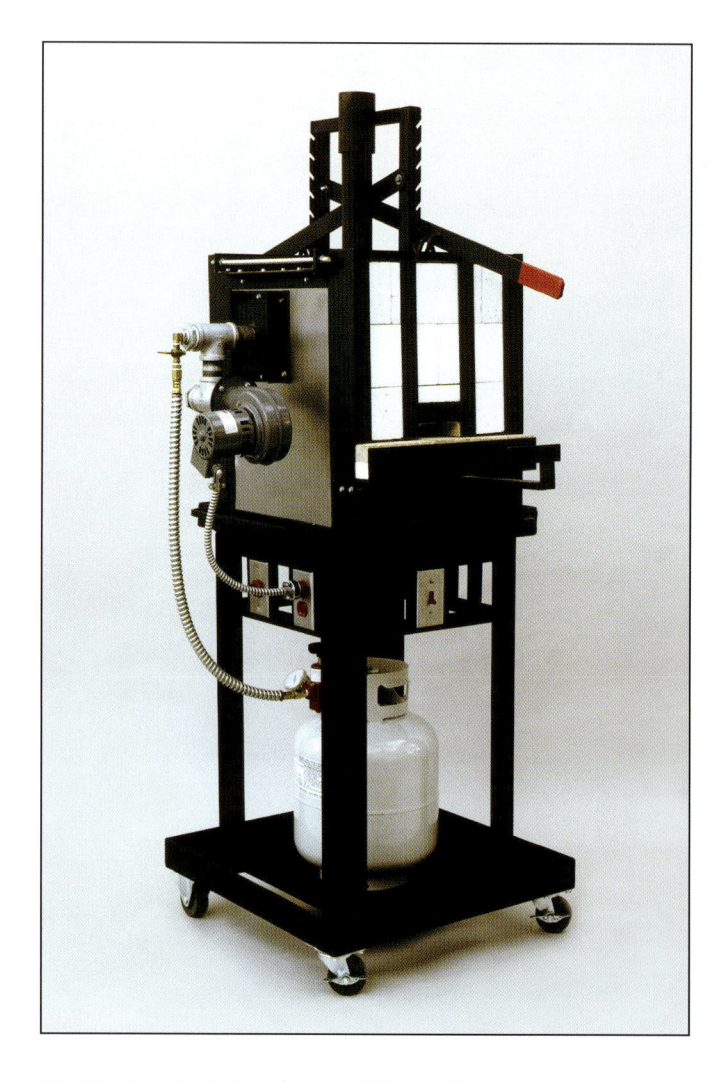

Electrical control of outlets and blower fan

Insulated to 2600 degrees for maximum heat retention and efficiency

Fold out arms to support metal stock

Guillotine doors for ready access

CONCLUSION

OH LIFE

BE STEADY AS YOU GO
HAVE FAITH IN YOUR COURSE
ONE FORWARD DEED BEGETS ANOTHER
OUT OF VOIDNESS COMES VOLUMES
ALL WAITING FOR COURAGE

LOOK BEYOND THE WINDOW OF THE CONSCIOUS
INTO THE VASTNESS OF THE UNCONSCIOUS
SEEKING THE KEY
RIDE THE EXPANDING CURVE
OF THE GOLDEN SECTION

TODAY AND EVERY DAY BRINGS YOU CLOSER
TO THE ONENESS OF ALL THINGS
THE ENERGY THAT PERMEATES THE UNIVERSE
THE PLACE FOR THE PSYCHE TO RESIDE
WHERE THE SQUARE AND THE CIRCLE ARE ONE

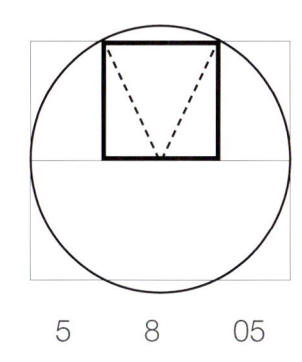

5   8   05   LOUIS O. ROBERTS

APPENDIX

WRITING

I was approached by a would-be author at my favorite gathering place who inquired about the creative process of writing. He had many concerns and misgivings as to whether he should pursue this career endeavor. Without any prior thought, I found myself answering him with the following comments, which may be of help to others – they were to me:

- When you write you **COMMIT TO IT** – you do it 5 days a week at the same time (as a minimum) whether you feel like it or not. Even if you do not think you are accomplishing very much – little bits accumulate over time.
  For example, when you wake up in the morning, you do not decide whether to go for a walk or not. If you have committed to it, you go – not letting rain, snow or sleet stop you.

- You first have to **DO IT FOR YOURSELF** – because you have to and want to. It is important that you write for your own fulfillment. Do not think about publishers, marketing, sales, money. These things will come, if you have something worthwhile to say.

- You say that there are so many really good writers out there – there are, but many of them have nothing to say. For the most part, they are focused on how well they write and not on content. **PASSION OF SUBJECT** will make you a good or at least a decent writer. This is also true in other fields with people who have an innate talent; they ride on their natural ability and often do not develop a deep understanding of the work.

- We all have **DOUBTS** – as to whether we can do what ever it is – write, draw, perform. This is a normal part of the human condition. As Herman Hesse wrote, "he. . . learned by experience that faith and doubt belong together, that they govern each other like inhaling and exhaling."

- Do not enter competitions – do not give away **YOUR UNIQUE IDEAS**. They are what separate you from all the other "good" writers out in the world. Limit exposure of your work to a trusted few.

- I find that **SELF PUBLISHING** is the best approach for getting the book in print, copyrighted and launched. In this way you have control over the content and design of the book, and limited exposure of your ideas. Use the best distributors and sales people. In addition, personally promote it to bookstores, libraries, museums and any other organization to which it might apply. If you have success, a large publishing company will pick it up from there.

DRAWING

I Have found from experience as a teacher that everyone has the capacity to draw. Below are a few excerpts from my lectures on creativity that may be of assistance. These are important concepts to be aware of when *drawing what one sees*.

■ Horizon

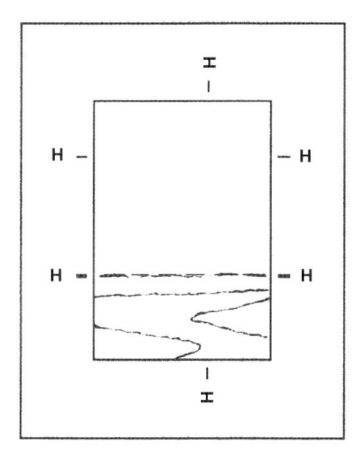

Avoid placing horizon in the middle of the drawing – can be boring / static

■ Vanishing Points

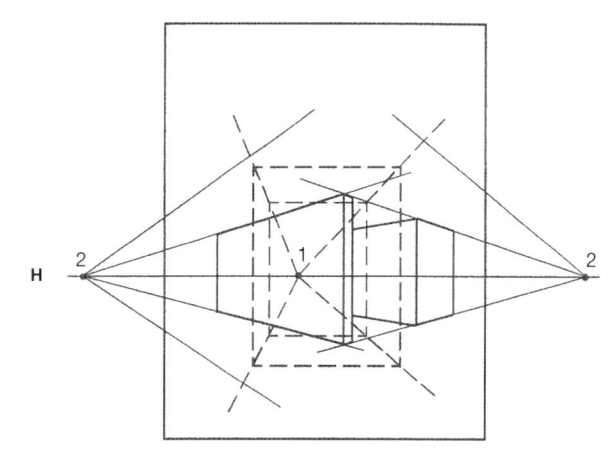

1 point perspective - - - -
or
2 point perspective ———

■ Line Extensions

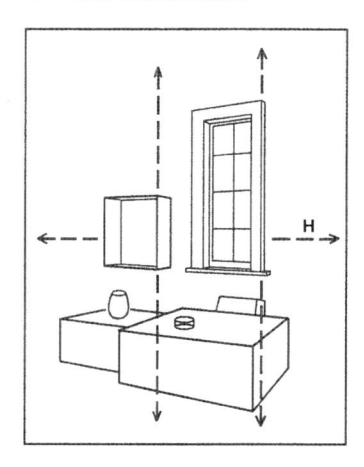

Extend imaginary lines from points in image relative to the paper's edge

■ Pieces of a Puzzle

The relationship of sizes and shapes proportional to the paper's edge

BIBLIOGRAPHY

Abbagnano, Nicola. *Critical Existentialism.* New York: Doubleday Anchor Books, 1969.

Allen, Edward. *Stone Shelters.* Cambridge, MA: Massachusetts Institute of Technology Press, 1969.

Ashihara, Yoshinobu. *Exterior Design in Architecture.* New York: Van Nostrand Reinhold, 1970.

Bachelard, Gaston. *The Poetics of Space.* Boston: Beacon Press, 1969.

Grayson, David (Ray Stannard Baker). *Great Possessions.* Garden City, NY: Doubleday, Page & Company, 1917.

Barrett, William. *Irrational Man.* New York: Doubleday Anchor Books, 1962.

Briggs, John. *Fractals: The Pattern of Chaos.* New York: Simon & Schuster, 1992.

Carver, Norman F., Jr. *Italian Hilltowns*. Kalamazoo, MI: Documan Press, 1979 / 1995.
-----------. *Iberian Villages: Portugal & Spain.* Kalamazoo, MI: Documan Press, 1981.
-----------. *Japanese Folkhouses.* Kalamazoo, MI: Documan Press, 1984 / 2003.
-----------. *Silent Cities: of Mexico and the Maya.* Kalamazoo, MI: Documan Press, 1986.
-----------. *North African Villages.* Kalamazoo, MI: Documan Press, 1989.
-----------. *Form & Space in Japanese Architecture.* Kalamazoo, MI: Documan Press, 1993.
-----------. *Greek Island Villages I.* Kalamazoo, MI: Documan Press, 2001.

Ching, Francis D. K. *Architecture: Space, Form and Order*. New York: Van Nostrand Reinhold, 1979.
-----------. *Interior Design: Illustrated.* New York: Van Nostrand Reinhold, 1987.

Christ-Janer, Victor F. *"Constituent Imagery" The Yale Architectural Journal - Perspecta 17* (1980): 8-17.

Corner, James and Alex S. MacLean. *Taking Measure Across the American Landscape.* New Haven: Yale University Press, 1996.

Csikszentmihalyi, Mihaly. *Flow; The Psychology of Optimal Experience.* New York: Harper, 1990.
-------------. *Creativity: Flow and the Psychology of Discovery and Invention.* New York: Harper-Collins, 1996.

Cullen, Gordon. *Townscape.* New York: Reinhold Book Corporation, 1968.

Doczi, Gyorgy. *The Power of Limits - Proportional Harmonies in Nature, Art and Architecture.* Boston: Shambhala, 1994.

Dubos, Rene. *A God Within.* New York: Scribners and Sons, 1972.
--------- . *So Human an Animal.* New York: Scribners and Sons, 1968.

Durrell, Lawrence. *Spirit of Place: Letters and Essays on Travel.* New York: E. P. Dutton Co., 1969.

Eliade, Mircea. *The Sacred and the Profane: The Nature of Religion.* New York: Harcourt, Brace, Jovanovich, 1959.

Fanelli, Giovanni, & Francesco Trivisonno. *Citta antica in Toscana.* Firenze: Sansoni Editore' 1982.

Frampton, Kenneth. *Studies in Tectonic Culture.* Cambridge, MA: MIT Press, 1995.

----------. *"Intimations of Tactility: Excerpts from a Fragmentary Polemic." Architecture and Body.* New York: Rizzoli, 1988.

Frankl, Viktor E. *Man's Search for Meaning.* New York: Simon and Schuster, 1959 / 1984.

Fraser, Douglas. *Village Planning in the Primitive World.* New York: George Braziller, 1968.

Freudenheim, Lesie M. & Elizabeth S. Sussman. *Building with Nature: Roots of the San Francisco Bay Region Tradition.* Santa Barbara: Peregrine Smith, 1974.

Germen, Aydin, ed, *Islamic Architecture and Urbanism.* Dammam, Saudi Arabia: King Faisal University, 1403/1983.

Giedion, Sigfried. *Space, Time and Architecture.* Cambridge, MA: Harvard University Press, Fourth / Fifth edition, 1962 / 65 / 67.

Gombrich, E. H. *The Story of Art.* London: Phaidon Press, 1995.

Grillo, Paul J. *Form Function & Design.* New York: Dover Publications, 1960 / 1975.

Hall, Edward T. *The Hidden Dimension.* New York; Anchor Books, 1969.

Heidegger, Martin. *Poetry, Language, Thought.* New York: Harper and Row, 1971.
----------. *Being and Time.* New York: Harper and Row, 1927 / 1962.

Hemming, John & Edward Ranney. *Monuments of the Incas.* Boston: Little, Brown and Company, 1982.

Hillman, James. *The Soul's Code: In Search of Character and Calling.* New York: Random House, 1996.

Isham, Norman M. & Albert F. Brown. *Early Connecticut Houses.* New York: Dover Publications, 1965.

Jung, Carl G., ed. *Man and His Symbols.* London: Aldus Books, 1964.

Kelly, Kevin. *Out of Control: The Rise of Neo-biological Civilization.* Boston: Addison Wesley Publishing, 1994.

Kepes, Gyorgy. *Language of Vision.* Chicago: Paul Theobald, 1969.

Kostof, Spiro. *A History of Architecture: Settings and Rituals.* Oxford, UK: Oxford University Press, 1985.

Lauer, David A. *Design Basics.* San Francisco: Holt, Rinehart and Winston, 1990.

Leich, Jean Ferriss. *Architectural Vision: The Drawings of Hugh Ferriss.* New York: Whitney Library of Design, 1980.

Levoy, Gregg. *Callings - Finding and Following an Authentic Life.* New York: Three River Press, 1997.

Lynch, Kevin. *The Image of the City.* Cambridge, MA: MIT Press, 1960.

Marc, Oliver. *Psychology of the House.* London: Thames and Hudson, 1977.

Moholy-Nagy, L. *Visions in Motion.* Chicago: Paul Theobald, 1947.

Morrish, William Rees. *Civilizing Terrains: Mountains, Mounds and Mesas.* Minneapolis: University of Minnesota, 1989.

Norberg-Schulz, Christian. *The Concept of Dwelling: On the Way to Figurative Architecture.* New York: Electra / Rizzoli, 1984.
------------. *Genius Loci: Toward a Phenomenology of Architecture.* New York: Rizzoli, 1979.

Oliver, Paul. *Dwellings: The House Around the World.* Oxford, GB.: Phaidon Press, 1987.

Owen, Stephen. *Readings in Chinese Literary Thought.* Cambridge: Harvard University Press, 1992.

Papadakis, Andreas, Catherine Cooke & Andrew Benjamin, eds. *Deconstruction: Omnibus Volume.* New York: Rizzoli, 1989.

Pennick, Nigel. *The Ancient Science of Geomancy - Man in Harmony with the Earth.* London: Thames and Hudson, 1979.

Quantrill, Malcolm. *Alvar Aalto: A Critical Study.* New York: New Amsterdam Books, 1983.

Rapoport, Amos. *House, Form and Culture.* Englewood Cliffs, NJ: Prentice-Hall. 1969.

Rilke, Rainer M. *Letters to a Young Poet.* New York: W. W. Norton, 1934 / 1962.

Rudofsky, Bernard. *Architecture Without Architects.* Garden City, NY: Doubleday & Co., 1964.
------------. *The Prodigious Builders.* New York: Harcourt Brace Jovanovich, 1977.

Russell, Bertrand. *Wisdom of the West.* New York: Crescent Books, 1959.

Saint Augustine. *Confessions.* Oxford: Oxford University Press, 1998.

Salvadori, Mario, & Robert Heller. *Structure in Architecture.* Englewood, NJ: Prentice Hall, 1963.

Salvadori, Mario. *Building: The Fight Against Gravity.* New York: Simon & Schuster, 1979.
------------. *Why Buildings Stand Up.* New York: McGraw-Hill, 1980.

Schumacher, E. F. *Small is Beautiful.* New York: Harper and Row, 1973.

Thompson, D' Arcy W. *On Growth and Form.* Cambridge, UK: Cambridge University Press, 1961.

Tillich, Paul. *The Courage to Be.* New Haven: Yale University Press, 1952.

Varanda, Fernando. *Art of Building In Yemen.* Cambridge, MA: M IT Press, 1982.

Vitruvius, Marcus. *Ten Books on Architecture.* Cambridge: Cambridge University Press, 1999.

Walker, Lester. *American Shelter.* Woodstock, NY: The Overlook Press, 1981/ 1996.

Whiteson, Leon. *The Watts Towers.* New York: Mosaic Press, 1989.

Williams, Christopher. *Origins of Form.* New York: Architectural Book Publishing Co., 1981.

Wright, Frank Lloyd. *The Natural House.* New York: Horizon Press, 1954.

Young, J. Z. *Programs of the Brain*. Oxford, Oxford University Press, 1978.

CREDITS

All creative works, drawings, photographs and diagrams are by the author except those listed below, credited either to the artist, the photographer or the copyright holder. In addition, each of these sources is noted adjacent to the work. Where the source is unknown (5), it is indicated below the image.

- P. 20: **Peter N. Mauss** (photo)
- P. 22: **Art Sinsabaugh** (2 photos)
- P. 24: *Architecture Without Architects* photos
    - a. © Armée de l'Air, Musée de l' Homme
    - b. © Instituto della Enciclopedia Italiana
    - c. © Gabinetto Fotografico Nazionale
- P. 25: **Bruno Zevi** (*Zodiac # 14* cover)
- PP. 26-27: **Jorn Utzon**, architect (5 drawings)
- P. 31: **Peter A. Clayton** (Pyramids photo)
- P. 35: **Jeffrey Becom** (Machu Picu photo)
- P. 39: **Bruce Miller** (Stadium Gates photo)
- P. 39: **Dana Levy** (whisk photo)
- P. 39: **Lee Fatheree** (table photo)
- P. 41: **Guenther Tetz** (2 photos)
- P. 42: **Leonardo da Vinci** (drawing)
- P. 44: **Sigmar Polke** (book cover)
- P. 45: **Olaf Veltman** (tree photo)
- P. 51: © MIT Press (Yemen Villages photo)
- P. 53: **Hugh Brehme** (lake photo)
- P. 58: **Morley Baer** (Kiva ladder photo)
    - © Special Collections, UCSC
- P. 59: **Jean Paul Gisserot** (megalith photo)
- P. 63: **Rembrandt van Rijn** (drawing)
- P. 63: **Bill Schoening** (galaxy photo)
    - © NOAO, Tucson, Arizona
- P. 64: **Marvin Rand**, Hon. AIA (3 photos)
- P. 65: **Jorn Utzon** (2 drawings)
- P. 65: **Balthazar Korab** (2 photo)
- P. 66: a. **Ezra Stoller** (Seagram photo)
    - b. **Timothy Hursley** (Disney photo)
    - c. **Joshua M. White** (model photo)
    - d. **Michelangelo** (David / library)
- P. 67: a. **Jan Vermeer** (2 paintings)
    - b. **Vincent Van Gogh** (2 paintings)
    - c. **Wolfgang Volz** (bridge photo)
    - d. **Michael Cullen** (Berlin photo)
- P. 68: a. **Edward Weston** (3 photos)
    - © Center for Creative Photography
    - b. **Cartier Bresson** (2 photos)
    - © Magnum Photos
    - c. **Ruth Bernhard** (2 photos)
    - © Princeton University
- P. 71: **Balthazar Korab** (left photo)
- P. 72: **Hugh Brehme** (tower photo)
- P. 73: **Prithwish Neogy** (chapel photo)
- P. 119: **Casper David Friedrich** (painting)
- P. 132: **Balthazar Korab** (church photo)
- P. 133: **John R Covert** (painting)
- P. 133: **Lyonel Feininger** (painting)
- PP. 171-177: **Jorn Utzon** (6 drawings)
- P. 181: **Hedrich Blessing** (2 Photos)
- P. 182: **Balthazar Korab** (Dulles photo)
- P. 182: **Alvar Aalto** (drawing)
- P. 204: **Alvar Aalto** (2 building plans)

We have tried our best to contact all copyright holders. In individual cases where this has not been possible, we request copyright holders to get in touch with the publisher or author.

ACKNOWLEDGMENTS

I want to pay homage to those glowing human beings who directly and indirectly cultivated my enthusiasm and interest in being creative, to explore and develop an architectural philosophy and to write this book.

The foremost of these would be **Mary Roberts**, my mother, who was always there for me and my brother. As a child, when I confronted a difficult or impossible situation, she would always tell me, "where there is a will, there is a way" – which still rings loudly in my mind. She prepared me for life with an "anything is possible" attitude.

Aldo G. Roberts, my father, who taught me the secret life of stone – its beauty, imagery and construction. He also instructed me to pay attention to the details in whatever I did; he was fond of saying, "do it right the first time and you won't have to do it again."

I have been very fortunate to have a few people who stood by me and have been supportive under all circumstances. None could surpass my wife, **Nancy**. I sometimes look upon her as an angel (if there are such things), who was sent down to look after me. She has been my major editor and sounding board for the thoughts and ideas herein. If it were not for her clear thinking, critical eye and encouragement this book might not exist.

Giulietta, my daughter, wise from an early age, made me realize that the source of knowledge is everywhere. Her natural creative ability has always been a wonder to me – uninhibited and flowing in all directions. She was a catalyst for some of my early ideas concerning creativity.

John Higgiston, my uncle, gave me confidence and encouragement when it was most needed. As I was coming into my teens, I admired him as the most intellectual person in my sphere. He had completed four years of college in three, and afterward was asked by the university to stay and teach philosophy. In retrospect, I look upon him as the most gifted teacher I have ever encountered. He could demystify and simplify any subject making it understandable to just about anyone. When he said you could accomplish something, you believed him. And, he employed a spare and powerful body language that captured your undivided attention.

Guenther Tetz, a friend since college, is a professor emeritus of visual communication and a world class graphic designer whose keen artistic sensitivity was available at two critical points. He gave me some guidelines early on and later at the end reviewed the graphics in this book with his discerning eye.

I worked in the architectural office of **Victor Christ-Janer** for two years prior to starting my own practice. At the time he was a professor of architecture at Columbia University graduate school.

Frequently he would come into the office and expound on existentialism, Martin Heidegger, Carl Jung and others – subjects and people that profoundly interested me. He fed fuel to my fire.

Gene Hicks, a long time friend and fellow architect, who has an adventurous spirit and inquisitive nature that I have always admired. No matter what the subject, he has an insightful perspective which encouraged me to expand my thinking.

Norman Carver is an architect, photographer, and writer who has been my major source of reference and inspiration. His books on indigenous architecture are some of the finest available with artistically sensitive photographs of significant structures from around the world. He gave me my first computer with publishing programs included – and was graciously available for many of my questions.

I am grateful to the numerous family members and friends who played a significant role in the various aspects of my life and / or assisted with this book in some way. I am sure you know who you are, but if you do not, your name is probably listed below:

Aldo J. Roberts, Louise Higgiston, Yolanda Lawrence, Robert & Lynda Cox, Sr. Leonora. Fr. Martin Hitchcock, J. Arthur Setaro, Otto Turderung, Marian Hancock, Jules Gauthey, Charlie Mathews, John Brundage, Herman Pundt, Peter Bodnar, Thomas Bates, Victor Kochel, Lois B. Roberts, Samuel Stelzer, Ronald Zocher, Art Sinsabaugh, A. Richard Williams, Robert Nelson, Alan Glass, Jay Kabriel, Ron Thomas, Hans & Rosemary Hoffmann, Gail Hicks, Christopher & Ghislaine Moomaw, John Ferris, John & Virgina Geils, Beau Hickory, Raymond Becker, Andy Schiltz, Lewis & Ethel Hurlbut, Louisa Calder, Stanley Mongin, Bruce Hall, Alan Dimen, Beverly Bense, James & Marjorie Rawls, Tamlyn Rawls, Nanette Sexton, Lisa & Gary Lucks, Yildirim & Aysil Yavuz, Robert & Alice Deering, Malcolm & Diane Wildsmith, Tod Lundy, Maura Lundy, Wayne Drummund, Hassan Al Nazhah, Aydin Germen, Murat Germen, Nezar Al Sayad, Vincent McCarthy, Suzie Parish, Fr. Chrysostom, Thomas Turman, Garry & Sylvia Bennett, Dorothy Mayer, Blaine Ellis, Michael & Trish McEneany, Jeffrey Becom, Sally Aberg, Lucas Blok, Barbara Ruzicka, Albert & Francis Paley, Christopher Winfield, Rodney & Betty Winfield, Hamish & Wendy Tyler, Kathleen Hamilton, Cole Weston, Davika Weston, Kim & Gina Weston, Mel Edelman, Gary Quinonez, Cecille Caterson, Ryan Drake, Hazel Lily Drake, Roger & Harriet Stribley, Meredith Stricker, Doug Picard, Kumi Uyeda, Mark Baer, John & Ann Day, David Salinas, Susan Bein, Francine Ellman, Roman Barnes, Andrew Durkin, Jason Christian, Beata Obydzinski, Jim Casteel, Richard Gadd, Gerrica Connolly, Dale & Cheryl Morrow, Harrison Faulkner, Margaret Butterfield, Charlie Craddock, John E. Warner, Susan Giacometti, Mary Wurtz, Sue Willaims, Robert & Pamela Green, Robert Blaisdell, David Williams, Stefani Esta, Rick Pharaoh, John Balcom, Robert Brownell, Amy Funt, Richard & Michele Ruble, Randy & Debbie Reinstedt, Sven van Rooij, Kevin Cardona, Brian George, Eefje Theeuws.

INDEX

Visual images in black.
Book titles in *italic*.

A

Aalto, Alvar 182, 204
    Finlandia Hall, Helsinki 204
    Seinajoki Library, Finland 204
    Shiraz Art Museum 182
Abbagnano, Nicola 81, 85
abilities, talents, traits and
    sensitivities 18
abstract art 186, 253
abstract thoughts and images 17, 201
acorn theory 28
actualization 88, 94
    faith . intuition . commitment 88
    wholeness 94
aesthetic
    creation 38
    factor 10
    identity 27
    judgments 69
    principles 198, 200
aesthetics and vision 9, 203
aesthetic vision notebook 69
Age of Reason 78
Agnoli, Val - architect 188
A God Within 28, 34, 40, 49, 58, 62
Al-Hajra Village, Yemen 191
Amalfi Peninsula 49
ambiguity 10, 190
analyzing the system 34
ancestral forces 18
ancestral past 58, 76
Ani, Turkey 128
archetypal images 63, 175
architectural expression 14, 70
    early human habitats 120–127
    forms in nature 110–119
    indigenous 128–131
architectural
    magnitude 74
    vision 6
    theorists 170
        Bachelard, Gaston 179
        Christ-Janer, Victor 179
        Frampton, Kenneth 175
        Giedion, Sigfried 172
        Heidegger, Martin 178
        Norberg-Schulz, Christian 174
        Utzon, Jorn 170
architecture 9, 12, 34, 38, 40, 41, 65, 70, 80, 188
    considerations 95
    contemporary 132
    expressions 206–220
        earth and sky 224–236
        earth - sky implied 216–220
    horizon, on the 52
    inspired by
        ancient man-made forms 210
        natural forms 206–209
    integration 74
    past / future 38
    poetic 189
    purposeful and reflective 38
    restatement of nature 70
    vision 9, 10
Architecture and Body, "Intimations of Tactility" 44, 75, 175
Architecture Without Architects 24–25, 184
arrowheads 18, 31
art 38–39, 66
art critic 38
art forms 38
artist 43
atmosphere 42
attitude 81, 82, 201, 204
Aurelius, Marcus - *Meditations* 94
awareness 27
    self 76
    of an idea 24
axis mundi 52, 74, 174

B

Bachelard, Gaston 44, 75, 179
Badlands of Alberta, Canada 207
Baker, Ray Stannard 81. *See
    also* Grayson, David
balance 34, 71, 242
    ecological 74
    point 34
balanced
    environment 8
    organism 34
    world 6, 9
Bamburgh Castle, England 51
Barrett, William 85, 87
battered walls 73
belief and creative art 38
Bennett, Garry Knox 39
Benson, Richard 198
Bernhard, Ruth 68
between earth and sky 44, 57
Bhutan
    Bhutan House 183, 185
    Dzong, Punakha 73
birth and evolution of an idea 18
Blake, William 201
book layers 6
Bosco, Henri 44, 75, 179
boundaries 175
Bourdon, David (on Christo) 67
brain, studies of the 38
Bresson, Cartier 68
building construction system 232
built form 188
burial mound 59
Burton, Joseph A. 189

C

"character ethic" 34
Calatrava, Santiago - architect 41
Camus, Albert 84
capitalism 34
Cappadocia, Turkey 35, 48, 120–121, 183
capturing the period 204
Caucasian mountains, Russia 89
cave 18
    entry 59, 203
    sky connected 172, 180
Celtic burial mound and megalith 59
Celtic dolmen, Pentre Ifan, England 53
central idea 44
Chaco Canyon, New Mexico 187
character, integrity, and honesty 78
characteristics of each individual 28
childhood 18
    experiences 27
    future relevance 60
    influences 204
    memories 24
    seeds planted 28
childhood images 19
    ancient dolmen 19
    lean-to construction 20
    stone walls 20
Chinese character 57
Christ-Janer, Victor 48, 58
    constituent imagery 179
Christo 67
    Pont Neuf, Paris 67
    Reichstag, Berlin 67
Churchill, Winston 41
Clovis Point arrowhead 31
clues to our direction 28
Coastal Cliff house 216
cocoon 24, 68
collective images 63
college 21
    architectural designs 24–25,
        Communication Center 104
        Golf Club 98–99
        Island Cultural Institute 100–101
        Railroad Terminal 102–103
    library 26
    notebook 12
colors and materials 242
commitment 89, 199, 258
concentration 199
    accidental / spontaneous 199
    structured 199
concept 201–203
    multi layered 242
    sketches 140, 202–203
Concept of Dwelling, The 74, 174
conclusion, book 256–257
Confessions 30
confidence 190, 197
Connecticut woods 18
connection to the earth 24
consciousness 62, 76
conscious realm 22
contemplation, controlled 199
continuum 30, 33, 40, 42
    contribution 30–31, 188
controlled guidance 190
conventional architecture 70
conversation and storytelling 62
cooking 197
Corfe Castle, England 186
cosmic roots 75
courage to act 88
Covert, John R. 133
craftsman style house 9
craftsmen's guilds 39
creating form 62
creative
    acts 31, 34, 62, 190, 194
    expression 24
    path 27
    process 6, 10, 201
        evolving organism 190
        flexible and fluid 188, 190
    work 42, 81, 88, 195
creativity 9, 10, 40, 195
    ambiguity 10
    exercising 10
    origin 18
    potential 10
    self realization 84
    source 60
    tools 197
Critical Existentialism 81, 85
cultural symbols 62, 63

D

dance 38
Darwin, Charles 190, 199
da Vinci, Leonardo 42, 78
Dechenlabrang Monastery, Nepal 131
de Laszlo, Violet Staub 33
democracy 76
Descartes 48
Desert School 202
design 197
    basic 200
    considerations 195, 201, 203
    priorities 195
    tools 197
determination, discipline, and faith 197
developmental lessons 18
direction 10, 12, 18, 24, 27, 110
Docheiariou Monastery, Greece 189
dolmen 19
dolmen entry, Bryn-Celli-D du, England 59
dolmen / megalith house 214
doubt / faith 196, 258
drawing 198, 259
    horizon 259
    line extensions 259
    pieces of a puzzle 259
    universal language 198
    vanishing points 259
Drew, Philip 74
    The Third Generation 74
Dubos, Rene 28, 33, 34, 40, 49, 58, 60, 62, 79, 83
Dulles Airport 182
Durrell, Lawrence 71

E

earlier life experiences 64
early expressions, architectural 98–104
early human habitats 120–127
earth 49, 70, 175
    anchor point 49

base element - foundation 49, 70
   food, water, shelter, and fuel 49
   integrated sketches 106–108
   physical and biological origin 49
   preservation 75
earth connected 24–25, 48–52, 70–71, 75, 114, 204, 206, 209
   contemporary architecture 132, 140–142
   elements 144–153
      planar forms 152–153
      sculptured earth forms 150–151
      wall forms 146–149
   forms 110–133
   highrises 220, 222
   indigenous architecture 128–131
earth expressed, sky implied 72, 216–223
earth-sky architecture 14, 206–207, 224–236, 242
   historical examples 27, 180–183
   reinforcing philosophies 170–172
earth-sky (vision) 44, 48–49, 57, 62, 70–72, 74, 170–179, 184, 196
   connection 48, 53, 69, 70, 203
   cosmic and terrestrial 173
   energy between 74
   expressed 73
   image 19, 133
   phenomenology of light 175
   image 19, 133
economic system 34
ecopsychology 35
ecosystem 196, 223
Egypt, Giza Pyramids 31
Eliade, Mircea 33
energy between earth and sky 19, 44, 52, 74
Enlightenment 79
equilibrium 28
eroded rock formations 45
essence 80, 97, 189, 195
   balance of forces 184–188, 189
events, life 18
evolution of a vision 10, 12, 18, 89, 97
   early expressions 98–105

   emerging path 134–138
   exploring ideas 144–156
   sources / influences 110–134
   studies / drawings 160–169
evolutionary experience 69
Exhibition Building - Nervi 40
existence 30, 84
existentialism 78, 84
   French 84
   German 84
   Italian 84
   positive 84, 85
   shadow side 78, 84
experiences, life 19
experiential past 28
experiential world 18
expressions
   architecture 206–245
   objects
      furniture 250–251
      mechanical 254–255
      sculpture 252–253
   urban planning 246–249

F

faith . intuition . commitment 88, 92
faith and confidence 69, 196
Falling Water 65, 71, 181
father 19, 20
fire 203, 213
firmness, commodity, delight 42, 200
flexible and fluid (mental attitude) 188, 190, 194, 196, 201
floating roof 26, 65, 73
folk art 65
forge, propane metal 254–255
form 9, 40, 201
forms in nature 110–119
Frampton, Kenneth 44, 75, 175
Frankl, Viktor E. 80, 81
furniture designs 250–251
future direction 12

G

Gaelic, term 52
gates, metal 39
Gehry, Frank 66

   Experience Music Project 66
   Guggenhheim Museum 66
   sculptural forms 66
Geils Residence 20, 134–137
genes 18
genius 10, 195, 201
Genius Loci 71
genius loci 18
Giedion, Sigfried 26, 43, 74, 172
   Third Generation 173
Giza Pyramids, Egypt 31, 183
going inward 28
golden section 42, 257, end pages
gravity 49, 74
Grayson, David 81. *See also* Baker, Ray Stannard
Great Possessions 81
Greece 35, 189
Green, Charles – James House 71
Guggenheim Museum in Bilbao, Spain 9, 66

H

"how" of life 30
Hawk Hill Residence 20, 238–243
   systems, architectural 242
   territories, floor plan 197
Hegel, George 84
Heidegger, Martin 52, 62, 72, 75, 84, 178, 201
hereditary characteristics 18
Hesse, Herman 196
highrise towers 220–223
Hillman, James 28
"hoodoos", Canada 207
horizon 21, 52, 259
   edge of sky 52
horizontal landscape 22–23
Hughes, Robert - art critic 38
human
   achievement 31
   behavior 34
   consciousness 38, 76
   continuum 30, 60, 62
   creativity 34
   homeostasis 38

psyche 22, 31, 48, 60, 73
    language of 57, 58
  spirit 30, 31, 38, 40, 42
Huneker, James G. 38
Hungarian farm house 185

I

"image ethic" vs "character ethic" 34
idea 10, 17–18, 82, 201
  abstract thoughts 17
  birth and evolution 18
  sketches 156
idea, evolution, reality 10
imagery 58, 62
  universal 70
  foundation 31
images 18, 58
  collective 63
  language 18
  recording 10
images and symbols 57, 189
indigenous architecture 128–131, 184, 185
  Abha, Saudi Arabia 188
Industrial Revolution 39
influences 18
  ancient dolmen 19
  lean-to construction 20
  people, places, events, and images 18
  plant 140
  stone walls 20
innate past 17, 28
inner forces and patterns 62
In Ruins 186
inspirational sources 186, 199
instincts and insights 28
internal and external forces 27
intuition 8, 28, 62, 69, 78, 80, 89, 201
Irrational Man 85, 87

J

Japanese cemetery 125
Jaspers, Karl 85
Johnson Residence 138
judging architecture / art 42, 200
Jung, Carl 28, 42, 61, 63

  uniqueness 10

K

Kahn, Louis I. 189
key information 22

L

L'Antiquaire 44, 75
Lake Patzcuaro, Mexico 53
Last Man Home - Tarjei Vesaas 174
Lauren, Henri - Aviator's Tomb 170
Lawrence, D. H. 39
lean-to construction 20
Le Corbusier 176, 181
Letters to a Young Poet 24
life / meaning 81
lifeblood 28, 60
Loarie, Richard 132
local cafe 41, 199
Lundy, Victor - architect 132
Lynch, Kevin 174

M

Machu Picchu, Peru 35
major themes, of book 9
Man's Search for Meaning 81
man-made in nature 48
Man and His Symbols 61, 63
man between earth and sky 44, 196
Man in the Modern Age, Jaspers 85
Marc, Oliver 45
Maslow, Abraham 80
materialism 34
Mayan temples 27
Medici, Religio 28
megalith, Champ-Dolent, England 59
megalith house 210
memories 28
mesa, Southwest United States 52
Mesa Verde, Colorado 131
Michelangelo 66, 69, 78, 199
  David 66
  Laurentian Library 66
Midwest Landscape #33 22
Midwest Landscape #97 22
Miller, Arthur 43
Milwaukee Art Museum 41

Mont Saint Michel, France 72
music 28, 62, 82

N

"natural" symbols 63
natural environment 9, 18, 34, 95, 203
nature 9, 12, 40, 195
nature and man 33, 34, 86
Navarro Ridge Houses 230–236
necropolis, Sinkiang, China 52
Nervi, Pier Luigi - architect 40
New England countryside 12
Nietzsche, Fredrick 79, 83
Nobel Prize 77
Norberg-Schulz, Christian 71, 74, 174
North Salem, New York 19
notebooks 198
note cards - 3 x 5 index 106–109, 197

O

Oakland Hills Residence 2, 224–229
office apprentice design
  County Government Center 105
oriental structures 27
origin, of a vision 18, 24, 28
  awareness 24
  beginning 18
  uniqueness 28
original thoughts 60, 61
overview 30, 34, 38
  art / architecture 38
  continuum 30
  society / world 34

P

Paley, Albert 39
past, present, future 30
perception 30, 64, 76, 200
perception of life / reality 24
performing arts 62
permanence and change 57
personal
  beliefs 194
  expression 204
  fulfillment 28
Perspecta #17 48, 58, 179
Pescara, Italy 129

philosophy 76, 77, 80, 84
    existence 84
    intellectual stage 76
    life / meaning 80, 81
    purpose 80, 82
    speculation 77
    suffering 82, 83
    wisdom / knowledge 76
photography 27, 68, 69, 198
Pichler, Walter - sculptor 82
Pinnacles National Monument 206
Pirelli Building 182
place (location) 71, 74, 184, 188, 203
place in time and space 30
planar forms 119, 133, 152–153, 223
plant Influence 140
poetic beauty 22
Poetics of Light 175
Poetics of Space, The 44, 75, 179
poetry 62, 72, 189
Poetry, Language, Thought 52, 72, 75, 178
Polke, Sigmar 44
Polo, Marco – "land ship" 64
Ponti, Gio 182
precedents, earth-sky 170–172
preferences and affinities 69, 200
prehistoric ancestors 76
prevailing conditions 30
primitive architecture 59, 184
primordial
    imagery 57, 63
    roots. 9
principles
    architectural 195–197
    design 197–204
    human 194–195
Programs of the Brain 38
prose and poetry 62
prototype earth integrated house 139
Psychology of the House, The 45
Pulitzer Prize 28, 33, 43, 81
purposeful and reflective art 38

R

raised platform 26, 65

reality 10, 34, 193
    perception of 64
    physical and psychic 70
realization of the past 24
recording tools 10, 197
    notes, drawings, photographs 10
recurrent images 22
reference code (book) 6
reference points 30
reflection of man 38
relativism 78, 79
Rembrandt's Philosopher 63
Renaissance 78
resurfacing influences 61
Rilke, Rainer M. 24
Roadside Service Complex 202
Roberts House 140–143
Robie House 65, 181
Rohe, Mies van der 66, 182
    Bacardi Office Building 66
    Seagram Building 66
romanticism 78
Ronchamp Chapel, France 73, 181
Roszak, Theodore 35
Roxbury House 20
Rudofsky, Bernard 24, 184
ruins 35, 173, 186–187
Ruskin, John 9
Russell, Bertrand 77
Russia, Western Caucasus 92–93

S

Saarinen, Eero 182
Sabatino (Sam) Rodia 64
Saint Michael Island, Cornwall, England 131
sanctuary - in a house 197, 203
Sartre, Jean Paul 79, 84
scandinavian farm 129
sculpture 69, 252
sculptured earth forms 70, 112, 150–151
Seagram Building 66
seeds planted 22
seed pod 68
Semperian formula 177
Silkeborg Museum 172, 176, 180

Simon Petra Monastery 35–36
Sinsabaugh, Art 22–23
    Midwest Landscape #33 22
    Midwest Landscape #97 22
site, of a building 74, 201, 203
Skara Brae, Orkney Island, Scotland 124
skeletal overhang 143
sketch cards - 3 x 5 index 198. *See also* note cards
sky 52, 72
    aerial element 53
    air 176
    implied 72
    light and heat 52
    rhythms of lives 52
sky related 45–47, 54–55, 129
    elements 154–156
    free forms 158
    geometric forms 158
    other forms 159
    planar forms 156–157
Snow, Dan – stone mason 20
So Human an Animal 79, 83
Soul's Code, The 28
source of creativity 60
Space, Time and Architecture 26, 74, 172
space-time continuum 30
Spanish aqueduct 72
spark that ignites creativity 17
Spirit of Place 71
spirit of place 24, 71, 184
St. Augustine 30
St. Loca, Amalfi Peninsula, Italy 49
stars - universe 63
stimuli, varied 17
Stinson Beach, California 188
Stone / Boulder house 209
stone formations 110–111
Stonehenge 32, 125–127, 183
Studies in Tectonic Culture 176
studio environment 199
style vs content 40, 43
subliminal recall 60
Sumela Monastery, Turkey 49
Sydney Opera House 9, 26, 65, 180

symbolic imagery 9, 58
   ladder 58
   language 9
   skulls 58
symbols / symbolism 58, 62, 189
   cultural 62
   gene encoded 62
   natural 63
   timeless 62
   universal 62
   visual, written, verbal, mental 62
synthesis / analysis 184, 204
systems, architectural 242

T

"temples of God" – flowers 18
table, art 39
Taktshang Monastery, Bhutan 56
talents and abilities 27, 195
Tantallon Castle, Scotland 187
technically competent 42
tension between earth and sky 19, 44
territories, concepts of 196–197, 203, 239, 244
Texas Residence 244–245
The Third Generation 74
thunder clouds 21, 44
time, concept of 30
   St. Augustine 30
   past, present, future 30
timeless symbols 62, 63
   archetypal images 63
tools 197–198
"to see what everyone else sees..." 24
total absorption 10
treasure, personal 10
treasure hunt 69
tree, as earth and sky image 21, 45
Trulli House, Alberobello, Italy 50, 185
truth 34, 76, 78, 79
tufa rock 35
Turkey 48, 49, 89, 120–121
Tuzigoot Indian Ruins, Verde Valley, Arizona 54–55

U

umbrella concepts

   concepts of territories 196
   earth and sky 196
   ecosystem 196
   scope 196
unconscious 8, 17, 38, 58, 60–63, 195, 199, 201, 204
   absorption of information 60
   access to 60
   creative tool 60, 190
   explore 63
   intuition 64
   lifeblood 60
   psychic reservoir 60
   source of creativity 60, 199
   two forces 60
unconscious awareness 63
understanding a system 34
uniqueness 8, 10, 12, 28, 64, 81, 195, 201
   aesthetic 28
   ancestral forces 18
   experiential past 28
   innate past 28
   view or vision 28
unity, of design 184
universal symbols 62
universe 34, 40, 52
University of Illinois 22
urban planning 246–249
Utzon, Jorn - architect 26, 65, 74, 170, 172–173, 180
   architectural vision 26
   Platforms and Plateaus 173
   Silkeborg Museum 172
   sketches 26–27, 171–172, 176–177
   Sydney Opera House 65
   World Exhibition competition 65

V

Van Gogh, Vincent 67
Vermeer 67
villages, Bani Murra, Yemen 51
vision 9, 10, 24, 27, 42, 44, 64, 69, 70, 190, 201
   architecture 70, 242
   beginning 24
   central idea 44

   multileveled 57
   perception 64
   symbolism 58
   wholeness 64
vision images 14
visual equilibrium 44
Vitruvian Man, The 42
Vitruvius' "delight" factor 74
Vitruvius, Marcus 42, 200
Voice of the Earth, The 35

W

"why" of life 30
wall forms 146–149
walls 20
   connected to the ground 20
   stone 20
water 203, 213
Watts Towers, Los Angeles 64, 82
Western Caucasus, Russia 92–93
Western Civilization 77
Weston, Cole - bust 252–253
Weston, Edward 68
wholeness 8, 12, 30, 34, 64, 86, 94, 95, 200
   achieving 190
   architectural 95
   balanced systems 94
   interconnectedness 190
window of the mind 17
Wisdom of the West 77
Woodward, Christopher 186
Wright, Frank Lloyd 65, 71, 181
   organic architecture 65
writing 27, 258
   prose and poetry 62

Y

Yemen
   Al-Hajra Village 191
   Bani Murra 51
Young, J. Z. 38

Z

Zodiac Magazine #10 170
                  #14 25, 172

271

Book – Golden Section Proportions

NHTI Library
Concord's Community College
Concord, NH 03301

8

5

5

0   1   1   2   3   5   8   13   21